D0840612

By the same author

The Confusion of Realms

Common and Uncommon Masks

Writings on Theatre 1961-1970

Common and Uncommon Masks

Writings on Theatre 1961-1970

Richard Gilman

Random House/New York

To my students

Rocco, Alan, Barbara

We must get behind the masks of common vision.

 —JERZY GROTOWSKI

❡Contents

III—Contemporaries

IV—Phenomena

V—Theatres

Contents

¶Introduction

If during my childhood I had answered the question of what I wanted to be when I grew up with "A drama critic," I'm sure I would have concurred in any decision of my parents about the need for therapy. Drama criticism is no ambition for the young: it scarcely ought to be one for the mature. Unless you write for one of a few large publications—the *New York Times* is the only one that really counts these days, and the *Times* wants reviewers, not critics—very little in the way of money, fame, power or even influence is likely to come to you.

What's worse, for the spirit addressing itself to a subject and not an institution, any hope you have of affecting the art with which you deal is rather quickly ground down, just as the theatre itself grinds down all but the toughest and most unassimilable talents. Literary critics can and have helped change the course of poetry or fiction, but drama critics, as Shaw, one of the best of them, remarked, find the theatre going on as though they had never spoken.

Drama as an art has never had very much status or cachet in this country, compared with literature when I was young and with films now. When I was coming of age intellectually, beginning to think and write, the drama in America had almost no position in the consciousness of people of sensibility or cultural aspiration. None of my friends or acquaintances went to the theatre, except on very rare occasions, when something like *A Streetcar Named Desire* came along (and then as much for Marlon Brando as for the play), when a British company like Old Vic brought Shakespeare here, or when some obscure troupe or other put on one of the infrequent and invariably inept productions of some contemporary European masterpiece.

Always European. There weren't any American dramatic masterpieces, although a few people I knew thought well of Thornton Wilder and the O'Neill cult was never out of hearing. But to me O'Neill was what you admired when you were eighteen and got over, the way you got over Thomas Wolfe and Romain Rolland. Everything else was Broadway, all those stars of middle-class culture, whose names I had first heard when, at around fifteen, I was discovering the connections between bright lights and power but was not able to separate the two from art or truth: Robert Sherwood, Sidney Kingsley, S. N. Behrman, Maxwell Anderson and the rest.

For there was no real alternative to the highly commercialized and formulary American stage. Off-Broadway didn't come into existence as anything significant until the middle fifties. The Little Theatre movement, which had flourished or at least asserted itself from World War I to the end of the twenties, was by now nothing more than a handful of quirky provincial enterprises. The war had put an end to the spasm of socially oriented and mostly government-sustained activity of the Depression years. And there was no acting in America that could ever have been said to have a life and style of its own.

All this meant, among other things, that if you were interested in drama you pursued that interest by reading plays, regarding the great dramatists, the Greeks, Elizabethans and masters of the modern European tradition beginning with Ibsen (later I was to discover that it had actually begun nearly fifty years earlier with Büchner) as figures in literature to be experienced in rather the same way as you did the great poets and novelists.

But even the so-called contemporary European theatre, the one you could be interested in at any rate, was made up at this time—the late forties—almost wholly of writers long dead: Ibsen, Strindberg, Chekhov, Pirandello. Brecht was only a rumor to me: I had never heard of Ghelderode, I'd read Cocteau's novels but not his plays. Nothing new seemed to be coming out of Europe: the reigning playwrights were Anouilh and Giraudoux, Terence Rattigan and Christopher Fry, all exemplary to me of drama as a now lifeless and so necessarily derivative art.

And then three things happened to me. They occurred with none of the shapely coherence and utter decisiveness that make so many intellectual memoirs suspect, but together they brought about a change in my attitude toward the theatre. The events were, in no particular order that I can remember, that I saw the first production in New York of *Waiting for Godot,* read Eric Bentley's *The Playwright as Thinker* and discovered the Living Theatre.

Beckett's play was and remains the most revelatory and consciousness-changing experience I've ever had in the theatre. I had known his work, along with that of Genet and Ionesco, only through a scattering of comments about them I'd read here and there. When I left the theatre that night in 1954 I took away not only the recognition that I had just witnessed the truest and most beautiful work of imagination of my generation but also a sense of possibility for the theatre as a place of art, of drama as a renewable form, such as I hadn't ever really had.

Bentley's book (which has never received quite the praise I think it deserves) gave me both a historical perspective on the modern theatre and an awareness of its intellectual complexity, as well as introducing me to important European dramatists I hadn't known. And the Living Theatre, which I went to see in its very early days in a loft near Columbia, revealed to me the possibilities of passion, dedication and imagination in acting and production. Their work was often inept or merely idiosyncratic, but they were quite literally the only enterprise in New York where theatre was conceived of as something more than bourgeois ritual.

Still, though my interest in drama grew, I had no special incentive to write about it, except for some passing references in my other work. By the end of the fifties I was writing literary criticism and reviews for various publications, most frequently for *Commonweal.* One evening James Finn, the magazine's literary editor, asked me down for a drink and took me entirely by surprise with the question, Would I like to be their drama critic? I told him, which he of course knew, that I had no background in theatre, had nothing but an amateur prospective on it, and he replied that the editors liked my mind and writing and thought those better qualifications than any sort of presumed expertise.

I began my weekly column in the fall of 1961 with a review (not reprinted here) of some production or other of *The Pirates of Penzance,* and went on writing for *Commonweal* for the next two and a half years, seldom missing a week and going to the theatre on the average of five nights a week. You didn't of course have to review everything, but I was indefatigable in those days.

Within a few months I began to be asked to contribute to other publications, which I did throughout my tenure at *Commonweal,* as well as at *Newsweek,* where I went in 1964. This meant that I was able to write the longer, more complex pieces which regular magazine reviewing ruled out. I wrote on drama, as I say, but also continued to write on fiction and ideas, and later occasionally on films, thereby breaking the law of specialization—drama critics, literary critics, film critics, all in neat boxes—which is a peculiarly American cultural phenomenon. It caused a good deal of mistrust of me in certain powerful circles.

I went to *Newsweek* for two reasons. The more pressing was that I very badly needed money. Unlike the majority of practicing critics, I was not a teacher (the first time I taught was in 1964–65, when I gave the big modern-drama course at Columbia, filling in for Eric Bentley and Robert Brustein, who were both on leave). *Commonweal,* for whom I had also been serving as literary editor, was a marvelous, spiritually generous publication to work for, but like all but a handful of magazines, paid its contributors and critics next to nothing. *Newsweek* of course paid better than I'd imagined anyone would want to. Even so, I hesitated before accepting their offer. What attracted me besides the money was the possibility of having an influence on an immeasurably larger readership and on the American theatre itself: what I feared, with not much originality, was being swallowed up in the vast machine.

My friends, among whom were several drama critics, urged me to take the job, on the ground that for the first time "one of us," someone with standards beyond the commercial, would be writing on drama for a mass magazine. (I remember a party at which Jules Feiffer kept whispering at me behind his hand, "Sell out, boy, sell out.") I finally became convinced that *Newsweek* meant what it said about wanting a serious critic and guaranteeing that there wouldn't be any censorship of or pressure on what I wrote.

There never was any censorship—I might knock eight big musicals in a row and there would be vague grumbling but no admonitory memo—but there was pressure of a subtle kind. I remember once telling a friend, who had asked me what the difference was between writing for *Commonweal* and *News-*

week, that in *Commonweal* I could simply quote Kierkegaard if I wanted to but in *Newsweek* I had to add "the nineteenth-century Danish philosopher." My audience at *Commonweal* had been a hundredth that of *Newsweek's*, but it was highly literate, compact and, most important, identifiable, even though it, too, didn't number the theatre among its salient interests.

Another pressure, the one which finally induced me to leave, wasn't directly *Newsweek's* doing, but simply an element of the situation I inhabited there. Nobody prevented me from being as harsh as I wanted to be about the general run of Broadway presentations, hits and flops alike, and about the inflated reputations of most of its practitioners, but even though I could say what I wanted to I had to say something. It was expected that I "cover" all major plays and theatrical events, the criterion for that being, naturally enough, "size," the money, power and publicity involved.

I found myself, as I think any honest drama critic will always find himself, growing desperate to think of ways of saying new things about unchanging evils or ineptitudes. Almost all Broadway musicals, for example, are bad in approximately the same ways: formula comedy defines in advance the observations you can make about it. And the surprises, the occasions when something original and exciting came along, usually off-Broadway, and toward the end of my work at *Newsweek* increasingly off-off, were simply not frequent enough to make the rest endurable.

More than this, I had had a notion, as I've said, of being able somehow to affect the theatre. Six years of writing criticism and reviews had instructed me in the naïveté of that ambition. The only effect I could discern, apart from the few minds I might have taught to see drama a bit differently, was that I had gained a reputation for being sour, hypercritical, an outsider ranting against the party to which he hasn't been invited.

There isn't anything one can do about such a charge; critics have always been subject to it. Not many people, not many insiders certainly, are going to believe anyone who says that he puts some vision of imagination and truth before anything else: the very words sound strained and self-conscious in our functional age. I had believed from the beginning,

with Shaw and against a writer like Walter Kerr, that the
drama critic owes his loyalty not to the theatre but to dramatic
art. Just because I cared about it I had to keep indicting what
I considered to be its delinquencies.

In any case, these are the reasons I left off being a drama
critic on any regular basis. I parted amicably with *Newsweek*
at the end of the 1966–67 season. I had thought more and
more about teaching, and after having been intimately associated for several years with the Open Theatre and done some
directing for them, about the latter activity, too. My colleague
and friend Robert Brustein had become dean of the Yale
School of Drama the year before, and now he offered me a job
there.

I taught at Stanford that summer, then went to Yale in the
fall. I'm there now, happy with the work and the students and
pleased to be associated with the Yale Repertory Theatre, for
which I directed a production last year, and which I think
is just beginning to come into something personal and organic.
I'm working on several books, and though I write an occasional
essay or review I can't imagine ever going back to drama
criticism as a regular thing.

All this as prologue to the present volume. It contains
everything I think worth preserving, the pieces that might be
of interest to others, from my writings on drama during the
sixties, except for a few essays which appeared in my book
The Confusion of Realms. I don't put it forward as any kind
of complete record of plays and phenomena during the last
decade, for of course it isn't one. It simply constitutes the
record of one man's sensibility, ideas and insights, along with
some anathemas and blessings, in response to what he was
called upon to judge and, less frequently, to explore.

As I read the pieces again I discover certain preoccupa-
tions and motifs. One is with the idea of repertory theatre,
which throughout the decade was at the center of a great
deal of hope and expectation, and if my own experience is
representative, of pretty severe disillusionment. Another is with
the problem of acting, not as a question of skill or its absence
or even of style, but in its role as the very basis, besieged
and problematic, of theatre itself. That the book ends with
the latest essay I've written, a long appreciation of Jerzy

Grotowski, who proposes and exemplifies the most radical overthrow of conventional and conventionally radical notions of acting, strikes me as most fitting, for Grotowski, better than anyone else in the theatre, suggests to me where I am now and want to go.

A final note: The majority of the reviews collected here are, as might be expected, from *Commonweal*, with perhaps a dozen from *Newsweek* and a few from the *New Republic*. The essays are from various publications, as widely separated as *Holiday* and *The Drama Review*. Thanks are due to the editors of all these publications for permisson to reprint.

One more note: I've changed almost nothing in the pieces, although the temptation to correct one's earlier lapses of style and to amend errors in judgment (the ones time points out) is nearly irresistible.

¶ Who Needs Critics?

A few weeks ago the Sunday *New York Times* theatre section carried a combined interview with and personality sketch of Jacques Levy, the director of Bruce Jay Friedman's hot new play, *Scuba Duba*. The piece might easily have been dismissed as a characteristically adolescent amalgam of fanmagazine biographical chatter and its subject's arch, offhand comments about art and life and the like. Yet Levy's peculiar new eminence and some of the things he had to say in the interview seem to me to be representative, as *Scuba Duba* itself is, of a phenomenon of much more than momentary importance, a cultural weather it seems accurate to call now the New Barbarism.

In the course of the article Levy laid down his principle of directorial procedure, in this play at least, which turned out to be a refusal to rely on any principle at all. The clearest point he made was that he did what he felt like, he did his "thing," to keep our terminology up-to-the-minute. In elaboration of this he cited the appearance of a female character with bare, dramaturgically irrelevant breasts, saying that he "just felt it ought to be that way." And he then went on to remark that he found "awfully funny" my own view (*The New Republic,* October 28, 1967) that the whole play and the production were pointless and tasteless since, he said, I obviously meant that it ought to have been "pointed and tasteful."

Now pointed is not the opposite of pointless, nor is tasteful the opposite of tasteless. *With point,* some kind of point—conscious illogicality, arbitrariness deliberately shaped, chance as a principle if that is what you want—is the opposite of pointless; and *with taste,* some kind of taste—bad taste as a weapon perhaps, inverted taste, revolutionary taste, but with some kind of aesthetic pressure applied—is the opposite of tasteless. What Levy was trying to do was confine me in some outworn, morally oriented critical position (I ordinarily get it from the other side: an inhumanist, an admirer of form without content, I'm mostly called) at the same time as he enlisted himself under the banner of a new and splendid freedom. But I am no more interested in having plays be pointed and tasteful, or having novels or paintings be for that matter, than he is; I am interested in art, however, and off *Scuba Duba* at any rate I suspect that Levy is interested in faking it.

For *Scuba Duba* is an ersatz play, a shopping-bag of attitudes and awarenesses plucked from others' shelves, not an act of freedom or a revolutionary move into a dimension that transcends previous categories of taste. If it were that, if it were an imaginative act on the order of certain new paintings or fiction of the type of Beckett's, or, to go back to drama, of some flawed but newly felt and conceived plays of the off-off-Broadway theatre, the kind of direction Levy gave to it might be justified, or at least its vulgarities might have felt less sophomoric and exploitive of a naïve audience's desire for titillation at the expense of experience. As it is, all the energy of Friedman's play is derived energy, all its structure is jerry-built, its whole imagination is tuned to the accessible, the comfortably outrageous, the predictably shocking.

This bad play might conceivably have been the occasion for a director to have used its badness deliberately, constructing a work, like certain pieces of camp or pop, which proclaim that their subjects' value lies precisely in their being available for art, like anything else, not in any intrinsic beauty or significance. He might, in other words, have used Friedman's text the way Lichtenstein uses comic strips. Levy half implies that he has in fact done this when he remarks that "content is the window dressing and style is what counts." I would prefer to put it this way: style, or form, is what any artistic work is about, content is what can be paraphrased from it. But the point here, the trouble with Levy's argument in this case, is that his directorial style, his imposition of a form on Friedman's script, is of a piece with the text, as derivative, debased and pseudo-sophisticated as it is.

What emerges most clearly from the *Times* piece is that

Levy doesn't want to be judged (who does?) and that his way of protecting himself is to declare all judgment irrelevant. I do what I feel like, I do my thing. It is in response to this that the whole question of criticism, its uses and justifications and even more its potential life, rises up. For the condition of art today, in which everybody is doing his thing, is such that criticism is in danger of finding itself without a subject, without, that is to say, a subject whose nature can define criticism's own being and purpose. Art on many fronts has moved past the old definitions and categories, leaving most criticism practicing in an abandoned house. In this way critics go on talking about tactile and compositional values in painting when painting is concerned with something else, or about character and plot in novels when the most interesting writing is doing other work.

"A new form," Alain Robbe-Grillet has written, "always seems to be more or less an absence of any form at all, since it is unconsciously judged by reference to consecrated forms." But that is just where the critic must start about his true business, which is to be conscious, to be, along with the artist and from another angle than his, by necessity the man conscious of new forms. And to be conscious of them, to know that they are there, with all their surprises, difficulties, precariousness and potential influence, so that they must be announced, clarified and protected, is what gives the critic his chief pleasure. There is a new freedom in art today, actually a renewed freedom such as art always wins for itself—and from itself—and the critic cannot be any less free than that.

As art changes, as it becomes less and less involved with directly humanistic concerns—the best new painting, the best new writing tell us nothing about how to live or even how to feel, but are constructions alternative to the ways we live and feel and thus sources of new pleasure—criticism has to change its bases, to move out of its own humanistic concerns. This doesn't mean that it is to be less *human,* but only less programmatic, for humanism in its historical career is and has been a program, not a strongbox of indissoluble values.

Less than ten years ago Alfred Kazin wrote an essay called

"The Function of Criticism Today," in which he argued most eloquently for the traditional role of criticism, which he saw imperiled. The tradition was that of *histoire morale,* it was concerned "explicitly, fightingly, with an ideal of man, with a conception of what man is seeking to become, with what he must become." And such criticism, Kazin argued, was coherent with literature's "classic functions of providing ideas central to social policy and moral behavior."

Yet if literature (or any art) is no longer doing that (if indeed it was ever its chief function) what kind of ideas and values can criticism concern itself with? It can, and has to, concern itself with the practice of the arts as *they* unfold: and this is the point at which I come back to Jacques Levy and the New Barbarism. Out of the shifts in art, the opening to change and the abandonment of previous bases, the technical revolutions which are at the same time moral ones, true works arise—newly true, not validated by "consecrated" criteria— but also novels, films, "events," plays like *Scuba Duba* and directorial acts like Levy's which are the simulacra of authentic works and get their borrowed life accepted because scandal and posture have become almost indistinguishable from true stances.

Jostling for attention with their "zaniness," and lack of principle, their mindlessness, their claim to be moral liberations because overtly sexual ones, their ugliness passing itself off as verve and their self-indulgence stepping out as expanded consciousness, such works hugely muddy up the terrain and make authentic art difficult to see. One of the tasks of criticism today is to distinguish them, to make distinctions between new forms and the lack of form, to adopt as a watchword the principle Coleridge laid down when he wrote that "every reform, however necessary, will by weak minds be carried to an excess, which will itself need reforming." The New Barbarism is one manifestation of Coleridge's "excess." For the critic today the job, as never before, is to keep excess seen as excess, as imposture and fraud, a task which is the unpleasant correlative of his major work of recognizing and elucidating the not yet consecrated. (1967)

¶ What Keeps Us Going

This is the time of year for recapitulation, but since in the present age of the theatre one season's summary is entirely interchangeable with another's, there is very little point in making one. From year to year the same sickness works at the root of everything, the same incompetence, vulgarity, pretension, mendacity and cowardice are on exhibit; and the same few exceptions keep us from giving up in absolute despair. That is to say, the same kinds of exceptions every year: plays or spectacles which against the tide and in crafty isolation—or fortuitous centrality, the "hit" that turns out to be art—possess their souls and are given adequate bodies to contain them.

Do we really have to say once again that the theatre is only alive today when it is being brash, irreverent (or imaginatively reverent), disturbing, antic, dangerous and even cruel? When it introduces cracks in the glacier of our public images and private fantasies? When it manages to leave off being a rear-view mirror? When it fills the air with rain, hailstones and flying objects instead of with fog or weak sunshine? It seems that we do have to keep saying it, over and over; saying it, telling the truth about the theatre's shame and boredom and death is very nearly the central activity and radical justification for a journalist-critic of drama in our time.

No doubt there are certain critics who enjoy being employed in this way, who like playing at policeman, internist or Jeremiah, holding the hand palm out, analyzing tumors, uttering "No!" in thunder forever, secure in the knowledge that there is never going to be a shortage of objects to thunder at, having only to keep their voices in good fighting trim. Well, it would really not be bearable, lacking this sort of temperament, unless one saw the profession, as some of us continue to do, as a service to one's public, whatever that is; a public which cannot know the truth unaided but which knows as well as oneself what to do with it when it is made clear. Even more sustaining, we see it, in all modesty, as a service to dramatic art, to the preservation of a hope for culture through the preservation of standards; resistance to the gross and the deceitful at least holds the way open for the shapely and the true.

And yet, even so, it would not be endurable to be a drama critic in these days if it were not for the exceptions, the accidents, sudden, unaccountable, miraculous in their power to renew hope and restore perspective. There seems to be a fixed number of them every season, no more than four or five, as though hope were meant to exist within a narrow, unchanging strip of territory, a running track around the central reservoir of theatrical staleness, lies and corrupt gestures. These accidents, these triumphs within a climate of defeat, are what make us able to go on. (1963)

¶Being a Critic

My dictionary defines a critic first as "a person skilled in judging the qualities or merits of some class of things, esp. of literary or artistic works," and then as "one who judges captiously or with severity; one who censures or finds fault." If I sometimes feel that I am swallowed up in the second definition more completely than in the first, I am comforted by the knowledge that for a drama critic of reasonable integrity there is simply no way of behaving more agreeably today. If anything, you have all you can do to keep from some act of total misanthropy, from letting your disgust at the continual degradation of the theatre's possibilities turn you into a machine that can only mutter no, no, no, forever.

If occasionally we still say yes, it is because sometimes in the suburbs of this moribund city of the theatre, more rarely in its center, something living is to be seen. Off-Broadway, for all its clumsiness, bungled opportunities and decrepit attire, and despite the paradox that it is at the same time rapidly acquiring some of the higher-level vices of its parent, still offers us most of what is vital and true on our stages. The lines it keeps open stretch back to the past and forward to whatever future there is for drama. Barring the Old Vic or a similar company, you won't see a single revival on Broadway this season, nor will you see anything revolutionary and unprecedented, unless, like *The Caretaker* it happens to possess ancillary qualities of a negotiable kind—obvious humor, an aura of easy profundity, or a queerness that can be read as sublimity.

What this situation means to the writer of periodical opinion on the drama, if not so much to the sequestered critic with the long view out his window, is that his task is complicated by psychological and social pressures of considerable weight. At best, his work is more difficult than that of the commentator on literature or painting, since he is involved, to an extent they are not, in a complex event unfolding immediately before and around him, full of vagaries, imponderables, adventitious facts and physical ambushes. But with a theatre that lies more than it tells the truth and that offends more than it pleases, how is he to bring the necessary steadfastness to the exercise of his judgment?

For most of us are unhappy in the role of Jeremiah; we would much rather sing a new song. And what this leads to is a relaxation of critical standards, greatest among the daily reviewers—where indeed there exist only the most infirm standards to relax—but to be met with in more serious quarters. We become oppressed by the negations we make, finding ourselves in the position of men who can never hold their peace at weddings. That the bride and groom are clearly not made for each other becomes at some point an intolerable observation to have to make, and we seize upon any chance to let the ceremony take place. One or two acceptable qualities, something plausible or inoffensive, and we join in the congratulations.

My review of *The Caretaker* was an example, if not of indulgence of mediocrity, then of too much praise for what is really only an interesting movement toward a revivified drama of essences and fundamentals. The animadversions I did make concerned the play's eclecticism and failure to maintain a consistent style; but what limits it more seriously is its lack of solid artifacts, its refusal of physicality at the same time as its adventures in language are not stringent enough. Samuel Beckett can get away with static situations because of his residence in a new country of the spoken word and his investment of *in-action* with ironic meanings; but Harold Pinter is not yet at these levels.

A Man for All Seasons is the other occasion upon which my weariness with a stance of opposition got the better of me. On reflection the play seems to me thin and attenuated, impelled by a conventional urgency, however laudable, and circumscribed by a dramatic imagination which will not risk breaking new ground. In this case, what led me astray was the seductiveness of Paul Scofield's performance. We are constantly in danger of forgetting that the play's the thing, in the face of acting as inventive and intelligent as Scofield's. And though such performances have of course their own beauty and justification, in witnessing them we are at best in the presence of only one element of the drama's total life, raised in cases such as this to a compensatory function. (1961)

¶ The Necessity for Destructive Criticism

It was George Jean Nathan who in an uncharacteristic moment of despair observed that drama criticism was probably the most useless activity in the world. Play *reviewing* obviously does have an effect, although almost never of an intellectual or aesthetic kind, but the criticism of drama seems to drop into the most soundless of voids. The journalist-critic writes his pieces—reasoning, cajoling, making analyses, presenting visions—and the machinery of the theatre grinds on in its heavy, automatic, self-perpetuating dream. Broadway listens only to its own voice or to those voices from outside which tell it what it wants to hear. And criticism is the one thing it has never wanted to hear.

And yet if asked, Broadway, represented nowadays by at least one negotiator who has gone to Harvard and who exhibits the weary patient smile of someone who has been through all the sociologies of taste and heard all the exhortations from Copeau and Artaud and Barrault, who knows the value or at least the price of Brecht and the maximum titillating power of Ionesco or Beckett, would more than likely reply that it certainly is willing to listen to criticism, only *constructive* criticism, if you please and if you are capable of providing it.

To which the critic, that horn-rimmed, golden-goose-killing neurotic, that Kropotkin of the weekly or monthly or quarterly press, can only retort that he doesn't please and isn't capable, for the simple reason that there is no such thing as constructive criticism, in drama or any other art, the virulent illusion that there is, or should be, being one of the chief reasons why the contemporary stage seems so entirely beyond redemption.

Some years ago Niccolo Tucci published a brilliant essay dealing with the fallacies and deceitfulness inherent in the notion of constructive criticism. His piece was about politics, specifically about the right and obligation of the citizen to call his government on the carpet for its derelictions or wicked acts, without necessarily having alternatives to put forward or anything positive to say. But his central point—that the people who insist that criticism be constructive are invariably asking that it be kind, indulgent, boneless and corroborative, that it not be criticism at all—was and remains pertinent to areas far beyond politics.

I want now to examine the implications for drama of Tucci's idea, and along the way to look into the relations of the theatre with those persons whose profession, or trade, it is to comment upon what happens on our stages. We may discover that what is "constructive" in the lexicon of the theatre had indeed no real existence, while the so-called "destructive" element works, oddly enough, as a source of light.

Before proceeding, I want to repeat a distinction I shall employ from now on, that between reviewers and critics. Snobbish, if you will, indecorous, probably quixotic. But it seems to me that we are never going to get out of the miasma of deceit, self-pity and wishful thinking that rises from the theatre in this country as it does from no other medium, unless we begin to accept those distinctions that operate in actuality—in our case between actors and stars, dramas and hits, art and artisanship—and critics and reviewers.

Perhaps the greatest irony in a situation bursting with ironies is the reiterated idea that the critics are killing the theatre. Now we all know that when theatre people or the public refer to the "critics" they almost always mean the New York reviewers. It is certainly true that the critics, those persons whom the dictionary describes as "skilled in judging the qualities or merits of some class of things, esp. of literary or artistic work," have long harbored murderous thoughts about the condition of our drama, but their ineffectuality as public executioners is legendary. The reviewers, on the other hand, come close to being the most loyal and effective allies the commercial theatre could possibly desire. But not close enough, it would seem—the thing constitutes a case of an absolute desire encountering a relative compliance.

As a corollary of its demand for constructive criticism the theatre insists on absolute loyalty, and clearly receives a very high degree of it from the reviewers, who are all "theatre-lovers" to one or another flaming extent. And that brings us to our second irony. For "loyalty in a critic," Bernard Shaw wrote, "is corruption." This richly disturbing remark comes near the heart of so much that is wrong in the relationship between the stage and those who write about it from seats of power or seats of romantic yearning. From the true critic the theatre generally gets what can only be interpreted as gross infidelity, the reason being, as Shaw and every other major observer of drama makes abundantly clear, and as our own sense of what is civilized should tell us, that the critic cannot give his loyalty to men and institutions since he owes it to something a great deal more permanent.

He owes it, of course, to truth and to dramatic art. Once he sacrifices truth to men or art to institutions he is corrupt, un-less, as is so frequently the case, he has never had any capacity for determining truth or any knowledge of dramatic art; for such men, corruption is clearly too grandiose a condition. But at least some of the reviewers are men of ordinarily developed taste and some intellectual maturity, and it is among them that corruption, in the sense not of venality or outright malfeasance but of the abandonment of a higher to a lower good, operates continually and in the name of that very loyalty which is worn like a badge of honor.

In "reviewerese," that peculiar language in which seven words—haunting, striking, gripping, charming, powerful, stunning and refreshing—do the heaviest duty, and in whose Golden Treasury the line "Momma, momma, momma, what a good solid show!" represents the ultimate in lyrical expression, the vapidity and perversion of values is spread out daily for all of us to see. But seldom has the dishonesty of popular stage reporting been so openly revealed and even trumpeted as it was by Walter Kerr, who is beyond question a critic fallen among reviewers, a man of wit, taste and useful ideas, whenever, that is to say, he is not busy sending telegrams to his mother.

With only the slightest indication that he was at all troubled by the matter, Mr. Kerr told a television audience that he felt he simply had to juice up his favorable notices, so that a mediocre work would come out entertaining, a passable one superior and a good one superlative. The reason was that if his language invariably matched his perceptions his readers, who were also of course potential theatregoers, would scarcely ever be encouraged to buy tickets.

Mr. Kerr left no doubt that he practiced what the naïve among us can only regard as a piece of high-level chicanery because of his passionate interest in the survival of the theatre. Such exclusive and truth-despoiling devotion is familiar to us in other areas, in advertising, for example ("my sometimes flagging faith that a dramatic critic is the servant of a high art, and not a mere advertiser of entertainments"—G.B.S.), or professional patriotism. We are forever coming up against this rationalization: if you want the theatre to survive, you have to lie on its behalf, you have to play the game, the name of which is "My-Theatre-Right-or-Wrong." How astonishing it is that the producers seem not to be aware that it is being played.

The truth is that their grievance against the reviewers stems from the fact that the game is not played as strictly as they would like. The reviewers do have standards, debased and flexible as they are, whereas the producers, with very few exceptions, have none, or at least none that are reliable. The result is that whereas each producer desires only that his particular offering be accepted and endorsed, the reviewers, some of whom may have to turn themselves into knots to do it, continue to judge plays and spectacles according to certain standards of professionalism, minimal criteria of humor, excitement, display, and quite shrewdly arrived-at norms of public acceptability and potential popularity (editors, Max Beerbohm wrote, "mostly engage for the criticism of plays men whose opinions coincide as nearly as possible with those of the public").

A double or elastic standard is better than nothing, which would seem to establish the public's debt to the newspapers for that much if nothing more. But the producers are also in the reviewers' debt, for without the latter's insistence that Broadway be Broadway, that it continue to serve, that is to say, a normative and exceedingly slowly changing idea of entertainment and popular enlightenment, the commercial stage would quickly enough degenerate into a condition of utter capriciousness, a flux in whose wash and roll the potential audience would find itself entirely without bearings and imposed on from every side.

What is much worse, from the managerial point of view, is that the sufferings and bewilderment of an audience from whom all guidelines have been snatched away, would eventually be translated into renunciation and flight. Just as its literary counterpart, the clientele of Womrath's, would largely give up reading if best-seller lists were to stop appearing, the Broadway audience, deprived of its caveats and assurances, its Hits, Smashes and Bombs, would give up going to the theatre rather than face the terrors of unpredictable experience and unheard-of sights. It would not be a question of merit: what is too good is surely as alarming as what is bad.

In fact, that is the point about the reviewers, that they exist, consciously or not, to keep Broadway functioning within staked-out grounds. They preserve it as the arena for theatrical enterprises which may neither rise above an upper limit determined by a line stretching between the imaginations of Lillian Hellman, William Inge and Richard Rodgers, nor beneath a lower one marked out by the inventiveness and sense of life of Norman Krasna, Harry Kurnitz and Garson Kanin. Whatever creeps into the spaces North or South of this Central Park of the imagination is adventitious, arbitrary, hermetic; if it is good, if it is art, if it is *Waiting for Godot,* its presence on the Street may confidently be ascribed to someone's idea of a joke that just might pay off.

Outside the theatre's hothouse, not part of its clubbiness, its opening-night ceremonies or its cabalisms, unconsulted about the honors it awards itself, and owing no more devotion to it than the literary critic owes to publishers or the art critic to galleries, the serious critic of drama is left free—to do what? To judge. "There is one and only one justification for the trade of drama criticism," Nathan wrote, "and that is to criticize drama and not merely apologize for it." And Shaw went further: "A critic is most certainly not in the position of a co-respondent in a divorce case: he is in no way bound to perjure himself to shield the reputation of the profession he criticizes. Far from being the instigator of its crimes and the partner of its guilty joys, he is the policeman of dramatic art; and it is his express business to denounce its delinquencies."

It is this idea of the critic as policeman that infuriates theatre people to the limit of their anarchistic temperaments. Their anger, as I have pointed out, is wrongly directed against the reviewers, who although they possess almost limitless powers of life and death are the Keystone Cops of the profession, whereas the critics, the FBI whose penal code is immeasurably severer and more uncompromising, possess almost no means of making their indictments stick.

Still, that may be a temporary matter. For there is a type of theatre person who senses that when the last shekel is in and the last platitude echoed, it will be the weekly and monthly critics, the best among them at any rate, who will have the last word, as Shaw wrote that posterity would remember the plays and performers of his time as *he*, and not the newspapers, evaluated them.

In whose pantheon now is Miss Hope Booth, "a young lady who cannot sing, act, dance or speak, but whose appearance suggests that she might profitably spend three or four years in learning these arts, which are useful on the stage"? And in which of our playhouses are the revivals of Sydney Grundy, Jerome K. Jerome and Arthur Wing Pinero, those manipulators of "dead machinery" who were the Inge, Schary and Chayefsky of their day? The nature of Shaw's "constructive" criticism was that it helped build tombs for all the lifeless drama of his time and thereby cleared the ground for something better.

Go through the three volumes of Shaw's criticism, cover-

ing as many London seasons, and you will find that not once
in fifteen or twenty times was he anything but indignant at
what he was called upon to see. Without pity he excoriated
the theatre of the nineties, which sounds so much like our
own, with its "dull routine of boom, bankruptcy and boredom," its performers' "eternal clamor for really artistic work
and their ignominious collapse when they are taken at their
word by Ibsen or anyone else," its lugubrious spectacle of "the
drama losing its hold on life." It was only when once or twice
a year something came along that did have a hold on life that
Shaw's critiques turned enthusiastic and positive. But not
"constructive"; you do not patronize or act generously toward
artistic accomplishment—you identify it.

For if the critic is not the maker of dramatic art, he is the
man most able to say what it is, and at the same time to establish the conditions in which it may flourish or at least gain a
foothold. By being negative, *destructive,* if you please, toward
everything else, he can help it outride the ephemera of
"smash" and "riot" and "socko." And he will do his champion-
ing nearly always in the teeth of the coiners of those inimitable descriptive terms. To the handful of great journalist-
critics the English-speaking stage has had—Shaw, Beerbohm,
Nathan (for all his crotchets and his Francophobia), Stark
Young and Eric Bentley—we owe most of our knowledge of
the permanent drama of our time, and in most cases we owe
even the opportunity to see or read it.

When the London reviewers were doing their best to drive
Ibsen back to the depraved Continent (*Ghosts* was "unutterably offensive," "revoltingly suggestive and blasphemous," "a
dirty act done publicly") it was Shaw, along with William
Archer, who fought brilliantly and implacably to keep open
the door to a resurrected drama. Later Nathan helped O'Neill
past the roadblock of those newspapermen who characteristically admired his "power" while being terrified of his thematic
and technical innovations. And more recently the truly heroic
work of Eric Bentley, both in introducing us to the most vital
contemporary and nineteenth-century European plays and in
promulgating standards for a potentially mature American

theatre, is a monument to the critical spirit at its untiring best.

Beerbohm once described what that critical spirit, which in relation to the stage seems never to be incarnate in more than three or four journalists at the same time, is perennially up against in its efforts to keep dramatic art alive. "My colleagues," he wrote, "have, for the most part, a primitive mistrust of strangers. They do not say, 'Here is new blood. Let us help it to circulate,' but, 'Here is new blood. Let us throw cold water on it.'"

Plus ça change . . . We know what it has been like trying to get our own new blood to circulate. The xenophobic response to the only interesting and significant works of the past fifteen years, the wretched, dismal inability even to begin to understand that a change is coming over some of the primary notions of drama as art, so that the stage may at least be enabled to catch up with painting and music and the movies—the whole depressing history is available to anyone who wants to spend a few hours in the newspaper branch of the New York Public Library.

Yet in reality it is not as depressing as it might have been, since it is relieved by one of those glorious streaks of irony which make the history and sociology of popular culture so much more entertaining than its products. The truth is that things do change; it is only the various kinds of spirit which remain the same. Thus the reviewers and the Broadway intelligentsia (the people who admire *J.B.* and keep one eye Off-Broadway for trends and applaud experiment whenever it is nonexperimental) have been considerably more open to the new drama than were Shaw's and Beerbohm's contemporaries to Ibsen and Hauptmann and Shaw himself. We may be forgiven for thinking it would have been a cleaner thing all round if they had remained closed.

After years of not getting Ionesco they discover him in *Rhinoceros*, his least characteristic and probably worst play. They recognize something in Beckett, but chiefly when Bert Lahr is around using his splendid talents to turn the piece into vaudeville; by now, having never understood him, they find Beckett old hat and yawn through all his newer plays. They haven't the faintest notion of what *The Blacks* is about, but extol its "theatricality" and ritualisms the way they would a Senegalese rain dance.

Having turned purple at *The Connection* and then been advised that it is the most interesting new work by an American in years, a number of them greet *The Apple,* an outstanding example of second-year jinx, with vastly increased respect. And they raise to demi-godhood the author of *Oh Dad,* and thereby demonstrate once again that to the eye of the freshman the sophomore is a dazzling sight.

But everything new, whether or not it is good and whether or not, if it is good, it is understood, is at the periphery. At the center the manufacturing and packaging of the familiar goes on, taking up most of everybody's time, including the critics, who have to come on the scene on second nights and prepare to undo, for their own readers and perhaps for posterity, what the reviewers have accomplished that morning. It may be the necessity of pointing out that *Gideon* serves a conformist idea of nonconformity and is full of spurious philosophy and neighborhood metaphysics. Or that *A Gift of Time* isn't merely "somewhat lacking in tension" but entirely ugly, with the ugliness that comes from substituting at every point the contrived and the debased for the living imagination.

Each season has its *No Strings,* the occasion on which the naked emperor is hailed as being most magnificently clothed, where the synthetic, the factitious, the false and the deracinated converge to form an exemplary reminder of the commercial theatre's flight from art and life *and* entertainment, if that was what you had modestly been looking for. (The fantastic dishonesty with which the racial theme is handled, and the consequent singling out of that very element for special praise, make for one of the best possible commentaries on our current situation; we are truly up to 1984 in the theatre, or a little beyond.)

Every season also has its tides of sycophancy on which float the reputations of certain star performers and against which the critic may want to throw himself as a minor counter-current, so that Jason Robards, Jr., and Maurice Evans and Barbara Bel Geddes will not think that the seas are all that smooth. Or, turning around, he may want to say a word, if not of praise then of comfort, for the kind of inept but unpretentious Off-Broadway effort upon which the newspapers habitually unload all the scorn and vituperation which their pusillanimity or thralldom prevents them from delivering to those big houses on the Street which can seat five or six times as many of the bilked.

Well, who cares? Who is listening? Already the new season is upon us, the posters are up, the excitement and renewed hope and smell of possible success are in the air. The forecasts and previews are in the Sunday sections. We see that Willard Flange's new play, *The Tongue at the Roof of the Mouth,* described as a "study of backbiting in a Nebraska town," will be the first major work to open. Lillabet Paradise has written a drama based on the life of Jessica Dragonette, and it will star Frieda Zeitz-Kochmann, who has been enticed from retirement. Three musicals adapted from *The Origin of Species* will open within four days of one another.

The Leopoldville Art Theatre will be at the City Center with entirely revamped stagings of the classic Congolese repertoire. Harold Frond's Bjornson cycle resumes at the Sixth Street with the seventeenth offering in the series. A boxing match between a three-year-old spastic and his father's common-law wife will be the highlight of *You Got It, You Keep It,* the much-heralded new comedy by Alec and Bill and Frannie and Hobart and Pru Turnbull, which is being directed by Zoltan and Imre and Miklos and Istvan Chardash, with sets by Hammacher and Jim and Schlemmer Hotley. And Saratoga Wilson reports that there isn't a single mean or depraved character in his new work, scheduled for the same theatre as the long-awaited musical based on the life of . . .

We will recover. The committees will name the prize winners, the producers will issue a statement saying that the critics are certainly going to kill the theatre, which could survive even them if only the entertainment tax would be lifted. A noted director will write an article allowing as how all the theatre needs is a few old-fashioned hits, and another will write one denouncing people who forget that the business of the theatre is entertainment. Three reviewers will call it the best season in seven years, three will call it the worst in eight.

And the critic, to whom seasons are the least of considerations, will recover himself in silence, cultivating his sorrow, his anger and his narrow hope. And keeping his powder dry. (1962)

¶ The Absurd and the Foolish

If we are going to continue talking about the Theatre of the Absurd, it might be a good idea to decide what we mean by the term. Richard Barr and Clinton Wilder, for example, were well-intentioned enough when they announced a series of plays under that awning at the Cherry Lane; the trouble was that scarcely half the works they presented qualified as in any sense "absurd," the others being merely unfamiliar, or vaguely experimental, or extreme in one way or another. Genet's *Deathwatch* is not an absurdist work, nor, strictly speaking, are Albee's *The Zoo Story* and *The Sandbox* (though *The American Dream* does get in under the wire).

Beckett's *Endgame* and Ionesco's *The Killer* are of course central achievements of the movement—movement of the recent imagination, let us say right here, not a marching society of like-minded dramatists—while Arrabal's *Picnic on the Battlefield* is a minor and not very successful product of the second or third wave, and Kenneth Koch's *Bertha* is a tiny, very amusing, offbeat but *sui generis* piece which to call "absurd" doesn't hurt but doesn't help much either.

The reason for this motley is hardly occult. It lies essentially in our ineradicable need for categorization—that process of inversion by which names, or labels, are called upon to cordon off and give actuality to objects and qualities, instead of taking their life from them, and that condition of cultural cowardice in which we debar the new and unexpected in the interests of safety or aggression, seeking habitations or delineated enemies. "I don't buy those absurdist plays," someone will say and thereby put under interdict anything beyond *The Miracle Worker*. Or else, "I'm dotty about the absurd," which means that the speaker is going to find himself in the kitchen with every lucubrator of the merely illogical or non-narrative and every head counselor of theatrical camping.

Now, if we go on using "Theatre of the Absurd," the primary justification is one of convenience, but we should keep in mind that its exemplars are only loosely united, as much by what they assert or bring forth as by what they oppose or depart from. Beckett and Ionesco are nearly as unlike as Ibsen and Chekhov, who have been similarly lumped together for their creation of a drama of new intentions and procedures. What we may safely say is that for a play to be absurdist it must, minimally, exhibit the overthrow of naturalism, the abandonment of straightforward narrative, a lack of interest in psychology and an abstract or fragmented conception of character.

Beyond that—and this is what makes it possible to distinguish the men from the boys, or the absurd from the merely foolish—there are certain positive characteristics of this kind of drama. Briefly, they include a pressure of literature and of intellectual history behind a work (a play like *The Apple* seems to have been written by an illiterate, albeit an energetic one), a pressure of ideas behind the language and a fusion of language and action in which neither is simply illustrative of the other but where speech constitutes an "action" in itself and actions are extensions of speech. And finally, there must be a sense that experience is not reducible to our formulas, resists our logic and patterns of conscious meaning, will not divide neatly into comic and tragic, or light and heavy, and is, in short, absurd in a metaphysical and not just a behavioral sense.

To return to the productions at the Cherry Lane. I didn't see them all, but the ones I did see displayed the weaknesses and inadequacies we might have expected from so jerry-built and indiscriminate an enterprise. The range was from passable to catastrophic. *Endgame* ranks near *Godot* in the Beckett canon, but the Cherry Lane offering was so badly done that I had to hold fast to my memory of the published play in order to endure it. The chief handicap was Ben Piazza in the role of Clov. Mr. Piazza always turns up in absurdist plays, but I wish he would go in for *Dr. Kildare* or *Gunsmoke,* since his granitic deadness of speech and total catalepsy of movement have maimed or murdered everything I have seen him in. Apart from that, I am not a fan of Sudie Bond and I didn't think Alan Schneider's direction was nearly as imaginative or taut as it could have been.

The Killer came off better. It is curious that in Europe this play is generally considered Ionesco's masterpiece, while here it has met with irritation and a peculiar condescension. I saw it described by one of our best critics as "tedious"—which is a matter of taste—and by a lesser one as having for its subject the existence of evil even in innocence—which is a matter of complete misconception. It is "about" the fact of death, the absurdity which death introduces into our days and also about the ruinous failure of our humanist ideologies to cope with it. In any case, the production wasn't too bad; the cuts seemed mostly useful, the pace was lively, and Brandon Maggart played Bérenger without much vocal distinction but with a country-cousin innocence and Jimmy Savo-like ebullience that were diverting and appropriate.

The Cherry Lane's program is over, but if you want to see a purportedly absurd work that is really a rather foolish one and thus exemplifies some of what I have been saying, *Oh Dad, Poor Dad, Mamma's Hung You in the Closet and I'm Feeling So Bad* promises to run for a long time. Arthur Kopit's play does have its engaging moments, but they are more a matter of performances and décor than of any intrinsic excellence. Jerome Robbins, in his debut as a theatre director, has staged the work with éclat and inventiveness, and some knowledgeable and skillful actors are in sight, notably Barbara Harris, a comedienne of vast resources and stirring madness.

But Mr. Kopit has of course written no more than a superb example of college humor, wherein the grotesque serves for the witty and the titillating for the revelatory. The comedy is almost exclusively physical and depends on extravagance—a pet piranha and tenderly nursed Venus's flytrap plants, a corpse in the bedroom—since verbally it has almost no existence at all, unless you consider this funny: "A Turkish Piastre, 1876, good year for Piastres"; or this: "Twelve months later [than the night of his conception] my son was born." There is no sense of ideas at work and there is assuredly nothing metaphysical, and nothing mysterious in this play which we might describe as the theatre of the absurd filtered through Harvard, Madison Avenue, a reading of certain European *farceurs* and maybe a few fond memories of the early Marx Brothers' films.

Apropos of the current tendency to confuse capers with creative imagination and misanthropy with aesthetic daring, there is this remark of Ionesco which *Oh Dad*'s author and admirers might reflect upon. "What is comical is the unusual in its pure state; nothing seems more surprising to me than that which is banal; the surreal is here, within grasp of our hands, in our everyday conversation." There is really no need to go so far afield if you want to effect a revolution in the drama. (1962)

¶ A Note on Ennoblement

Time magazine recently had its say about the Theatre of the Absurd. The playwrights of the absurdist school, *Time's* nameless writer said, after bestowing some faint left-handed praise (the key honorific was "theatricality"—a word used by critics who may not either enjoy or understand but are aware that something lively is going on), are ultimately failures because they do not do what playwrights are supposed to do. That is to say, they fail technically because they disobey the laws of drama and morally because they do not "ennoble" us.

There isn't much one can say about the first part of the indictment, except that the charge has been made against every original dramatist since the theatre began (its counterpart having perennially been used to try to put down new movements in all the other arts) and that people who insist on plays obeying the "laws of drama"are hopelessly unable to tell true drama when it appears. Actually, it isn't too much to claim that every significant play, as every significant painting, poem or piece of music, breaks "laws" as an essential aspect of its creation. But of course what it is breaking are not laws at all, but precedents.

The second accusation, that of the failure to ennoble man, is more difficult to combat, though no less pitiful a revelation of the bourgeois mind: in Berdyaev's sense, a mind encased in rules and materiality, with a skin of radical sentimentality. For what are we to say to people who crave *to be* ennobled, by art or anything else? Did the Greeks attend their tragedies in order to have nobility served up, for reassurance? Or did they attend as participants in a celebration and ritual unfolding of an action which was noble *in itself,* and precisely because it dealt courageously with ignoble matters, painful matters, terrifying and shameful ones?

What the anonymous *Time* writer and the millions he presumably speaks for really want is to be told that man is good, wise, enduring, loving, reliable, predictable, profound, clean and dignified, above all dignified. As though Oedipus was dignified, with his bloody eyesockets and his hideous memories!

"Positively abominable play . . . infecting the modern theatre with poison . . . a dirty act done publicly . . . Offensive cynicism . . . Melancholy and malodorous world . . . Mass of vulgarity, egotism, coarseness and absurdity . . . Unutterably offensive . . . Scandalous . . . Revoltingly suggestive and blasphemous . . . Morbid, unhealthy, unwholesome and disgusting . . . A piece to bring the stage into disrepute and dishonor . . . A wicked nightmare . . . As foul and filthy a concoction as has ever been allowed to disgrace the boards. . . ."

The Balcony? Happy Days? The Connection? No, *Ghosts,* after its first London production in 1891. Doubtless a similar compilation could be made from the Paris newspapers of 1830, after Hugo's *Hernani,* or of 1896, when *Ubu Roi* made its devastating appearance. " 'Indecent' is too often a synonym for human," Mauriac has written; and the history of efforts to make the stage more human, to sweep away the platitudes, frozen responses and lifeless gestures of a theatre bent on repetition and the maintenance of self-satisfaction, is that of a series of outcries, predictable, instinctive, filled with that inverted shame and strange violence we see in men whose illusions have been threatened.

And always the chief illusion is that things are basically well, that the beast has been tamed and man is in the saddle, that we get what we deserve and deserve what we get, that reverses are reversible, that we understand (although better by and by), that virtue triumphs and love conquers all. But we're not sure, so tell us again.

A child being comforted against the dark. But it happens that we are right to be frightened of that darkness. Contemporary man has known almost no light at all, and if contemporary man, like man of any other era, is noble, it is to the extent to which he faces the darkness, moves into it and keeps his eyes open. And this is true whether he is a religious man or not. What is true in any case is that if we are noble we do not need to be told about it, and if we aren't we cannot be made so by being told about it.

But of course the bourgeois theatre, the theatre of *Theatre Arts, Time* and Marya Mannes, the *serious* bourgeois theatre as distinct from all that crass commercialism, is not really interested in ennoblement, but in optimism. When Miss Mannes scolds Tennessee Williams for his sordidness, or when Howard Taubman hopes that Genet will someday write about blacks and whites who love one another, we are in the presence of those old balloons filled with the gas of middle-class propositions about life.

It simply can't be that difficult, irrational, bloody and opaque (it can't be that funny, either!). We have a vision of existence as moderately difficult, moderately irrational, moderately bloody and moderately opaque: we see, we see, oh noble crown of moderate apotheosis set on man's deserving brow, we see—*Gideon!*

One more word. If optimism is what's wanted (the modern equivalent of faith and hope), there's a chance that the playwrights of the so-called absurd can give us better grounds for entertaining it than Chayefsky or MacLeish. That is, if we can accept the notion that there is something encouraging in looking into the abyss and not flinching. If we can, then Beckett's tramps waiting in intolerable anguish are encouraging and so are the words of Bérenger at the end of Ionesco's *The Killer:* "Oh God! There's nothing we can do. What can we do . . . What can we do. . . ." The fact that there is no question mark is exactly why it is so encouraging: the statement, summing up and crystallizing the entire astonishing and valorous play, tells us what our condition is. The nobility may or may not follow. (1962)

¶About Nothing—
with Precision

The Sunday *New York Times Magazine*—that repository of everything that has been said better elsewhere—recently carried one of those "debates" about the theatre and the movies which leaves us wondering if our cultural despair is as deep as it should be. Tyrone Guthrie argued for the stage and Carl Foreman for the screen, each man displaying an extraordinary masochistic yearning to make the other look good. Mr. Guthrie said that theatre was more "live," that the movie actor "can't pull out all the stops and stun an audience . . . battering it like a typhoon," and that he personally had never seen a movie that wasn't mere journalism. Mr. Foreman said that films were more visual, that plays were just full of "words, words, words," and that since the movies were so much cheaper you could bring the children.

Any more such interchanges and the end is of course in sight, but penultimately we may find it desirable to choose. As for me, despite the fact that as a drama critic I might have been expected to have lined up behind Guthrie, I found myself rooting for Foreman—or being willing to root for him had he exhibited a grain of sense and had the game been rather different; had it been, that is to say, not a question of which medium was intrinsically better or more important but which was giving us more present satisfaction, more truth and more art. Posed this way, I think the debate can have only one outcome: the movies, whatever they may have been or may become, are currently filling the emptiness left by our theatre's abdication from anything we can recognize as our experience. And only snobbism, professional investments or myopia can prevent us from seeing that.

A handful of movies are filling the space: six, eight, per-

haps a dozen in the last few years. Three or four are filling
more of it than the rest. As for the bulk of films, someone has
said that mass tastes belong more to sociology than aesthetics,
a dictum as applicable to Broadway as to Hollywood. Most
plays are bad, most movies are bad; it has simply been my observation that almost nothing in the recent theatre has been
nearly so good as some of the films of the new Frenchmen, of
Bergman, Kurosawa and Fellini, especially of Resnais and
Antonioni.

Before going on, I should set down some propositions.
The first, which should already be clear, is that the movies
are an art, full-fledged, conscious, of legitimate birth and
needing no more defenses or rationales. The second is that,
while cinema is not so different from theatre as is sometimes
thought, what does separate them is important enough for us
to be able to locate in it some of the reasons for the movies'
present superiority. And the third is that it may be possible to
maintain an admiration for the contemporary screen without
fatal prejudice to a belief that drama possesses the means to
affect us more radically and more durably, whatever its almost
complete failure in recent years to affect us at all.

Still, I wouldn't line up any trumpets to proclaim this
belief in the theatre's historical and renewable powers. Thirty
years ago Antonin Artaud, writing about the kind of theatre
he wished to compel into being, said that it "did not intend
to leave the task of distributing the Myths of man and modern
life entirely to the movies." If we shift to a less apocalyptic
plane in order to substitute the word "metaphors" or "recogni-
tions" for myths, we who love the theatre remain in the same
position as Artaud, except that we have so little of his at least
partially efficacious thunder. The movies are more than ever
undertaking our commerce, conducting our transactions, while
our desire to get back into the field grows more pious and
statutory every day.

I write from the boundless unhappiness and ennui induced
by a theatrical season in which I saw more than a hundred
plays and spectacles only three of which roused me to a more
than temporary acknowledgement of some isolated and her-

metic act of skill or passion. There were times when there
came over me the raw craving to see a movie: in one mood,
any movie, as on those Saturday afternoons in childhood; in
another, a movie that might be able to put me back in touch
with the world, after the deracinations and exiles of our theatre of repetition which cannot find a new tone or gesture in
any of its bags.

In any but one, I should have said, and such poor hope as
we possess comes from it; it contains the only objects we can
dare pit against those beautiful and strange new films that
have occupied the strategic angles of our vision. I am growing
more and more to dislike "Theatre of the Absurd" to describe
the kind of play that breaks, by means of new languages,
parody and mockery, innocence, despair and painful fantasy,
with everything that is moribund or dead in our theatre—
which means nearly everything besides itself. But the term
helps isolate what I mean.

"Meta-theatre," "anti-theatre," perhaps "infra-theatre," if
we have to have a name. It doesn't matter, except that the
"absurd" invites the foolish, asking for Arthur Kopit and Gelber's slipping out of his connection, and that such theatre is
only absurd, on the occasions when it is, if you use an old
logic to measure it by. In any case, this sort of drama, whatever its future (and I believe the theatre itself has none unless
it is somehow along these lines) provided me with the few
evenings on which I didn't feel suffocated, when the air was
stirring around me so that I didn't have to go to the movies
to discover that new and original dramatic shapes are still
possible to make.

What is so suffocating about almost all theatre today is its
unshakable attachment to and nearly unbroken consecration
of what has ceased to exist. The stage throws back at us
gestures, inflections, rhythms and grammars that have lost
their right to serve as descriptions of ourselves—we are no
longer like that, even if the forms persist mechanically. At best,
nostalgic reminders of our past; at worst, deadly repetitions of
a present we are seeking the means to shake off. Unless we
want to note that the theatre also sends us Chayefsky or Mac-

Leish-style mythograms, which are messages from the future, dispatched from areas of aspiration none of us has any intention of ever occupying.

There is a future which we do want art to colonize: the area of our next moves, our forthcoming utterances. The art of the present is always partly predictive, since it tells us what we are about to be. Artaud wrote that the theatre can renew our sense of life by being the arena where "man fearlessly makes himself master of what does not yet exist, and brings it into being." But that is exactly what certain movies are doing instead. When I first followed that long, disconsolate, abandoned search in *L'Avventura*, that arc of despair that led to truth, I knew that it traced what I had been prepared to feel next; that from then on it would be impossible not to see existence with the same narrowed, dry-eyed, precipice-crawling intentness as Antonioni.

La Notte takes us to the same place, by a different route. Here Antonioni leads us into the city, into concrete, walls and reflections in glass, after the rocks, great spaces, sea and terraces of *L'Avventura*. And here the search (or movement; films *move*, are a tracing of movement, and in Antonioni, as in Resnais and the best moments of the others, the movement is everything—events, narrative statement, meaning) comes to the same end, or a fractional distance beyond. The acceptance is made of what we are like; it is impossible not to accept it as this film dies out on its couple shatteringly united in the dust, because everything we are not like, but which we have found no other means of shedding, has been stripped away.

I think this stripped, mercilessly bare quality of Antonioni's films is what is so new and marvelous about them. The island criss-crossed a hundred times with nothing come upon; the conversations that fall into voids; Jeanne Moreau's head and shoulders traveling microscopically along the angle of a building; unfilled distances; a bisected figure gazing from the corner of an immense window; the lawn of the rich man across which people eddy like leaves; Monica Vitti's hand resting on Ferzetti's head in the most delicate of all acceptances; ennui, extremity, anguish, abandoned searches, the event we are looking for never happening—as Godot never comes, Beckett and Antonioni being two who enforce our relinquishments of the answer, the arrival, two who disillusion us.

When Antonioni visited the studio of Mark Rothko he is reported to have told the artist that "your paintings are like my films—about nothing, with precision." An alarming remark, calculated to throw the film theoreticians and the significance mongers into a cold sweat. (Film criticism has always struck me as mostly having the tone of Samuel Goldwyn trying to talk his way in to see Immanuel Kant.) Yet there is no reason to be dismayed. Antonioni's films are indeed about nothing, which is not the same thing as being about nothingness.

L'Avventura and *La Notte* are movies without a traditional subject (we can only think they are "about" the despair of the idle rich or our ill-fated quest for pleasure if we are intent on making old anecdotes out of new essences). They are about nothing we could have known without them, nothing to which we had already attached meanings or surveyed in other ways. They are, without being abstract, about nothing *in particular*, being instead, like most recent paintings, self-contained and absolute, an action and not the description of an action.

They are part of that next step in our feelings which art is continually eliciting and recording. We have been taking that step for a long time, most clearly in painting, but also in music, in certain areas of fiction, in anti-theatre. It might be described as accession through reduction, the coming into truer forms through the cutting away of created encumbrances: all the replicas we have made of ourselves, all the misleading because logical or only psychological narratives, the whole apparatus of reflected wisdom, the clichés, the inherited sensations, the received ideas. In *L'Avventura* the woman says: "Things are not like that . . . everything has become so terribly simple. . . ."

Irony, parody, abstraction, reduction: they are all forms of aggression against the traditional subject, against what art is supposed to deal with. They are, much more than the direct violence which we also use, our most effective means of liberating our experience, releasing those unnamed emotions and perceptions that have been blockaded by everything we have been taught to see and feel. What excites us about these new movies, what causes us to call each other up about them as we no longer do about plays, is the sense they communicate, in one degree or another, of extending the areas of freedom —troubled freedom because a price is paid when you are always half engaged in repudiating your erstwhile captors— that we have gained from the other arts.

I don't think it too much to say that the movies, having come into their maturity, are giving us more, or more useful, freedom than any other form. It may be evanescent, or simply data for more permanent structures to be created by other means, but it is being given to us, a week scarcely passing without some new accession. It ranges from the narrowest and most preliminary liberation such as is bestowed by British movies like *Room at the Top, Saturday Night and Sunday Morning* and *A Taste of Honey,* with their mostly traditional procedures but temperamental and thematic rebelliousness, to the far more solid and revolutionary, because more purely cinematic, achievements of Antonioni.

In between are the films of the Frenchmen, Chabrol, Godard, Truffaut, with their neo-existentialist adventures, proceeding by non-motivation and arbitrary acts, the camera jiggling or running along at eye-level or freezing fast, in not entirely successful visual implementation. And there is Bergman, with his new, not entirely convincing legends, his preachy discontent but also his powerful and clean images and isolations of immortality in a context of abrasive psychology and harsh weather. And Fellini, whose *Dolce Vita* I thought vastly overrated because of its obviousness and mechanical application of its ideas, but some of whose earlier films—*I Vitelloni* and *La Strada*—were full of lucid, plangent vision.

I want only to add, passing over so many others and not even touching on the purely abstract film or the work of the American underground (I am an amateur moviegoer, with no compulsion to study everything and no breviary of the medium), a word about Alain Resnais. He seems to be only just below Antonioni, perhaps not so central, but doing with time what the latter does with space, if the distinction is admissible, since film is preeminently the fuser of time and space. But as metaphors the words might serve.

L'année dernière à Marienbad, Resnais has said, is "a mechanism differing from the usual spectacle, a kind of contemplation . . . it is about greater and lesser degrees of reality." And the reality is that of time, of memory and anticipation, the mechanism distributing our ordinary categories, mixing past, present and future, the images from each realm advancing and retreating, fading, reemerging, repeating, coalescing and finally coming to exist simultaneously, the way the mind actually but unavowedly contains them. It is a great film, a "new kind of fiction," as Robbe-Grillet has remarked; when its heroine asks, "What life would you have me live?" we are ready to answer, "This one, because it is truer."

If the movies are providing us with this truer life, this more real fiction, I don't think it has anything to do with the boldness of its themes compared with the theatre's. I think the reason lies, beyond the accidents of genius or circumstance, precisely in the fact that the screen is more abstract than the stage. That is to say, I see the decline of the theatre as rooted in its profound physicality, its being of all the arts (dance is speechless drama) the most nearly incarnate, the most committed to the palpable gesture and the actual word. And it is there, in our gestures, our emotions really, and our speech that we have become most atrophied, most devitalized and false.

What this means for drama is that, being wedded to our bodies and our language, it finds it all but impossible not to drag along with us, imitating our spent movements and utterances. But the film is only the reflection of our movements and statements, and reflections can be *arranged,* selected, reanimated through juxtaposition, interpenetration, *editing.* André Malraux wrote that "the means of reproduction in the cinema is the moving photograph, but its means of expression is the sequence of *planes.*" And planes are outside us, geometries beyond our power to turn into clichés.

When the movies obey their highest nature, turning from being merely another teller of stories to the creation of visual equivalents of our experience, records of our presence among objects and patterns of our occupation of the world, they enjoy a freedom and an authority that the stage has almost lost. Whether it will recover them is not easy to say; there is no magic in our protests that the theatre is perennial, that its loss would be unthinkable, and so forth.

Because our theatre depends so heavily on language, in which so much of our ineffectuality, deceitfulness and untruth is locked, I think it will have to be redeemed mainly by language, despite Artaud's fiery wish that it be redeemed in other ways. And the theatre cannot create a new speech by itself, especially when there is almost nobody willing to listen.

The three plays I saw last season that give me any hope were all works which while not bereft of a reinforcing *mise en scène* were primarily achievements of language, parodic, ironic and outside our formulas. They were Beckett's *Happy Days*, N. F. Simpson's *One-Way Pendulum* and Kenneth Koch's *George Washington Crossing the Delaware,* and none ran for more than a few weeks. I know it is being said that anti-theatre is on the way out. But I can't imagine what will replace it, except something that has learned from it and continues its general action. And I believe we won't have a "total" theatre, the kind of positive, multi-leveled new Elizabethan age certain tiresome critics keep calling for, until we have gone through a great deal more fragmentation, narrowness, indirection and painful jest. Nor will true theatre be anything but a minority enterprise for a very long time.

Meanwhile the movies, with their distance from our skins and breath, their power to make our reflections obey a transforming and arranging will, their eyes less jaded than our own, are beginning to reconstitute our experience. Far-flung, anonymous, their meetings held in shadowy caverns, they are becoming the community of vision that theatre once was. Actuality may be the highest good; when actuality becomes unreal we will settle for true shadows. (1962)

II/Classics

¶A Timid Mother Courage

Now that Bertolt Brecht's *Mother Courage and Her Children* is more or less firmly ensconced between *Mary, Mary* and *Mr. President* perhaps we can stop talking about it as a "major theatrical event," a "stunning evening of adult drama," a "triumph of art over commerce" and other self-congratulating and conscience-appeasing phrases of this kind. Whatever truth there is in them, there is a melancholy under-truth: that one of the greatest plays of our time should first be presented on Broadway nearly twenty-five years after it was written; that something uncompromising and mature should be so rare in our theatre; that art should win over the "culinary" (Brecht's word for commercial theatre) once in a hundred times. Besides, the play is not done nearly well enough to justify any complacency, and, finally, almost nobody among the tub-thumpers seems to have more than a sophomore's idea of what it is about.

It seems that *Mother Courage*, to discuss the play before the production, is being taken as a grim antiwar document or a testament to human endurance or an amalgam of the two. It is not that these interpretations are entirely wrong but that they are inadequate and reductive; they do no sort of justice to Brecht's complex vision and they tend to turn the piece into propaganda or sentimental affirmation of the kind our national magazines are so anxious to obtain from the arts. But Brecht's play is at least as much anti-*peace* as antiwar and at least as much despairing as affirmative. It is in the equilibrium between these ostensible opposites that its true life exists, just as the true life of its central character exists in the tensions and balances of her conradictory impulses toward love and exploitative commerce.

It is a root mistake, however, to think of the play as primarily a study of individualized character in the manner of psychological drama. Its title is, after all, *Mother Courage and Her Children,* and Brecht, as Walter Sokel has said, never "begins with the individual but with the problem." That is what epic theatre is about. The problem here is death, destruction, suffering, rapacity, the cloud that hides the little and powerless man—most men—from history, the very organization of society on such ferociously competitive lines as to make the difference between war and peace only a matter of degree. "I'm not in love with war," Mother Courage says, but she lives off it as a sutler because that is the only way she can live; the deeper implication is that since social life is a war one can only exist by participating in it on its terms, thereby suffering the corruption and human losses it mechanically imposes.

The play is set in the Thirty Years' War, which Eric Bentley has reminded us, is "in German history . . . the *locus classicus* of death—the death, not of individuals, but of cities and populations." But as is true of all Brecht's work, *Mother Courage* is outside historic time or local setting, dealing as it does with a perennial human condition and approaching, in a way that has simply not been noticed, a truly tragic statement. The tragedy lies in the fatality with which the tough, avaricious, ingenious woman of the title is ground down and, more especially, in the inevitability with which goodness and virtue are rendered useless and brought low at the same time as they continue anguishedly to assert their claims and to thrust up their contours to our sight.

In the loss of the three children—whom Mother Courage's sleazy, haggling, cold-eyed selling of supplies to the army from her wagon is precisely designed to protect and preserve —we are shown the immense irony of the way in which "making a living" destroys life, how the process of preservation brings about the ruin of that human substance which is being preserved. Eilif, the valiant son, dies because he does in a brief interval of peace what he had been honored for doing in battle; Swisscheese, the simple and honest son, because his virtues are inimical to a world of appetite and plunder; and Kattrin, the dumb *Kindernarr*, the doter on children and possessor of a breast anxious to receive love and bestow comfort on suffering, because there is no time, room or air for their nourishment. She can only indicate that she possesses love by sacrificing herself and thereby losing the actuality of love; as one of the prefatory legends says, even the stones must speak, but they then go back to being stones in the silence of death.

In all this we are intended to see, beyond Brecht's Marxist analysis and comment on society (Brecht's Marxism, we are finally coming to understand, is continually being transcended by his dramatic sense, his *prédilection d'artiste*) a comment on, or rather a great passionate but at the same time rigorously cool and controlled vision of, the eternal contradiction between man's impulses and aspirations and his fate. Whether or not one accepts Brecht's truth as decisive and complete, the play is marvelously effective and deserves to have its effectiveness seen in the right light.

As Brecht himself wrote, his "merchant-mother" is a "great living contradiction who is disfigured and deformed beyond recognition." In her, "antitheses in all their abruptness and incompatibility are united." She is not an image of "the indestructibility of a vital person afflicted by the inequities of war," but quite the opposite: one of the destructibility of humanity no matter how tenacious, muscular and energetic. As she wearily hitches herself to her cart once more in the play's final scene, she may impress us with a sort of indomitability but she also leaves us—or should leave us—shaken by her monstrous dehumanization and intolerable losses.

How well does the current production incarnate and exemplify these meanings and qualities of the play? The first thing to say is that it is an honorable effort. Jerome Robbins is a director of much smaller stature than the play requires, but he has at least not tried to hoke it up, he has stayed faithful to its form and broader values. Eric Bentley's adaptation is an exceedingly good one, preserving the special fusion of the colloquial and the abstract that Brecht's German is built up from; the sets by Ming Cho Lee are simple and effective, consisting mainly of an earth-colored curving backdrop and some portable properties; and the Paul Dessau music in its toughness and jagged but not jazzy rhythms is consistent with Brecht's intention.

Nevertheless, if the production isn't an offensive one, it is curiously pallid and inert, as if all the people concerned in it were so overwhelmed by the occasion that they backed gingerly up to it, remembering some shreds of Epic Theatre Theory and keeping one uneasy eye on the Broadway audience, which is only too likely to be scared out of its wits by something so honest and biting as *Mother Courage.* Beyond this, there is a basic lack of subtlety, of dimension; the play proceeds on the surface, so that most of what I was describing before has to be guessed at, and a failure of modulation and pacing, the effect of which is to run everything together in exactly the way that Brecht, with his alternation of active scenes with reflective ones, of songs with speech and straightforward expression with biting irony, tried so strenuously to avoid.

Finally, there is the matter of the cast. With one or two exceptions—Eugene Roche, Louis Guss and John Harkins in minor roles; Zohra Lampert in a major one—it is just not up to the demands of the text. Miss Lampert is especially good as Kattrin (it is interesting that Robbins should have given her so much useful and impressive physical material to display; the characters who *can* talk tend to stand around twiddling their thumbs), and the scene when she dies beating a drum in order to save a town from an approaching army is a highlight, if a virtually indestructible piece of theatre.

But it is Anne Bancroft as Mother Courage who exists as the production's weakest element. Miss Bancroft is an actress of considerable force and vitality, but apart from being far too young for the role, she almost entirely lacks the range, subtlety and intelligence the part requires. Her Bronx speech is annoying, but even more irksome is her Bronx *manner;* when we hear her say, with head cocked to the side and crisp, subway-learned gestures, "Swisscheese, I've brought you up

honest because you're not very bright, but don't overdo it,"
the image irresistibly rises of a mother urging her teen-age
son, in their apartment on the Grand Concourse, to feel free
to cheat a little on his exams. Miss Bancroft is, of course, a
name. What *Mother Courage* needs is a person, an actress of
depth and that particular sort of courage that consists in being intelligent and taking chances. I don't blame her for her
deficiencies, nor Robbins for his. I just wish that when we
speak of notabe events in the theatre we would hold up higher
standards of execution.

But *Mother Courage* on display, however inadequately, is
better than in mothballs or avant-garde collections. I recommend seeing it, then reading it to fill out the picture. (1963)

¶ Weep No More
for Brecht

If there were any lingering fantasies along Broadway that Brecht could be made to pay, the catastrophe of *Arturo Ui*, taken off the boards before a week had passed, should have settled the matter for good. There is certainly nothing to mourn in this; at least the air is clear now, and it is probably the first reason we have had to be grateful to David Merrick in his entire career.

Broadway has always suspected that if you do Brecht right you will lose the mass audience, but now, after last season's *Mother Courage* and Mr. Merrick's abortive *Arturo Ui*, it presumably realizes that if you do him wrong you will lose everybody. This is not to say that the commercial theatre has any choice: it only knows how to do Brecht wrong, as it only knows how to do any uncomfortable, more-than-routine playwright wrong. But we can be confident that it isn't going to try to get away with it in Brecht's case for a long time to come.

Brecht is simply not wanted on Broadway and there is no way to make him palatable. The entrepreneurs are surely correct in thinking that their pleasure-seeking middle-class audiences will not tolerate a dramatist who offends them technically as well as spiritually, in their taste, expectations, self-esteem, image of each other and sense of the way the world goes. So why should we lament these failures and travesties of production? Is it anything but a gain to see Brecht drop out of the hands of the packagers, to be picked up eventually, we may hope, by other hands which will know what to do with what they have? When and if we have an equipped, viable, continuous non-commercial but professional theatre whose precise reason for being is to do Brecht and his peers with fidelity and imagination, we will possess him again.

Meanwhile, let us pray that this will be the last post-mortem.

Arturo Ui is one of Brecht's distinctly lesser works, a self-styled "gangster show" which he wrote in 1941 but which remained unproduced until after his death in 1956. It is an almost exact parallel of Hitler's rise to power, set in the Chicago of the late twenties and early thirties and told in terms of a mobster who in alliance with local businessmen organizes a protection racket and fastens his grip on the city. Throughout, the events are the central ones of Hitler's early career—his dealings with Hindenburg, the Reichstag fire, the murder of Ernst Roehm and his SA lieutenants, the undermining and later annexation of Austria. In case anyone misses the parallels, they are spelled out in titles flashed on a screen after every scene.

As a historical document *Arturo Ui* suffers from the reductiveness of which Brecht sometimes was guilty; his businessmen play too large a role, anti-Semitism and the general irrationality of Nazi modes and attitudes play too little. As a drama it suffers from an uncertainty of tone and wobbliness of mood, from an obviousness of strategy and, most centrally, from its very desire to appropriate history in order to warn against its perversions—the play's full title is *The* Resistible Rise *of Arturo Ui.* What this means is that if it is going to work at all it has to be given an especially brilliant and inventive production, one that imposes a definite stylized line, such a production as the one the Berliner Ensemble, where it is now a centerpiece of the repertory, has been giving it. One European critic described that production as being fugue-like, precise and abstract, while Kenneth Tynan, in a complementary response, said that it added to the script "a fever, a venom and a fury."

The Broadway offering may be said to have added to the script a head-cold, a bad taste and an irritability. It was a masterly demonstration of the theatrical arts at war with one another and an incomparable illustration of how to divide the responsibility for an assassination. That hetman of dramatic emasculation, George Tabori, has rendered Brecht's language into an American idiom, the subtlety and contemporaneity of which should be sufficiently indicated by "That's the way the cookie crumbles" and "When ya gotta go, ya gotta go." Tony Richardson, who is rapidly becoming the Cecil B. DeMille of the serious theatre, directed the work in seven different styles, with seven different moods and paces, and one consistent belief—that if you make enough irrelevant noise and blink enough lights people will think that something important is happening. And Jule Styne wrote a Tin Pan Alleyist's notion of a Brechtian score, tuneless, pseudo-ragtimey, excitable, something superbly suited to a white matron's plans for a mad, mad party up in Harlem.

How it was allowed to happen we shall never know, but out of the carnage rose Christopher Plummer's diverting performance in the title role. It may not have been what Brecht had in mind, but to have been faithful to Brecht when all around were playing Benedict Arnold would have made the evening more of a disaster than it was. In any case, Plummer took off on his own, playing Ui with Chaplinesque gestures and Runyonish speech, inventing as he went along, antic, telling and original. He could no more hold up the play than Tabori or Richardson could let it go, but he left an image in the memory that wiped out perhaps a quarter of the pain. (1963)

¶Two Ways of
  Looking at Brecht

There have been complaints that considering our present condition of theatrical scarcity the appearance of two different
productions of the same play is wasteful and supererogatory.
Yet after seeing the Living Theatre's and the Masque Theatre's versions of Brecht's *Mann ist Mann* on successive nights,
it occurred to me that the opposite might be true: that one
real dramatic imagination seen several ways is worth more
than any number of unreal ones seen a single way each. This
leads me to a proposal that we set aside a month or a season
in which only one good play may be presented, in as many
conceptions as are brought forward.

Thirteen ways of looking at a blackbird. Well, the point of
that was to teach us about the imagination's relation to its
material, and the point of having one play in two or thirteen
or thirty-nine versions is much the same: to instruct us in the
liberating truth that real multiplicity and differentiation lie in
the area of form, not subject. And the usefulness of that, simply on a practical level, is that it might help put an end to all
the nonsense we spout about meaning and idea and theme
in drama; it might keep us from continuing to think of *Macbeth* as a play about ambition, or *The Blacks* as one about
Negro-white tensions, or *The Bald Soprano* as a study in the
failure of communication.

To see two different sets of sensibilities at work upon
Brecht's play is to understand again that dramatic imagination is everything, that if we believe a play to be "about"
something other than its own action and composition it is by
that token inferior, a paraphrase of some order of reality other
than the dramatic. Which is why, if *Mann ist Mann* exists as a
work of stage art, it cannot be about brainwashing or Com-

munism or Capitalism or even the individual vs. society, though these things may enter into it the way syphilis entered into *Ghosts*. The beauty of having the two productions coming on each other's heels last week was that in comparing them we could get beneath notions of subject matter or theme to the underlying theatrical reality, the rhythms, arrangements and colorations.

It is true that the Living Theatre's production uses a text revised by Brecht in 1953 from his play of the mid-twenties, while the Masque stays with the original. But the revisions were small and not consequential. Both versions—the Living Theatre's *Man Is Man* and the Masque's *A Man's a Man*— agree substantially in subject and theme. What they don't agree on is procedure, tone, spirit and vision. They therefore end up being "about" different things—different spirits, visions, tones and ways of dramatic procedure. And that is the paradox of the form-versus-content dichotomy.

Neither production is anywhere near satisfactory, I'm afraid, but the Masque's, whatever you may have heard, is inferior to the Living Theatre's. The Masque had several advantages: Eric Bentley's translation of the original text is much more lively and unfettered than Gerhard Nellhaus' of the revision, and John Hancock worked with a cast and company whose professional attainments seem well beyond those of his rival. And indeed Hancock has directed a considerably more professional show than Julian Beck, if by professional you mean—and you will have your spectator's license revoked by our stage authorities if you don't mean—slickness, consistency and propriety; everything is in its place, each bit of business clicks off at the right speed, and no effort is spared in hewing to what is considered the Brechtian line.

Yet what is the Brechtian line if it is not outside the formulas? In the Masque's superficially coherent and briskly moving but strangely flat, prim and daunted production, Brecht's fantasy is reduced to the level of English music-hall entertainment, or rather to our neighborhood-theatre idea of that. When are we going to get over *The Threepenny Opera* and understand that that is only one minor aspect of Brecht and that, even so, you had better do it with rankness and brutality and an ugly kind of insouciance? The Masque people have mounted a bourgeois Brecht, as my colleague Robert Brustein remarked at intermission; they have given us Bob Hope and Harry Lauder instead of Chaplin and the Keystone Cops.

The Living Theatre's *Man Is Man,* on the other hand, for all that it works in a number of diverse styles, bogs down rather catastrophically in the final scenes (which it might not be irreverent to remark are rather confusing and insufficiently realized as they come to us from Brecht) and is marred by some totally inept performances, but it does at least offer us what we can believe was Brecht's intention. And that was to present the transformation of the laborer Galy Gay into a fighting machine, in a mode of fantasy, low comedy, pathos and savage wit, with a sexual component which the Masque's superficial bawdiness doesn't come near expressing and a distance from naturalism which that production's revue style is not the proper instrument for attaining.

As Galy Gay the Living Theatre's Joseph Chaikin is a great deal superior to the Masque's John Heffernan, because although he is a less accomplished actor he plays the part right, which is to say he tries to maintain the oblique, artificial style —the *gestus* of Brecht's theory—that reinforces the play's position beyond either farce or naturalistic satire. Again, the Living Theatre's Warren Finnerty plays Bloody Five with far more imaginative scope than the Masque's Michael Conrad, who resembles someone out of *Marty;* the L. T.'s satanic William Shari is a much better Uriah Shelley than the Masque's coy Harvey Solin and its Benjamin Hayeem a more resourceful and amusing Wang than the Masque's Maurice Edwards. Only the two Widow Begbicks are standoffs, both Judith Malina and Olympia Dukakis being interchangeably hopeless.

I shall close with reference to one scene that seemed to me to indicate the difference between the productions. At the Masque, Galy Gay's trial and humiliation are conducted in a straightforward, thoroughly uninventive manner; at the Liv-

ing Theatre he is inserted up to his neck in a latrine and remains with eyes closed throughout. I think Brecht would have
given his nod to that, as well as to as many more productions
of his play as we will require before we get with it much more
robustly than even the Living Theatre does. (1962)

¶The Drawing Room and Beyond

Rosmersholm is one of the subtlest, most intricate, and—although not necessarily for these reasons—most important of Ibsen's plays. In 1886 he was almost halfway through his last and major phase. Nine years before, *Pillars of Society* had broken with the intentions of the bourgeois stage; after *A Doll's House* and *Ghosts,* his first, somewhat uncertain thrusts into the true unknown, he had worked off his disappointment and anger at their reaction in *An Enemy of the People* and had come into full possession of his total theme and identity with *The Wild Duck. Rosmersholm* was a turning point, and at the same time a summation and a source for what was to come.

In it Ibsen put the governing impulses of *A Doll's House* and *Ghosts* into a wider frame, freeing them from some of the specificity of idea and action—their problematic aspect—that had cramped them there. His dilemma had always been to find ways of anchoring his imagination; the bourgeois theatre had no place for *Brand* or *Peer Gynt,* so he accepted the burdens of naturalism, the box set and the events of the parlor, and made them serve the earlier visions, from which he never ceased to draw. The immense subjects with which his art was concerned—the past as hound of the present, the ideal as corrupter of the actual, with the human soul caught between in illusion and self-deception—would from *Rosmersholm* on unfold in the most precarious equilibrium between poetry and fact, myth and statement, symbol and prop.

That is what makes all of Ibsen's later work so difficult for us; we are forever falling into the naturalistic trap, on the one hand, and the symbolic one on the other. The plays before *Rosmersholm* are reduced to the social problems with which they ostensibly deal, the very last dramas are seen as "poetic fantasies," and are thought to be proofs of Ibsen's waning and self-indulgent powers, since they are obsessional and ritualistic, lacking the sociological fervor and polemical force which we have decided are Ibsen's suitable qualities, at the same time as we find them dated.

We are not at all sure about *Rosmersholm*. There is its sense of fatality going beyond strict events, there are evident symbols and a feeling of indefiniteness, a shifting between the psychic and the moral and metaphysical, tremendous compression, allusiveness, a highly wrought texture of reference and implication. It is a "hidden" play. And yet there are still "problems" and external issues, the action is essentially within the naturalistic framework, there are no scenes on the mountaintop or on high towers. So we play it uncertainly, having trouble with this tragedy in the drawing room which resists familiar intonations and colloquial gestures but which is not a high tale about the death of kings either.

We are especially likely to get Rebekka West wrong. James Huneker's idea of her is the one we continue to hold, and it is a jaw of the naturalistic trap. She is, Huneker wrote, "as cunning as Becky Sharp, as amorous as Emma Bovary, as ambitious as Lady Macbeth . . ." The reviewers repeat this fractional truth and the academic surveys perpetuate it, along with their notions of Chekhov's "undramatic" drama and Shaw's ideational one. There are still such women around, one newspaper asserted last week in order to validate the play, the way novels are validated by our being assured of the possibility of meeting their characters in our streets.

The point about Rebekka is that you will not meet her in the street; she is not transferable from the play to reality; she is Ibsen's woman, not ours. If she is cunning, amorous and ambitious, the qualities serve a purpose other than that of a courtesan or career woman, and they are in any case, partial and temporary, data for transformation, for dramatic development, and do not come close to defining her. She is in the play to be one element at the scene of a tremendous struggle from

which moral revelation arises; and the "design" she carries out
is not to trap a man but to snare a truth. The difference is that
between Ibsen and the well-made play.

The truth of *Rosmersholm* comes out of the confrontation
of entire realms of being and faculties, as all Ibsen's truths do.
Rosmersholm, the place of inherited morality, of ideality and
unchanging destiny, against the North, the open, the untrammeled. Rosmer himself, the man of received conscience, who
suffers from a lack of effectiveness due to innocence and the
enervations of purity, Rosmer the *representative*, against
Rebekka, the new, the unhistoric, the self-created, the *personal.* And the great central movement that constitutes the
tragedy: the mutually mortal blows they deal in the attempt
to fuse antitheses, to merge into a new being that shall be capable of transforming existence.

Of all the ways in which David Ross's current production
fails, the one from which everything else comes is the inability
to get past the drawing room, the surface of the drama, to the
tragic rhythm beneath. To do this you have to direct your
actors in the job of playing together in a way that transcends
the simple ensemble—which is necessary even on a naturalistic
level—so that they may participate in a total movement and
vision instead of in the stages of a narrative. You have to maintain the tension between detail and verisimilitude on the one
hand, and the more spacious action, the metaphysical movement if you will, on the other. You have to subordinate your
characterizations, the Huneker kind of thing, to the creation
of a single organism.

But what happens is that Mr. Ross's cast doesn't even play
well together in drawing-room fashion: there are scenes,
especially some between Kroll and Rosmer, in which there is
such declamation, so much sing-song alternation of speeches,
that we wonder why there are no rostrums and individual
water glasses. And there is a pervasive lack of larger implication, a steady dragging down of the play to the level of domestic tragedy, with the wider effects, the mystery and the
fatality, being sought for in tightenings of the lips and sudden

glances around, in overrapid movements, and in the hoarse, passionate, neurotic interpretation of Rebekka by Nancy Wickwire.

Miss Wickwire is a good actress but she is a bad Rebekka because she plays her *à la* Huneker. "I don't think I can be said to be particularly high-strung," Rebekka tells Kroll at one point, and he agrees. It is a vital pointer to what she is: an *agent* of aspiration and destruction, whose relation to Rosmer simply uses the facts and emotions of their story to go beyond it. For example, their closing scenes, the developing *Liebestod*, have to be played with a sense that it summarizes a movement of the imagination and not merely an ill-fated romance, and with an ironic awareness of the limitations of the kind of language Ibsen had to use but which he was constantly pressing past.

But the last scenes of Mr. Ross's *Rosmersholm* feel like *Camille*, and Miss Wickwire and Donald Woods embarrass us because of it. Mr. Woods had embarrassed us previously with his tight-lipped, inexpressive Rosmer; he fails because he doesn't do enough, as Miss Wickwire fails because she does too much. Only Bramwell Fletcher's Brendel is right; only in that small but essential role do we see the play triumphing over its difficulties and achieving its perilous equilibrium through being acted in a style that remains bound to events yet makes the signs accomplishing poetry. And Mr. Ross has chosen to make his highest percentage of cuts in just that place. (1962)

¶ The Search for Ibsen

After attending a performance of Ibsen's *Wild Duck* Rainer Maria Rilke wrote to a friend that he had come to know "a new poet to whom we shall go by path after path." Ibsen, he went on, was a "man misunderstood in the midst of fame. An entirely different person from what one hears."

Just so. Things haven't changed much. Rilke's Ibsen is very like our own: the unexpected arrivals at his door when we had imagined all the approaches to have been blocked off; the misconceptions coupled with the classic status; the discrepancy between the popular image and rumor and the actual man and art; perhaps most relevant of all the truth, which Rilke was one of the first to perceive, that in Ibsen we have to do with a poet, not a philosopher or controversialist.

One can almost use Ibsen as an infallible test of critical acumen. When our leading reviewer, Walter Kerr, attaches Ibsen firmly to the "drama of ideas" and then defines that as a "drama in which people are digits, adding up to the correct ideological sum," one can taste the sourness of understanding gone wrong, or never having gone anywhere. When Mary McCarthy writes of Ibsen that his work is "repetitive and inchoate," that his plays "grow more grandiose as the symbolic content inflates them," and that "his career appears as a series of false starts and reverses in an interior conversation that keeps lapsing into reverie," one possesses a compendium of all that it is possible for insensitivity, arrogance—and I am tempted to add, malice—to accomplish: the quintessence of mis-Ibsenism.

There is something profoundly ironic in our professions of weariness with Ibsen, when one considers that at the rate his dramas are produced here it will take approximately until the year 2023 for us to see the dozen "social plays" once each, with only a prayer that *Brand* and *Peer Gynt* might come along as widely spaced *lagniappe*. But we *are* tired of Ibsen, everybody says so; nobody seems to have anything else to say except Eric Bentley and Francis Fergusson, who are still unaccountably bothering to work at the Norwegian and who send up from time to time eccentric findings pertaining to his greatness.

I must confess to feeling about Ibsen like a lover whose beloved draws mostly unappreciative stares. I can't imagine why everyone doesn't see what I do, and I conclude that they are simply not looking at the same person. That is to say, I think the weariness is really with an Ibsen who never was, the Ibsen shackled to Victorian furniture and Victorian gestures, to the well-made play, to an outworn posture of muckraking, to theses and to William Archer's English-language versions. With such an Ibsen we can indeed be bored to insensibility.

That there is another Ibsen can be discovered in more direct ways than by reading Bentley and Fergusson. New York has had a *Hedda Gabler* which is splendid in every way but one—its leading lady, whose style and vividness unfortunately can't compensate for a serious misreading of the part and a consequent throwing of the entire play out of whack: Hedda is not a femme fatale or a study in neurotic behavior as much as she is a locus for energy turned in upon itself, an arena for the struggle of being with nonbeing; in other words, the part calls for an actress with more intelligence than is common. Yet the other performances in the Fourth Street production and the English they speak (I believe the Michael Meyer translation is being used) go a long way toward overcoming some of the impediments to our grasp of the nature of Ibsen's art.

We have actually had quite a few good new translations of Ibsen lately (I trust this doesn't undermine my thesis about the prevailing lack of interest) of which the best I've seen are those by Meyer and by another Englishman, James Walter McFarlane. Oxford is putting his out, in handsome volumes which contain enough besides the texts themselves to make any Ibsenite rosy with gratitude: introductions, commentaries, early drafts of the plays, a compilation of Ibsen's pronouncements about them, material on their contemporary reception, a list of Ibsen productions in English and a thorough bibliography.

But the translation is of course what counts, and in the second volume of the series, which has just been issued, we can see just how far from Archer we have come. The book contains *Pillars of Society, A Doll's House* and *Ghosts,* the first three social plays chronologically and, the latter two at any rate, without doubt Ibsen's best-known works, as well as the dramas chiefly responsible for the Ibsen-image in all its obstinate wrongness and inadequacy.

Here is a scene from Act I of *Ghosts* in Archer's translations:

MRS. ALVING: Can't I really persuade you to stay the night here this time?

MANDERS: No, no; many thanks all the same; I will put up there as usual. It is so handy for getting on board the boat again.

MRS. ALVING: Of course you shall do as you please. But it seems to me quite another thing, now we are two old people—

MANDERS: Ha! Ha! You will have your joke! And it's natural you should be in high spirits today—first of all there is the great event tomorrow, and also you have got Oswald home.

MRS. ALVING: Yes, am I not a lucky woman! It is more than two years since he was home last, and he has promised to stay the whole winter with me.

MANDERS: Has he, really? That is very nice and filial of him; because there must be many more attractions in his life in Rome or in Paris, I should think.

MRS. ALVING: Yes, but he has his mother here, you see. Bless the dear boy, he has got a corner in his heart for his mother still.

MANDERS: Oh, it would be very sad if absence and preoccupation with such a thing as Art were to dull the natural affections.

And in McFarlane's version:

MRS. ALVING: Can't you be persuaded even yet to stay the night in my house?

MANDERS: No, no, Mrs. Alving, thanks all the same. I'll stay down there again as usual. It's so handy for catching the boat.

MRS. ALVING: Well, have it your own way. All the same, I really do think a couple of old things like us—

MANDERS: Dear me, you will have your little joke, won't you? Well, of course you must be feeling extremely pleased with yourself today. First the celebrations tomorrow, and then having Oswald home.

MRS. ALVING: Yes, just fancy! Isn't it marvelous! It's more than two years since he was last home. Now he's promised to stay with me the whole winter.

MANDERS: Has he now? There's a nice dutiful son for you. Because I imagine the attractions of living in Rome or Paris are altogether different.

MRS. ALVING: Yes, but you see here at home he has his mother. Ah, my dear darling boy . . . he still has a soft spot for his mother.

MANDERS: I must say it would be a sad thing if leaving home and taking up Art and all that interfered with his natural feelings.

I have deliberately chosen an extremely low-keyed section for my comparison, because something more "drastic" might obscure the point I wish to make. Surely the difference between the two passages, beyond McFarlane's redemption of Ibsen from "filial" and "natural affections" and that awful corner in the heart, is that in the one case we have a living conversation and in the other we simply haven't. And the prime benefit of that, the increment earned every time Ibsen is put into an English (or a French or German or any language) that someone somewhere might speak, is not so much a greater realism as a greater poetry.

For his poetry is not a matter of "poetic" language—the absence of that is precisely what the antirealists keep lamenting —but of a total dramatic vision; it rests in the intricate, endlessly subtle and astonishingly concentrated relationships of his characters, in the rhythms flowing beneath their actions, in the cross-weaving and cross-hatching of their effects upon each other—all of which closely resemble the relationship of words in a poem. And these structures of interconnection in Ibsen's dramas, these swiftly unfolding patterns of crucial human experience, are maintained under an aesthetic pressure of such intensity and delicacy that the slightest injury to the sense of life they communicate can send the whole thing into collapse, like a performer tumbling from a high wire.

As with the question of Ibsen's poetry, so with his dramatic structures. What has worked against him lately is our habit of blaming him for the very wellmadeness of his plays, as though he were only a super-Scribe from whom all the limitations of recent prosaic and gimmicky theatre flow. Short of taking up the matter full scale, I only want to say that one of the major elements in the extraordinary tension and rich ambiguity we feel in Ibsen's mature plays stems from the conflict between his poetic vision and the narrow theatre of realism which was the only one open to him. He took a system of dramaturgy which in lesser hands was, as Bentley says, "a toy . . . an end in itself," and made it yield him, sometimes grudgingly it's true, qualities much beyond itself.

The truth, as has been observed, is that Ibsen's theatrical artifices, his letters in mailboxes, burning orphanages, shots in the attic and sprung secrets, are designed to disguise and at the same time make possible a deeper artifice—that of his dramas' "life." They are the lies that lead to truth, the ruses by which the audience is made to enter and remain within a world it would otherwise execrate, because it does that to everything that might change it. In understanding Ibsen a rule of thumb to follow is that the mechanics of the plot always set free a denser meaning and imaginative substance than they literally contain, just as the "ideas" with which most of his plays are presumed to deal are never the deepest concepts which govern them.

How Ibsen has suffered from our everlasting nonsense about the drama of ideas! When are we going to see that *A Doll's House* is not so much a play with a thesis about women's rights as one with a perception about human rights and the despotism of most relationships—Bentley has said that the play would remain valid if Torvald were the wife and Nora the husband—and that *Ghosts* does not deal at its deepest level with the notion of the evil effects of heredity but with the tragedy of the spirit enmeshed in fact? We are probably not going to see it until we see again that *Antigone,* for example, concerns the idea of man's obligation to his humanity and that the political conflict in the play only serves that theme as occasion and springboard.

That is to say, all significant drama functions on two major levels, a perennial truth which we perennially forget. I am of course schematizing dreadfully, but let me describe these as thesis-occasion-plot and idea-vision-action. A play's thesis is not the same as its controlling idea; its occasion or specificities are not coterminous with its vision; its plot is not identical with its action, these movements of the spirit and psyche that go on in it. As Fergusson has written about *Ghosts,* "Mrs. Alving is tragically seeking; she suffers a series of pathoses and new insights in the course of the play; and this rhythm of will, feeling and insight underneath the machinery of the plot is the form of the life of the play, the soul of the tragedy."

If we feel that compared to most of the later work *A Doll's House* and *Ghosts* and especially *Pillars of Society* are flawed, it isn't because they are more purely "thesis" plays but because in them idea and imagination, vision and dramatic means are as yet imperfectly fused, and because the sacrifices made to the exigencies of the realistic stage are greater here. *Pillars of Society,* the play with which Ibsen broke with the past, suffers particularly from its obtrusive apparatus and even more from its avoidance of tragedy or that state of suspended judgment and ambiguous possibility that so often in Ibsen, as in Chekhov, constitutes the threshold of tragedy.

But *A Doll's House* and *Ghosts* stumble too. The former takes too long getting to the point where it will leave the well-made play behind—that is, where Nora's intrigue gives way to her discovery of Torvald's real nature and the drama becomes a moral quest. *Ghosts* cannot find a conclusion of the same depth and clarity as its preceding parts; Mrs. Alving's horrified cry offers us only the sound of tragedy, not its crystallization or summarizing image. But from one play to the next we can see Ibsen's mastery growing, as his ideas find their fitting analogues in actions and his devices become more and more instruments of revelation. Thematically, too, the plays are a progress, documenting, as McFarlane says, "a process of emancipation by ordeal," growing always more severe and un-compromising. "*Ghosts* had to be written," Ibsen himself de-clared. "I couldn't remain standing at *A Doll's House;* after Nora Mrs. Alving . . . had to come."

And everything else had to come after that. "In every new play I have aimed at my own spiritual emancipation and puri-fication," Ibsen wrote, and after *Ghosts* or once *An Enemy of the People*—his answer to the critics of *Ghosts*—was out of the way, each new play, coming at that relentless pace of one every two years, marks a deepening of this journey into the self and this search for spiritual wholeness that are at least as far-reaching and courageous as anything in our literature. At the end, with the so-called symbolic plays, Ibsen reaches the uttermost limits of art, where it questions its own *raison d'être* and thereby questions life most radically. In the severity and nobility of its undertaking, *When We Dead Awaken* is com-parable among recent works of this kind only, I think, to Mann's *Dr. Faustus.*

And there, stretching back from that last anguished state-ment to the first heroic step that replenished our resources, it all lies. Northern, cramped, hard, swift, perverse, unsparing, poised on knife-edges, in subject matter often "massively com-mon and middle-class," as Henry James said, but as he also said "never trivial and never cheap . . . the perfect practice of a difficult and delicate art." The theatre has rightly flowed past Ibsen in half a dozen directions but he has not been superseded, any more than Shakespeare and Sophocles have. For he gave us, in Shaw's words, "not only ourselves, but our-selves in our own situations." Have we really exhausted the substance and implications of that gift? Have we ever really accepted it? (1961)

¶ The Special Quality
of Joan

We are pretty well agreed that *Saint Joan* is a very good play, perhaps a great one, but there is no sort of agreement as to where its excellence lies. There is not even much consideration of the matter. *Saint Joan* rolls into town every three or four years and the reviewers, whether or not they like the particular production, roll out their adjectives to meet it—"stirring," "warm," "compassionate," and the like. But they use those words about Anouilh's *The Lark* and did about Maxwell Anderson's *Joan of Lorraine*, with no sort of discrimination. They cannot or will not say why Shaw's play is so much bigger and aesthetically more impregnable than Anouilh's, nor why *The Lark*, in turn, is such a long jump beyond Mr. Anderson's variation.

Ordinarily, plays on the same subject need not be judged by comparison with one another, since there are legitimately differing approaches to almost anything. Yet in Joan's case we do feel impelled to compare treatments, one reason being that she is by now so normative a myth, so commonly held an imaginative possession of mankind, that we have certain expectations concerning any use made of her story. Another reason is that the fact of half the drama's having already been written—splendidly in the court records and contemporary accounts—severely limits the playwright's freedom to invent, at the same time as it gives him a huge initial impetus.

The story, then, is essentially unchanging, though a particular aspect may be stressed, as in Dryer's film *The Passion of Joan of Arc*, or the opera *Joan at the Stake*. What is still free is the use that may be made of it. Following much the same course of events, the plays of Shaw, Anouilh and Anderson are distinguished from one another by intention as well as by craft: Anouilh celebrates "man" triumphing over abstraction, producing what is basically a pleasant poetic image; Anderson apostrophizes some bourgeois notion of "ultimate" values in a poetic prose of unpleasant pretentiousness; and Shaw—well, Shaw writes a drama.

Saint Joan has its faults. Eric Bentley has commented on how stale the anti-English jokes are and on how the first part of the play, what Shaw called its "romance," is inferior to the later scenes. But there is a case to be made for its being, along with *Heartbreak House*, Shaw's greatest achievement, the nearest thing we have to a quintessence of Shavianism. For Shaw was fundamentally a dialectical thinker, a writer of dramas for the mind (something quite different from mental dramas), and in this play the clash of truths is on a heroic scale.

Those truths have nowhere been better stated than in the preface to the play, and nowhere more succinctly there than in the letter Shaw quotes from a Catholic priest. "In your play," the man writes, "I see the dramatic presentation of the Regal, sacerdotal and Prophetic powers in which Joan was crushed." A simpler way to put it is in terms of the individual against the collectivity, which is the way it is usually seen. But Shaw does something far greater than merely defend or exalt the individual, as Anouilh, for instance does.

The priest's letter continues: "To me it is not the victory of any one of them over the others that will bring peace and the Reign of the Saints in the Kingdom of God, but their fruitful interaction in a costly but noble tension." To which Shaw remarks that it could not be better put. For a priest to have seen so early that Shaw was not engaging in anti-Catholic polemics (as Anouilh certainly is) is remarkable, but it is even more astonishing that he should have seen how very useful the play is precisely for those to whom Joan is a saint and not only a heroine.

The usefulness is that of all art to correct the imbalances and evasions of abstract intelligence. For the Catholic, if he is honest, there is a persistent difficulty with the double truth that the Church condemned Joan and then canonized her.

Theology cannot really satisfy on the point, but art, Shaw's lucid, unafraid, *secularized* art is able to. Joan had to be condemned and had to be declared a saint: that is the truth of the play, and it is what lifts it above all those other approaches to Joan which see her as victim merely or as hold-out and exemplar, the free soul brought down by the enemies of freedom.

"A costly but noble tension." *Saint Joan* is concerned with that. Subdivided, the tension is of several kinds: between Church and State and between their institutional necessities and those of the individual; between change and tradition; and, finally, in its internal structure as a work of art, between tragedy and comedy. The two modes do not simply alternate but attain that creative fusion which is the mark of the best drama of our time, and we see it perhaps at its most intense point in the Epilogue, which so many misunderstanders of Shaw continue to disdain, the Epilogue whose dominant note is irony—a stance which participates as nearly equally in tragedy and comedy as any we can take.

All this (itself of course the sketchiest of notes for an essay) is prefatory to a judgment of the Old Vic's production of *Saint Joan*. There is not much to say about it; like most productions it has no center, like most, its Joan is not up to the image we have formed from the text. Barbara Jefford is strong but without style, without that capacity to modulate through all the degrees and kinds of being that Shaw's heroine possesses. And the company isn't good enough, the director not intelligent enough, to work for that highly wrought condition of balance and sanity that is Shaw's great gift and the special quality of *Saint Joan*.

When an audience is found laughing with disbelief at certain of the speeches of Warwick and Cauchon, it may be a faulty audience but it is just as likely to be a faulty production, one which itself doesn't believe in the fact that, as Shaw went to such lengths to insist, there are no villains in the piece. "Normally innocent people . . . in the energy of their righteousness burned Joan," he wrote, and the proper way to play his drama is to keep them normally innocent while keeping Joan herself in that notch above normality and that committed

space just above mere innocence which make for her true
glory. To screw her persecutors down and screw Joan up is to
turn the play toward what it is assuredly not—a melodrama.
(1962)

¶Between Anger and Despair

> And there, there overhead, there, there, hung over
> Those thousands of white faces, those dazed eyes
> There in the starless dark the poise, the hover,
> There with vast wings across the canceled skies,
> There in the sudden blackness the
> black pall of nothing, nothing,
> nothing—nothing at all.
>
> —ARCHIBALD MACLEISH, "The End of the World"

Like an enormous fake elephant, an inflated contrivance to elicit oohs and ahs from the children, Eugene O'Neill's *Strange Interlude* has come into view again on Broadway, after having been in storage for nearly thirty-five years. And the children have responded beautifully, walking around the astonishing object with awed faces, in loving patience and with a sense of privilege, as if everything else on display in the world could now only be thought of as an illusion next to this thick, gray reality. Ah, children, Jumbo is back. Ah, dear children, when are we going to see you grow up?

Bernard De Voto once wrote *apropos* of O'Neill that *"Lazarus Laughed, The Great God Brown, Marco Millions* or *Dynamo*—one or another of them must be the silliest play of our time." Just so. But I would nominate *Strange Interlude* for more refulgent honors: as the most atrociously ill-written and ill-conceived play of our time, as the falsest "masterpiece" in the theatre, as very likely the worst play that has ever been written by a dramatist with a reputation. And what makes its current revival such an occasion for outrage is precisely the reverent atmosphere surrounding the event, the fact that as the first offering of the Actors Studio, that *soi-disant* savior of the arts of the theatre in America, it is being presented as

Revelation, crammed as full of stars as the Milky Way and made to blot out by its sheer pretentious gaseous bulk, its surrogate presence, any glimpse we might have had of an area of hope for maturity on our native stages and among our audiences.

I beg my readers' indulgence. I can't decide which is greater, my anger or my despair, and I can't be temperate. There is a process which psychiatry calls abreaction, the "release of psychic tension through verbalizing," and I ask to be allowed to engage in it. Oh, the unrelieved horror of that evening, which began at six, was interrupted at eight thirty for a dinner break (during which strong-armed waiters from nearby restaurants hustled the "Interlude crowd" to tables and thrust "Interlude Specials" in front of us) and continued on until half past eleven, although long before that hour the experience had taken on the quality of bitter, hopeless eternity. Bathed in the piety and idiot enthusiasm of that audience for whom O'Neill is holy writ, assaulted in our intelligence, aesthetic faculties and simple hope of physical survival, we came as close to conceiving an irreparable hatred for the theatre as only such a misuse of it as this can bring you to.

The despair sets in immediately, from the moment Marsden, the effete novelist, utters the play's first line—"How perfectly the professor's unique haven!"—and all the dim memories of the impossible language revive and sicken you with foreboding. It is a commonplace to speak of O'Neill's verbal deficiencies, but in *Strange Interlude* they are at their most flagrant because the play is literally nothing but talk—grotesquely artificial dialogue and those intolerable asides which have been seen as a profound theatrical innovation but which instead constitute one of the most colossal dramaturgical evasions on record.

The asides either tell the audience what it already knows or serve to choke the action of the play; the one thing they never do is contribute to any understanding of the characters that could not have been gained through direct speech, if O'Neill had been capable of that. It is just the playwright's task to make dialogue illuminate inner states, to fuse expression with the not-to-be-expressed. And indeed the fantastic ineptitude of *Strange Interlude* can be seen by measuring it against any work by Strindberg, the master whom O'Neill plundered and so badly misunderstood, and who in seven minutes on the same themes of sexuality, repression and the ravages of passion could convey precisely through dialogue unfathomably more than O'Neill in his four-and-a-half-hours of mutterings.

Quarter-baked Strindberg, tenth-rate Freud—the play is a vast mine of reductive psychologizing, spurious philosophy, adolescent mysticism, unrealized emotion and sentimentality on an epic scale. I have the space and the remaining sanity to quote only these examples from its endless wind-tunnel of false, foolish language:

"Yes, he's dead—my father—whose passion created me— who began me—he is ended. There is only his end living—his death. It lives now to draw nearer me, to draw me nearer, to become my end!"

"Oh, afternoons . . . dear wonderful afternoons of love with you, my lover . . . you are lost . . . gone from me forever!"

". . . and what has their loving to do with me? . . . my life is cool green shade wherein comes no scorching zenith sun of passion and possession to wither the heart with bitter poisons . . . my life gathers roses, coolly crimson, in sheltered gardens, on late afternoons in love with evening . . . my life is an evening . . . Nina is a rose . . . my rose. . . ."

Is it possible that this can really be taken seriously? Does the Actors Studio all-star cast take it seriously? Yes, indeed, for it gives these self-indulgent, arrogant performers a mighty opportunity to exhibit themselves in all their panoply of mannerism, artiness and self-myth. And José Quintero has directed them in exactly the way which will best give the lie to the Studio's professions of belief in ensemble playing: as a group of discrete individuals who occupy their respective areas of the stage as though they were independent and self-sufficient fiefdoms.

In the role of Nina, Geraldine Page has lapsed back into

her archest peculiarities, the breathiness, curled lip, portentous pauses and Mona Lisa smile which were splendid properties for a starlet on the way up. As Darrell, Ben Gazzara wears the same coat hanger under his suit that has always determined his mannequin movements; as Sam, Pat Hingle capers frantically around in order to convey the Natural Man; as his mother, Betty Field exhibits an astounding consistency in maintaining a piercing nonstop one-note delivery; as Nina's father, Franchot Tone seems in imminent danger of collapse; and as Madeline, Jane Fonda is her usual obnoxiously ingénue self. Only William Prince as Marsden seemed to me to come off with a shred of dignity. In this most absurd of all these absurd roles he managed to hold out a truth of his own which beat back the nonsense that O'Neill had written. It was a handsome performance, one that overcame all those references to his mother fixation and the murderous lines about purity and passionless love.

And so that is the scene. I have eased my rage and frustration in describing it to you, but you may wish to subject yourself to it nevertheless. If you are a masochist, there is nothing I can say, I have in fact helped you. But if you merely wish to subject yourself to O'Neill, out of unresolved confusion or lingering respect, I suggest you choose instead the film of *Long Day's Journey Into Night*. In that play, as in a few others of his last years, O'Neill broke through, became an artist and found the form for his vague floating passion for the "big things." In *Strange Interlude* the big things have no form, no language and, finally, no existence whatsoever. (1963)

¶Mr. O'Neill's Very Last Curtain Call

With *More Stately Mansions* we have apparently come to the end of the "lost" O'Neill manuscripts—which means that nothing is likely to turn up now as a new element in our judgment of his achievement and place. That judgment, it has to be repeated, is a continuing critical effort in the face of the acts of piety and apotheosis which go on being celebrated at O'Neill's shrine in the center of our established theatre.

We need O'Neill to be our greatest dramatist because, as Eric Bentley remarked of his cult some years ago, what are we to think of our native drama if he is not? From such local considerations to certain absolute ones is, however, a seductive step, and it never stops being taken.

If there is one point around which hard critical opinion, as distinguished from chauvinistic rhetoric or inarticulate zealotry, has coalesced it is that O'Neill's last plays constitute his strongest claim to permanent stature. It is a thin claim when measured against the accomplishments of his European contemporaries such as Shaw, Brecht or Pirandello, or his immediate predecessors like Ibsen, Strindberg and Chekhov. But at least *The Iceman Cometh* and *Long Day's Journey Into Night* do not have to be ashamed in that company, whereas we have been made increasingly aware of how inexorably the plays of O'Neill's middle period, upon which his aggrandizement has chiefly been built, are slipping out of consciousness, literature and indeed any reality except an antiquarian one. The recent intolerable productions of *Strange Interlude* and *Marco Millions* provide all the evidence anyone can want.

More Stately Mansions, which has never been performed here, belongs to O'Neill's penultimate period. It is one of the two plays—*A Touch of the Poet* is the other—which remain from the projected nine-play cycle about an American family that O'Neill called "A Tale of Possessors Self-Dispossessed."

The history of the project is a complicated one, but we do know that O'Neill completed four of the plays and was partway through three others when out of some unrecorded dissatisfaction he destroyed everything but the two works we now have. These were given after his death by his widow, Carlotta Monterey O'Neill, to Dr. Karl Gierow, the director of the Royal Dramatic Theatre in Stockholm, where they were first staged—*A Touch of the Poet* in 1957 and *More Stately Mansions* in 1962. Dr. Gierow, a prefatory note informs us, had to reduce the latter play from a script that would have taken nine or ten hours to perform to something under half that, and it is his shortened text, along with some further minor editing by Donald Gallup of the Yale library, which this volume offers us.

O'Neill's cycle was to have chronicled the history and moral fate of an American merchant family from the Revolution to 1932. *More Stately Mansions* (the title is from a poem by Oliver Wendell Holmes) was to have been the fourth play in the series, its action beginning where *A Touch of the Poet* left off. The latter work was centered on the figure of Con Melody, the rough, handsome, dreaming Irishman who ran a tavern in Massachusetts and affected to scorn the American aristocracy he really feared, and on his daughter, Sarah, who accomplished a breakthrough into that aristocracy's precincts by winning one of its scions. In the new play Melody is dead and Sarah is married to Simon Harford, heir to a commercial fortune and a man whose "touch of the poet" is destined to be replaced by a moral stain.

He is the arena for an epic struggle between the sundered halves of the American nature—its idealism and its materialistic impulses—which were also, of course, the major elements in O'Neill's always dangerously schematic grasp of activity. Beginning as a fervent champion of human rights (he is supposed to be working on a book outlining the principles of a future classless society), Simon is gradually transformed into a merchant prince caught up in the self-perpetuating and self-justifying acquisitiveness of an expanding nation. From a belief, "with Rousseau," that "at bottom human nature is good and unselfish," he comes to announce that "the only moral law is the strong are rewarded, the weak are punished . . . all else is an idealistic lie . . ."

But his hardening into a physical absolute and instrument of power is accompanied, like a nemesis, by sapping of his will and consciousness. The entire process is presided over by two women, his wife, Sarah, and his mother, Deborah, between whom the great monoliths of O'Neill's thought and emotion are divided. The women do battle for possession of him, the wife in the interests of her animal vitality and hunger for position and solidity, the mother out of a romantic flight from possessions and a need for the illusory consolations of "art." In the end the wife wins, but the cost is Simon's reduction to a dependency, though O'Neill clearly wished to make the denouement a liberation.

Throughout the play O'Neill's desires outrun his capacities, as they do almost everywhere in his work until the last phase, when through a reduction of scope and what we might call a localization of language he was able to fuse his moral and aesthetic intentions, to find a rhetoric which did not escape like a balloon from his feeling and a structure in which his thought did not appear dwarfed.

But here the fusion is not achieved; the moral and metaphysical critique and vision exist mostly as a series of statements and isolated confrontations which lack an organic base and a coherent impulse. As elsewhere in O'Neill there is a strenuous attempt to compensate for this condition through an atmosphere of portentousness, a heavy air of "high" poetry, apocalypse, fervid declamations and mysterious psychological irruptions. The following passage is typical, down to the exclamation points:

"But how stupid! These insane interminable dialogues with self! I must find someone outside myself in whom I can confide, and so escape myself—someone strong and healthy and sane, who dares to love and live life greedily instead of reading and dreaming about it!"

In this and other respects, *More Stately Mansions* is closer to plays like *Strange Interlude* (which it further resembles in its use of spoken thoughts) and *Desire Under the Elms* than to *The Iceman Cometh* or *Long Day's Journey* or, for that matter, to *A Touch of the Poet*. From time to time, it does reach that work's colloquial strength and unforced emotion, but much more often its urgency disappears in *sturm und drang*, and it never attains the clean simplicity, circumscribed ground and manageable ambitions of the other play in the cycle.

O'Neill, if we needed any more proof, was the victim of his ill-defined encounter with "Tragedy" and the "Soul," forever trying to embody them in works which, like this one, could not be compelled into clarity or convincing life; when the coercion stopped and he gave form to what his imagination had truly known and not merely aspired to, art at last became possible. (1964)

¶ "One Thing after Another"

"I have every cause to grow red with shame where History is concerned," Georg Büchner, the astonishing genius who died in 1837 at the age of 23, once wrote to a friend. In *Danton's Death* Büchner dealt directly with the shamefulness of history, which he saw as a record of human corruptibility and personal powerlessness. In *Woyzeck* his imagination focused on a single man, a humble but violent representative of the soul's own anguished history. Yet both plays are at once public and private indictments of man's institutions and lyric outcries against his perennial fate. Between them they constitute the fountainhead of most of the significant drama of the modern age.

Last week the Bavarian State Theatre offered New Yorkers a *Woyzeck* of all but perfect rhythms and proportions. (A simultaneous translation from German into English was provided by individual transistor receivers.) On its first visit to the United States the Munich-based troupe, which is subsidized by the Bavarian state government, prefaced Büchner's masterpiece with a short play by Goethe, *The Accomplices*, a dusty museum piece about adultery and light-hearted domestic malfeasance. But when the curtain went up at last on *Woyzeck*, all lovers of drama in the audience came fully awake.

Measuredly, carefully, with the utmost restraint and simplicity, Director Hans Lietzau allowed Büchner's play, which was left at his death as a series of fragmentary scenes, to shape its somber but infinitely resonant life on the stage. The single set was composed of dirty, flaking gray brick walls, a broken-down staircase and rickety platform—a scene out of an urban hell. If anything was lacking it was a sense of diversity; there was a certain monotony about some of the staging and a running together of scenes, which might have been more effectively separated by a greater use of music.

Yet the very absence of theatrical "touches" contributed to the implacable reality of the play, which is both fable and case history. Büchner based it on an actual event, a soldier's murder of his faithless mistress. The historical event had occasioned a lengthy debate about the man's sanity, but Büchner lifted the question to one of absolute universality: the nature of existence itself, which seemed to him mad, intolerably painful and without redemption.

Woyzeck, the murderer, brilliantly played by Heinrich Schweiger, is half oafish victim, half supersensitive judge of an aberrant universe. He is tormented by military bullies, made into an object of medical curiosity, mocked and derided by all the powers that compose the universe. Most tormenting to him is the power of sex; to be betrayed by his lover is the full revelation of the abyss. "God," he cries in anguish, "blow out the sun and let them roll on each other in their lechery! Man and woman and man and beast! They'll do it in the light of the sun! They'll do it in the palm of your hand like flies!"

Then, as the flayed Woyzeck drags himself up the stairs after being savagely humiliated, he mutters, "It's one thing after another." Such powerful alternations of tone occur throughout the play, which abandons traditional narrative and thematic development for a ritual procession of images. "I get so dizzy around such people," someone says of Woyzeck. Tragic, profound and prophetic. *Woyzeck* is a dizzying plunge into the whirlpool of truth.

¶ Our Trouble with Strindberg

If it is difficult to do Ibsen properly on our stages, it seems almost impossible to do Strindberg in the right way. Of course even the Scandinavians find Strindberg's fantasies and expressionistic dramas to be slippery propositions for directors and actors, but in this country we can't seem to get at his "naturalistic" dramas either. Everything has a way of coming out wrong: tone, pace, color, relationships, meaning. And the result is that Strindberg remains known to us in a literary mode chiefly, as a great imbalanced founder of the modern imagination, a precursor whose effect it is possible to trace in the textbooks but whose creations we never take hold of or allow fully to take hold of us.

Of the three great works of his main naturalistic period in the late 1880's—*The Father, Miss Julie,* and *Creditors*—the last would appear to be the one which would be least likely to make us flounder. It is, after all, an astonishingly concise and structurally coherent play, perhaps Strindberg's masterpiece in this respect, and, as a "tragi-comedy," it is neither so turbid with partly unclarified and undramatized emotion as *The Father,* nor so grimly "destructive" and intent on combining personal and sociological disaster in a single body as *Miss Julie.* Still, the three works do have one difficulty in common.

The trouble is, of course, with Strindberg's kind of naturalism. Even more than Ibsen, he confronts us with the spectacle of plays which while seeming to adhere to naturalistic conventions communicate a sense that something quite beyond naturalistic intentions is being carried forward. It has less to do with action than with character, even though an unsettling change has come over plot as well. As Strindberg wrote in the great preface to *Miss Julie,* "What will offend simple minds is that my plot is not simple, nor its point of view single. In real life an action . . . is generally caused by a whole series of motives, more or less fundamental, but as a rule the spectator chooses just one of these—the one which his mind can most readily grasp. . . ."

But inherent in this is the truth that plot and character are aspects of one another, so that if one changes the other must. You cannot have a new dramaturgy without a new conception of character, and for Strindberg, uniting as he did the age's increasing awareness of psychic complexity and social dissolution with a private set of torments of both psychic and social origin, it was the idea of character in drama that underwent the first transformation. In fact, we trace the thing that muddies his work and sometimes keeps it from the light of absolute art to his never-resolved struggle to find forms for this new, abstract conception of character; a conception which recent theatre has carried to one of its ultimate conclusions.

"Because they are modern characters, living in a period of transition more feverishly hysterical than its predecessor at least, I have drawn my figures vacillating, disintegrated, a blend of old and new." More than this, Strindberg's characters depart from what the stage had been used to by their lack of clear outline, their existence less as persons than as aspects of the psyche and soul, shifting foci of feeling, impulse and will. Inserted as they are into "real" contexts in the naturalistic plays, they strain against these limits and set us the problem of so staging the works as to keep them from flying apart, on the one hand, and to preserve them from the heaviness and darkening effect of detail, narration and verisimilitude on the other.

All this is by way of preface to the judgment that the current revival of *Creditors* does not come off. Its failure is due to the usual causes. It is played as a piece of naturalism, with precise settings and individualized characters. But at the same time, because it has been sensed that something is there that demands liberation from story and straightforward presentation and the illusion of actuality, it is played in an orotund, declamatory style by one of its three actors, in a hoarse, brooding manner by another, and in a half-kittenish, half-tigerish one by the third, all three performances working at cross-purposes in their attempts to shake free of the costumes and the surface of realism.

During the first act (the concession to our short attention span and need to smoke is deplorable: Strindberg made much of the play's being a single integrated act, and it does, after all, take only an hour and a half to perform) Donald Davis declaiming as Gustav and James Ray brooding as Adolf never once make contact with each other or with us. Only when Rae Allen's sharp and intense Tekla comes on stage does the play break into any kind of life, even if it is never quite the right sort. Miss Allen does at least suggest, by her subtleties, improvisations, charged pauses and abrupt transitions, the complex, wayward vision Strindberg intended—a vision of implacable forces within us and in our relationships, the "creditors" who exact payment for our hungers and our thrusts beyond our limits.

It is difficult to say what has to be done to allow plays like *Creditors* to continue to exist in, or to be revivified for, our theatres. One thing is certain; as Eric Bentley has remarked with his unfailing perception of why things go right or wrong, you have to play Strindberg's naturalistic dramas furiously, Dionysiacally, the comic aspects as well as the tragic. For it is fatal to allow even a trace of the drawing room to creep in.

But beyond that, is it too radical to suggest that dramas like these might be presented entirely outside the naturalistic skins in which they were first created? Presented with their passions abstracted, as it were, on bare stages and in modern or symbolic dress, with everything cleared for the emergence of those underlying essences, those dreams and nightmares that are still attached here to particular minds and souls but that push unceasingly toward existence in their own right? It will of course not be Strindberg in technical purity, but it may be more of Strindberg than we have been getting. (1962)

¶Pirandello to Perfection

In his preface to *Six Characters in Search of an Author* Pirandello tells us that he has the "misfortune" to be a philosophic writer. The complaint is for the most part a disingenuous one, since he acknowledges that it is just the philosophic or metaphysical impulse in his work that gives it its force and special nature, that this is what distinguishes him from those writers who simply describe or narrate. Yet Pirandello was not being wholly disingenuous; in the light of the artificial and crippling distinctions that are made between philosophy and art, between thought and drama, to be considered a philosophic playwright can indeed be a source of real misfortune.

The evil can show itself in several ways. You can regard Pirandello as so abstract, so immersed in a purely intellectual game that you miss entirely the deep passion of his work, a passion set apart from its traditional treatment in drama by its fusion with intellect, its being made to rise out of intellect and especially from the clash of mind with itself and with the enigmas of existence. Or you can deliberately play down the metaphysical aspects in order to release the sheer theatricality, turning the work into physical farce, the way Tyrone Guthrie did a few years ago in his rambunctious and soul-killing production of *Six Characters* at the Phoenix. Only when you understand that to see Pirandello whole means to see ideas and action in the most thoroughgoing fusion can you do his work justice in the mind and in production.

William Ball is a director who does see Pirandello whole and who has the taste, wit, mind and inventiveness to mount what he sees with nearly flawless beauty. His production of *Six Characters* is by far the finest I have ever seen, nor have I any hesitation in saying that I cannot imagine there ever having been a better one in this country.

He has used a new translation by Paul Avila Mayer, which

gets him off to a flying start, since the English version that has most frequently been used up to now, the one by Edward Storer, is stiff and in many places archaic and is, moreover, based on a text which does not incorporate the changes, especially those affecting the final scenes, which Pirandello continued to make. Mayer's rendering is based on one of the late texts; its English is immensely lively and accurate, colloquial where that is called for and grave, lyrical or declamatory when those qualities are required.

On this floor Ball has constructed a miracle of subtle staging. The key to *Six Characters* is of course in the relationships and interplay between the troupe of actors and the family that has come to get its "story" performed. Ball handles this interplay with brilliant craftsmanship, creating an extraordinary rhythm of speech, gesture and movement, maintaining through the most imaginative and finely paced groupings the tensions and ambiguities that hold the two "casts" in equilibrium with one another, just as imagination and actuality, the play's subjects, are held in the richest balance.

In a production so beautifully of a piece as this one is, it seems superfluous to single out individual scenes for praise. But two retain a special resonance in my memory. One is the first appearance of the family, who after a momentary failure of the lights on the stage where the company is rehearsing, are revealed in a compact group at the rear, swaying silently from side to side and bathed in a thin light; it is a shattering moment. The other scene is that in which the stepdaughter pleads with the absent author to "write our play!" and his presence is overwhelmingly evoked.

The performances are on a level with the direction, and indeed in some cases seem to have been elicited by the direction like a genie from a bottle. Jacqueline Brooks, for example, has never been noted for more than routine capacity in the classical roles she has been assaying, but she plays the stepdaughter with truly splendid verve and ferocity. As the director of the acting company Michael O'Sullivan is superbly the figure of Pirandello's intention: vigorous yet whimsical, put upon, diplomatic and long-suffering, a hard-headed man of the theatre who is nevertheless swept up into a new dimension of experience. Among others I might mention are David Margulies and Anne Lynn of the acting troupe and Richard A. Dysart as the father. But with the exception of James Valentine's somewhat strident and oratorical conception of the son, the performances are deserving of nothing but admiration.

In case I have failed to make it clear enough, I will say again that this *Six Characters* is not to be missed. You are not likely ever to see Pirandello presented with greater imagination and vivacity or with greater fidelity to his complex vision of the relationship between levels of truth and his passionate inquiry into the nature of reality. You are not likely, for that matter, to see any play this season which comes close to matching the pleasures and excitements of this one.

It pains me to have to add a note of warning about another Pirandello work being presented Off-Broadway these days. It is an extremely minor caprice of its author, something which has been translated as *Call it Virtue*, and its one-joke, one-conceit equipment very quickly runs down. But even considering the material he had to work with, its director, Amnon Kabatchnik, comes off terribly; he is, on the basis of this work at least, as shabby a director as William Ball is a resplendent one. (1963)

III/Contemporaries

¶Earliest Ionesco

Eugène Ionesco has for some time now possessed the status of a contemporary master. One of the founders of a new dramatic sensibility and one of the architects of a changed mode of theatrical procedure, he is almost as centrally located in the present landscape of the serious drama as Pirandello and Shaw were in the previous one and Ibsen and Chekhov in the one before that. Of living playwrights only Beckett and Genet have a comparable influence and only they elicit the same kind of admiration—an admiration reserved for those who have altered our ways of seeing and rediscovered for us a lost or interred aspect of existence.

The three came to our awareness about the same time, a dozen or so years ago, and in looking back it would seem that Ionesco has traveled further from his beginnings than either of the others. Beckett has largely remained within the territory of *Waiting for Godot* and *Endgame,* mining their quarries and refining what he takes out; Genet has become more complex and apocalyptic, but the forms of his imagination and his attitude toward reality have not changed much. Ionesco, on the other hand, has come a long way, both imaginatively and technically, from his first small plays, those astonishing exercises in the terrors of logic and the vertigo of reason which announced a radical overthrow of dramatic conventions and an end to psychology and emotional commerce on the stage.

What was being displayed to those tiny audiences who attended the first performances of *The Bald Soprano* and *The Lesson* was, as Jean Vannier has written, "a drama of language, wherein human speech is put on exhibition." The clichés of the first play, which Ionesco was inspired to write by his dizzying encounter with an English phrase-book, and the deadly logical flights of the second, were the dramas themselves, not simply means of advancing some anteriorly conceived "action" or of illustrating character or even, as the chief dignified misreading of Ionesco would have it, of mocking the orderly processes of social existence and celebrating an absurd counterpart.

To see a new production of *The Bald Soprano* and *The Lesson* is to be chiefly struck by how thoroughly they do depend upon language and, especially, upon language employed for specific insurrectionary ends at a certain moment of cultural time—language rebelling against previous uses, against exhaustion, misdirection, a too great weight of expectation, against, precisely, its own perennial tendencies and fate.

It is not that these first plays are purely verbal; from the start Ionesco showed himself a master of movement and stage business, and even more a great arranger of rhythms larger than those of speech, rhythms for speech to be contained in, as that of the professor in *The Lesson* is contained within the diapason of the total furious work. But at first everything of this kind is subordinated to the vision of language on its own, self-condemning, ludicrous, pitted against its past and pointing to no sort of future except that of an intensification of its present state of outrage and murderous self-arraignment.

Ionesco, however, had a future, and it was to go beyond the exigencies and fatalities of language, although they were always to remain a condition of his work. His later plays are richer and more complex; in them new lyrical and philosophic modes develop, humor becomes less a matter of linguistic sport than of the tension between appearance and reality, the dramatic consciousness spreads to include fuller states of being and more inclusive attitudes toward the horrifying, the banal, the metaphysically unjustifiable. In his greatest plays— *Amedee, Victims of Duty, The Killer*—Ionesco has written works of the same solidity, fullness and permanence as his predecessors in the dramatic revolution that began with Ibsen and is still going on.

"To feel the absurdity of the commonplace and of language—its falseness," Ionesco has remarked, "is already to have gone beyond it. To go beyond it we must first of all bury ourselves in it." In the light of this we can understand why *The Bald Soprano* and *The Lesson,* for all their durability in comparison with the bulk of recent theatre, are not durable enough. They are not so much dated as superseded, their achievements have been absorbed into the larger accomplishment of the stage in our time, and they appear to us now, only a decade after their arrival, to distill a faint but growing air of remoteness and historical curiosity. In these plays Ionesco buried himself in the falseness and absurdity of language and shocked us into recognition; they provided a central, necessary moment in the reeducation of the contemporary sensibility, but the moment, perfect and inimitable, has passed.

Yet the plays are worth seeing again and certainly worth seeing for the first time. The present production Off-Broadway is an adequate one, at least on balance, since its *Bald Soprano* has a good many weak spots and its *Lesson* almost none. The former is being done in what its entrepreneurs describe as the "original Paris style," and if a stylization of the English interior and its denizens along Edwardian lines and an incantatory, anti-naturalistic method of acting constitute fidelity to the original, then I suppose the description is legitimate. But whether or not it is, the cast is only fitfully up to the job, only Gerald E. McGonagill as Mr. Smith striking me as completely sound and nearly beyond reproach. But Ronald Weyand as the professor in *The Lesson is* beyond reproach, by far the best of the four actors I have seen in the role and a perfect interpreter of Ionesco's demented, salient early dream. (1963)

¶Beckett's *Happy Days*

If Samuel Beckett's new play is rather less successful than its predecessors, its virtues are nevertheless many and its effectiveness undeniable. That question of effectiveness, far more than the meaning of the plays—which are really far less arcane than we have been led to think—has always been to me the interesting one to ask about Beckett's theatre. How does it manage to achieve its high intensity and complete conviction —how, really, does it *reach* us—after its apparent abandonment of most of the traditional means of dramatic communication?

Beckett is of course a master of certain classic procedures, especially of the more low-down and kinetic kinds; it is a commonplace that his plays draw from farce, vaudeville, the circus and Chaplin, and that, on the other hand, he carefully, if marginally, observes the dramatic unities. But like Kafka, who created a prose in which realism was a deceptive sea where the strangest fish could swim, Beckett puts the conventions he utilizes into the service of an unheard-of dramaturgy. It is a dramaturgy which appears to be a repudiation of the ordinary purposes of the theatre but is actually a miraculous resuscitation of those purposes through a process of purification, deepening and a change of ground.

The miracle lies in the fact that here every element that has been thought to be necessary to the theatre's conquest of life—plot, character, movement, linear revelation, the resolution of struggle—has dwindled to a set of notations and gestures, if anything at all remains; and yet life continues to rise from Beckett's stage as it does from few others.

Happy Days is Beckett's furthest move so far in the direction of absolute stillness, of a kind of motionless dance in which the internal agitation and its shaping control are descried through language primarily and through the spaces between words. On an otherwise bare stage, under ferocious light, the woman Winnie sits buried to her waist in a mound of earth throughout the first act, and to her neck throughout the second. Behind the mound we occasionally see the man Willie's head or hand. Near the end, however, Willie crawls round and at last comes fully into the sight of the audience in the play's only major physical movement.

There are a good many minor movements, mostly having to do with Winnie and the contents of a large bag. From it come various objects of everyday use—toothbrush, a comb, a mirror, a bottle of tonic—and her business with them imparts both humor and that minimal stir and palpability without which even so marvelous a theatre of language as Beckett's would lack its necessary anchor. But the language, and the anti-language (one of Beckett's chief supports, as well as one of his main themes is the tension produced by the struggle between speech and silence and by the double thrust of words toward truth and lies) do most of the work.

It is almost all in a monologue delivered by Winnie (who is played by Ruth White in a virtuoso performance of impressive dimension and nearly perfect fidelity to Beckett's intentions, as a glance at the published play will confirm; Willie's vastly smaller role is only adequately handled by John C. Becher). In it she laments her youth, praises "the great mercies," is by turns frightened, coy, reflective, bitter, aloof, anguished, ironic, joyous, angry and serene. And from it arises a sense of life apprehended in its utmost degree of non-contingency and existential self-containment, with all its cross-purposes, vagaries, agonies and waste, its oscillation between hope and despair, affirmation and denial—a new enunciation of Beckett's special vision.

But Beckett's theatre, as has been observed, is one of pairs —Gogo and Didi, Pozzo and Lucky, Nagg and Nell, Hamm and Clov, Krapp and his taped voice—and in *Happy Days* Willie's presence serves Winnie as one of the poles of her address and the distant source of her sorrow and joy. One could say that the theme of the play is their relationship—we know them to be married—and that Beckett is commenting on the abyss between them. Yet, in his theatre, relationships are never explored for their own sakes, not even as archetypes; what is explored is the nature of a reality where everything, including every relationship, is in doubt and tension.

In any case, the slight feeling of disappointment with which I left the play stemmed, I felt, from the inadequacy of Beckett's treatment of Willie. He has none of the contrapuntal quality that we find in the other linkings, and he is too likely to turn the play toward satire or parody. Besides, he is made to perform, in the play's penultimate action, a disturbingly obvious and sentimental bit of business, the only one I have ever found in Beckett.

Still, *Happy Days* survives, a light in the season and a minor brick in the edifice being raised by the playwright who is to me the most valuable we have. If I were asked to identify that value, I could do no better than quote Jacques Guicharnaud, whose essay on Beckett in his *Modern French Theatre* is unsurpassed. After remarking that *Waiting for Godot* is not an allegory, he says what it is in words that apply equally well to each of Beckett's works: "It is a concrete and synthetic equivalent of our existence in the world and our consciousness of it." How rich are we in those? (1961)

¶ Pinter's Hits—and Misses

The thing hardly anybody seems to have noticed about the plays of Harold Pinter is that what is so effective about them is also the source of much that is unsatisfying. At his best, Pinter is a dramatist of high urgency, clear color and unimpeachable intentions. He has the right kind of dissatisfactions and impenitences, the accurate chimeras, the anxieties, hungers and vertigos proper to our time. And he has a high degree of freedom from the expectations of audiences, an aloofness from the theatre conceived of as a place of mutual congratulation, a toughness, or blessed innocence, to resist most of the pressures to make his plays serve other purposes than their own—to prevent them from "commenting" on our condition, or offering explanations or providing us with solace.

· He is among the most talented playwrights of the English revival, along with N. F. Simpson and John Arden, neither of whose work, however, we have seen enough of to be able to judge as confidently as we do Pinter. He has done what Edward Albee has only half done—he has broken through to a new dimension of drama, which means a present dimension of experience. The theatre is so suffocating today because it continues for the most part to take up and arrange what we no longer feel, or are involved in only anachronistically. Pinter's plays introduce us to a reality we do recognize as our own, though it is one which we cannot truly know until someone like him gives it its proper telling shape outside us.

Yet in Pinter the action is not in fact much more than an introduction, the beginning of recognition and affect and change. The shapes he creates are skeletal and unfinished, as though they have known what not to be but do not yet know what to become. Having stripped away much of what is exhausted in conventional drama, having made a psychology that confirms or explains yield to a metaphysics that invokes, and having made the logic of narrative continuity yield to the terrifying arbitrariness of the way we really experience the world, Pinter hovers still on the threshold of a theatre of new events and new portrayals. Unlike Ionesco and Beckett, in whose light, especially the latter's, he has so clearly worked, he has been unable to do more than present the *reverse* side of existence, the underskin of emptiness that sheaves our habitual gestures and spent meanings.

The Caretaker, with its strange terrors and pities and hints of significance within a scene of almost total bareness, and yet with its central failure to remain consistently in its chosen genre—the revelation of Aston's shock treatment betraying Pinter's fall from the high wire of a refusal to *explain*—exhibits his special gifts and deficiencies on a much larger scale than the two one-acters now being presented in the Village. But at least one of the latter, *The Dumbwaiter,* just because it is earlier, shorter and purer than *The Caretaker,* gives us an especially direct sense of what he intends and strives for but cannot quite achieve.

The other play, *The Collection,* is Pinter playing Pinter, a lapse from his originality and severity of purpose, a schematic exercise which results in a thoroughly unintentional sense of parody. It purports to be an examination of the nature of reality and illusion, somewhat reminiscent of the Japanese *Rashomon,* in that the participants in an event have conflicting stories to tell. But *The Collection* is more pretentious. A married woman did or did not have an assignation with a young man in a Leeds hotel. If she did, why does she deny it? If she didn't, why does she say she did, and, moreover, give several versions of what happened? And why does the youth similarly alternate between confession and denial? What really happened?

There is of course no answer. What there is, hopefully, is the communication of an experience of doubt, a breaking down of categories, a vision of fluidity and insubstantiality in our relation to the truth. But Pinter doesn't trust his vision enough to allow it to exist in the very grain and substance of the play. As in all his work, the air is thick with menace, but here it is factitious and imposed. Instead of arising from our being made aware of the abyss between the world and our means of apprehending it, the menace is manufactured, distilled from a great deal of reductive stage business, knife fights, mysterious phone calls, sudden reversals of behavior and cryptic smiles. We are not left with a sense of having witnessed orders of experience or faculties of the self come into collision, but with the fragments of a philosophic melodrama in which the thought and the action never fuse.

In *The Dumbwaiter* Pinter is strong, unschematic and effective. There is no working out of a philosophy, or an antiphilosophy, no "explanation" that there is no explanation. In a shabby basement room two hired killers await their next victim, who is unknown to them and whose arrival will be signaled by their shadowy employer. To pass the time they comment on items in the newspaper, discuss previous jobs, quarrel over whether one "lights the kettle" or "lights the gas" in making tea. Their trivial, banal conversation is of the order of that in *The Caretaker*, although less deliberately stripped and denotative.

Yet its basic effect is the same: an intensification of the alarm we feel at our failure to match our language to our true experience. Similarly, when the men discover a speaking tube and a dumbwaiter in the room and begin to receive orders for exotic dishes to be sent up (the place had been a restaurant) the absurdity of our categories of action, the division between the "serious" and the trivial, becomes farcically and disturbingly heightened. The men try desperately to placate the unseen powers, shoving canned food, biscuits, chocolate bars onto the dumbwaiter, while their impending job of murder hangs menacingly over everything.

In the end one man goes to the washroom, the other receives word that the first person who comes through the other door is to be shot, the door opens and in staggers the killer who has just left; he is the intended victim.

The play is greatly interesting for its fusion of terror and farce and for its movement beyond naturalism into a climate of indirection and metaphysical implication. (It is played here a little too broadly, too much like Laurel and Hardy, by John C. Becher and Dana Elcar, with the result that some of the dread is dispelled; *The Collection,* on the other hand, is acted tautly and effectively, especially by Henderson Forsythe and James Ray.) But it remains on the edge of fullness; it is less a complex equivalent of our experience than a taut and suggestive minor fable about it. When Pinter comes to fill in the space he has hollowed out by scooping away the expected, the connotative and the logical, when he locates the unexpected and illogical in an incontrovertible atmosphere of its own, he may astonish and transform us, instead of simply unsettling us and giving us a glimpse of new avenues, rare and valuable as that is. (1962)

¶Straightforward Mystification

During the first half-hour or so of Harold Pinter's *The Caretaker* I found myself thinking that this might be one of those revelatory occasions in the theatre when something entirely new and liberating takes place; I remembered my feelings on that evening in my youth when I had seen *Six Characters in Search of an Author* for the first time, and I thought of that wild opening night, full of dislocation, light, stupor and derision, when *Waiting for Godot* made its apple-cart-tipping appearance among us. But though *The Caretaker* remained original, true and substantial to the end, the sense of astonishment, of sitting in on a major breakthrough of the dramatic imagination, left me after a while and nothing could bring it back.

I hated to see it go. "An interesting soup but not a great soup," the child in the cartoon declares, and defines our unrest; we go on tasting every dish in hopes that the great thing will turn up. Still, we are told that of all the arts the theatre has the most problematic standards of absolute triumph, and with that in mind I left *The Caretaker* comforted by the probability that there will not be many superior plays this season, nor any whose acting, staging and direction so faultlessly conform to its substance.

To judge from both the response of the audience on the night I was present and the published comment so far, *The Caretaker* has been received here with a maximum of pleasure and a minimum of understanding. In Pinter's native England the same thing seems to be true. On both sides of the ocean his theatricality is praised, people speaking of "tension," "grotesque humor" and "subtle characterization," at the same time engaging in labored attempts to find parabolic or allegorical interpretations for the mystifying activities that go on in his dramas. They would do better to believe him when he protests that his plays, in intention at least, are direct, unsymbolic and crowded with actuality.

Which is of course not to say that *The Caretaker* is a straightforward drama. It is in fact an antidrama, or at least an antiliterary one, stemming, as so much that is interesting seems to these days, from Beckett, and with a more remote ancestry in the novels of Dostoevsky, Joyce and Kafka (another ubiquitous presence in the contemporary theatre of wit, dream, daring and anguish). There are not many clues to behavior, almost no psychologizing, few explanations and only the most tenuous and static of denouements. And the language moves from deliberate banality to parody, to the utmost simplicity of denotative speech, which is itself, of course, a parody of traditional stage rhetoric.

In one filthy room of a lower-depths London rooming house three men enact a charade of misunderstanding, thwarted love and appetite, and hopeless attempts at escaping from isolation. Davies, a tramp, the scurviest tramp imaginable, is befriended by Aston, who owns the house together with his brother Mick and who has vague plans for renovating it. From the beginning we are aware that there is something the matter with Aston; his speech is slow and dreamlike, he either stands gazing upon some unseen vista or tinkers endlessly with a broken clock, though he also speaks feelingly of a shed he is building with "good wood" in the yard.

Davies, on the other hand, is very much there, an incarnation of greed, envy and absurd pride, filled with the empty belligerence of the dispossessed and entirely ungrateful for Aston's kindness in taking him in. And Mick is also there; he is active, loquacious and strangely malevolent, baiting the tramp with outbursts of savage irony that are in extreme contrast with Aston's demeanor. The "action" of the play consists in the interplay among the three, in Aston's ultimate regretfully taken decision that Davies' presence is intolerable and in the latter's reduction to a condition of supremely naked, piteous need to be allowed to stay on.

It isn't hard to see why *The Caretaker* should have been

interpreted as a morality play in which Davies is Everyman, Aston Christ and Mick the Devil. But it won't do; the characters are far too actual for that, the play has too many incongruities and excrescences, there is too much movement beneath the surface. I think it far more to the point to consider the three men as constituting a triad roughly on the order of the brothers Karamazov—the major faculties of man's being, appearing as a triple irruption from the depths of the dramatist's imagination. And like Dostoevsky's brothers the characters of Pinter's drama are not therefore symbols but mysterious new creations; their reality is self-contained, so that they do not so much indicate meaning as irradiate it.

What then is wrong, or rather, less than magnificently right about *The Caretaker?* The final image is achieved: of unbearable loneliness, of war in the members of the body, and yet also of a persistent blind movement toward communion and authentic life. Under Donald McWhinnie's direction the cast, especially Donald Pleasence—who makes of Davies a superlatively realized figure for whom our compassion is as great as our repugnance—contributes everything necessary and adds nothing superfluous.

And yet there is a weakness somewhere, an ultimate failure of *establishment,* a final deprivation of fullness, of the sense of inevitability and of the vision of reality freshly apprehended. It seems to me that all this is due not to Pinter's untraditional dramaturgy but to the fact that he is not untraditional enough. That is to say, his play is too much a thing of jarring styles, characterizations and motivations, not a consistent piece of relentlessly exhibited discovery, such as we find true in the work of Beckett and in most of Ionesco.

Davies is too full-bodied against Aston's incorporeal virtue and Mick's free-floating intellect. Anecdote too frequently breaks the mood of nonspecific, noncontingent pity and alarm (there is a long monologue by Aston in which he describes an operation performed on him years before; it was in the nature of a lobotomy and it helps explain his current behavior but at the same time partly reduces him to a case history). And finally there is the existence of the parody, the irony and the inversion of accustomed attitudes, not as the very substance of the play but as discrete fragments separated by moments of direct, and therefore disconcerting, experience.

I would like to see Pinter more, not less, "absurd," to see him relinquish his anchors in the kind of truth which says what it is itself so that it resists new shapes and expression. (1961)

¶ The Pinter Puzzle

In all his plays, from *The Room,* which was written in 1957 as a more or less naïve exercise in the kind of drama Beckett and Ionesco had already made known, to his latest work, *The Homecoming,* Harold Pinter has been engaged with the question of what drama really is. It might be thought that the playwright, of all people, would know; yet if twentieth-century aesthetic developments have taught us anything, it is that the artist, rather than the public—which knows what it knows—is in continuing doubt about the nature of art. And since the theatre is the most immovable of all the arts, the most resistant to change, it is the playwright who has had to struggle most strenuously for new forms, against the heavy, unyielding conviction of nearly everybody else that there is no mystery about what plays are.

Plays are sequences of imagined events, recognizable to one degree or another as analogous to the events of life, and these events are participated in by "characters," whose interest and credibility are also measured by their potential actuality, their being possible to imagine in one or another way as existing in the world outside the drama. Beyond that, plays must "develop," must move steadily along, generally to a "higher" or "deeper" level, and must not, on pain of murderous responses from the audience, stop at any point—to give opportunity for reflection to gather new kinds of momentum, to simply be still, circular, without linear progression. What plays must do (the last stronghold of realism) is to trace a parabola for which life is thought to have provided the model.

Such, tightly stated, are the sovereign notions that still rule audiences, reviewers and commonplace playwrights alike. They learn nothing from the fact that nearly all the interesting drama of any period has taken place outside the textbook definitions. The complaint is still made against a play like

The Homecoming that it is slow, illogical, unlifelike, wasteful of its opportunities—which are to be fast, logical, lifelike—and that its characters are not the sort one would expect or want to meet on one's daily round. (Get me Ivan Karamazov: Ivan, baby, we're having a party and we'd love you to . . .)

In Pinter's growth as a dramatist, which in a central way means progress toward colonizing hitherto unconsidered territories of the dramatic, shaping a redefinition, *on the stage*, of character, plot, action, etc., he has come unevenly but significantly to re-direct procedures and techniques that had early threatened to congeal into mere negatives. His capacity for extracting ranges of implication from the most conventional varieties of speech themselves—incantatory, often, dreamlike yet anchored in the sharpest accuracy about how people really talk—his use of the most commonplace objects to undermine our complacency about the material world: all this was for the most part unsupported by any imposing intellectual structure, any more solid knowledge or intuition than that traditions of perception and experience were not to be relied on.

From his first impact here, by way of rumor and the published early plays and then through *The Caretaker* when it arrived, we spoke of Pinter as a new presence, the master of striking if not quite trustworthy, because seemingly autonomous, effects. The world, his plays announced, is arbitrary, everything menaces, nothing is what it seems; he had broken into a new universe of drama, one in which language seldom coheres with gesture, terror is the obverse of humor, and habits of action conceal other kinds of action we can sense but never know.

In this universe, he once wrote in a program note, "there are no hard distinctions between what is real and what is unreal, nor between what is true and what is false." It is precisely its tendency to assume at some point that it knows what is real and unreal (which means what has up to now been *considered* so) that compels every art including drama continually to remonstrate with its own past, to repudiate its own inertia. This is the least that so-called avant-garde art does—but it has to do more. The peculiar giddiness, the sensations of disequilibrium and disturbed orientation which Pinter induced through his dislocations of the familiar—these, while enormously valuable, were not fully satisfying. For what was being let in through the holes he had punched in conventional dramaturgy? Not what meaning but what new and substanceful drama of his own?

The Homecoming, though flawed and marked by aesthetic problems not yet overcome, is the impressive culmination of a subtle process of change that set in midway in Pinter's career. It was toward a seemingly greater realism, a filling in the vacancies, in which abstract menace and unspecific fear lurked, that had resulted from his abandonment of accepted thematic developments, of ordinary psychologies and sociologies and the sequential narratives in which the stage has traditionally encased them. But this realism had nothing to do with an imitation of life or the conventions of popular drama, except that, in the latter case, it made a canny and partly ironic use of them.

The shift can be studied through Pinter's changing *mises en scène.* Moving into domestic settings, usually middle- or upper-middle class, he largely withdrew from those alarming locales of his earlier plays—the basement room of *The Dumbwaiter,* the seedy rooming house of *The Birthday Party,* the dementedly cluttered room of *The Caretaker.*

These theatrical sites were objectively disturbing, menacing in their own right, physical metaphors of violence which meant that their atmospheres tended to carry a disproportionate share of the plays' effects, tended in fact to consolidate those effects as the very essence of the works.

The setting of *The Homecoming* still possesses disquieting features in its great gray sparsely furnished room. But something crucial has happened. This new Pinter room no longer largely dictates what is to happen to its inhabitants but only reflects what has happened and will happen to them; its walls and furnishings have soaked up their emanations, for the center of dramatic reality has passed to them.

Yet it doesn't lie in them now in any way which we can organically connect with what we think of as domestic drama.

If you think during the opening moments that you are watching a familiar battle scene, on the order of *Virginia Woolf,* or *Cat on a Hot Tin Roof,* you will be unprepared for what is to come and you may grow disgruntled, having expected, in the second act, denouement, completion, some satisfying rich ripe finale. But the play moves to its own logic, and is not a tale; its characters are only tactically engaged in representing potentially real people, their strategic task being to incarnate, along the lines of the "characters" in *The Brothers Karamazov,* certain human faculties, dividing among themselves fundamental possibilities of attitude and approach to existence. They are their figures in a drama of the mind, which is not to say an intellectual drama, but one which makes no pretense (or only a pretense) of being a replica of actuality.

The relationship of the four men who occupy the stage at first is savage, almost cannibalistic, at the same time that it is self-lacerating. "Mind you she wasn't such a bad woman," Max, the roaring foul-mouthed old man, says of his dead wife, "even though it made me sick just to look at her rotten stinking face, she wasn't a bad bitch." And he berates his coldly ironic son Lenny, the master of a stable of prostitutes, for "talking to your lousy filthy father like that."

Yet however straightforward, if extreme, their dialogue seems at first, its purpose is not to frame character or psychology, not as an English critic has pointed out, to reveal "inner life or intentions." Pinter's marvelously funny, splendidly violent or consciously banal dialogue is a matter of *kinds* of speech and therefore archetypes of being, warring with one another—Max's scatology, Lenny's wit, Max's pallid brother Sam's pinched rhetoric—as the faculties incarnated by the personages of the play similarly war. And the dialogue is there to serve the play, to serve its mostly immobile, nonanecdotal, ritualistic vision, not its presumed thesis, its "story" or concatenation of events.

That there is to be no plausible story quickly becomes apparent with the entrance of Teddy, Max's oldest son; a philosophy professor at an American university, he is returning for the first time in six years, with his wife Ruth, whom the others do not know of. Coolly elegant, enigmatic, sensual, Ruth immediately shifts the play to a new dimension. In the most Pinteresque of scenes, where language, objects and gestures unite to reinforce one another's elliptical and mythic condition, Ruth and Lenny clash. "I'll take it [a glass of water he has given her]," Lenny says, unaccountably threatening, to which she replies with deadly calm, "If you take the glass . . . I'll take *you*."

From then on the play is about who takes whom, that is to say, whose presence triumphs or yields, who, in the game of existence—not in that of society—are winners or losers. What loses most decisively is onlooking, spectatorship, the propriety of consciousness when pitted against the absolutism of the physical self. In a world beyond morality, what is being sought for is a condition of authenticity, an immersion in what is. And to accomplish this, the play now leaves irrevocably behind it (the point at which the public grumbling starts) all verisimilitude, all pretense of being about a family, a social situation, people like you and me. Pinter is at the heart of his vision here, and if we follow him into it—attending to these characters who can no longer be mistaken for types or personalities but only seen as incarnations of possibility, of desire and refusal—we will have overcome our deadly habit of wanting what we expect.

When Ruth engages Lenny, and afterwards Joey, the naïve strongboy younger brother, in a sexual embrace which Teddy, her husband, watches with pipe-smoking professorial detachment, and when later the family proposes that Ruth stay with them, working for her keep as a prostitute—a proposal which leaves Teddy as unruffled as before—we are not in the presence of social behavior but of a dance of death—and life. Ruth's acceptance of the proposal is a movement toward the greater authenticity of the family, their closer proximity to genuine being. For Teddy is an abstract man, a figure of pure consciousness, an observer, while she is almost pure instinct and physicality.

In the key monologue of the play, the central speech which, as in all Pinter's work, offers the one irradiation of intention to light the rest of the play, Teddy tells the others:

"You wouldn't understand my works . . . You wouldn't appreciate the points of reference. You're way behind . . . It's nothing to do with the question of intelligence. It's a way of being able to look at the world. It's a question of how far you can operate on things and not in things . . . To see, to be able to *see!* I'm the one who can see . . . [I have] intellectual equilibrium . . . You're just objects. You just . . . move about. I can observe it. I can see what you do. It's the same as I do. But you're lost in it. You won't get me being . . . I won't be lost in it."

It is a brilliant piece of writing, one almost no other English-speaking playwright would be capable of. Fusing the most exact and compressed meanings with the most intense feeling, colloquial at the same time that it stretches to a more inclusive and nonrealistic level of speech, it exemplifies what is never considered in our public chatter about the theatre: that language can itself be dramatic, can *be* the play, not merely the means of advancing an anecdote, a decoration, or the emblem of something thought to be realer than itself.

Teddy's speech is followed by a longer one of Lenny's, an equally masterly piece of writing, opposing another rhythm and another mode of language as action to its predecessor. In it Lenny, the wit, the implicated observer, moral consciousness corrupted but still alive, throws at Teddy an image of America which, in the conditions of the play, entirely transcends social criticism to become the truest kind of poetic fact:

"I will say you do seem to have grown a bit sulky . . . I'd have thought that in the United States of America, I mean with the sun and all that, the open spaces, on the old campus, in your position, lecturing, in the center of all the intellectual life out there, on the old campus, all the social whirl, all the stimulation of it all, all your kids and all that, to have fun with, down by the pool, the Greyhound buses and all that, tons of iced water, all the comforts of those Bermuda shorts and all that, on the old campus . . . I'd have thought you'd have grown more forthcoming . . . Listen, Ted, there's no question we lead a less rich life here than you do over there . . . We lead a closer life."

In the final movement of the play, this closer life is revealed to be partly one of fantasy. There is something crowded, rushed into being, somewhat arbitrary about this last section. Ruth takes command, promising in the manner of a contemporary fairy godmother to be whatever the men want her to be: for Joey a madonna figure, for Lenny a whore, for Max a young and rejuvenating wife. A whole allegorical structure now rises shadowily into view. But it is too late, it has not been fully prepared for and therefore comes as an afterthought. Yet the main action of the play has been completed with Ruth's move toward the family and Teddy's devastating acceptance of it; to wish to do more, to want his dense, specific, precisely nonallegorical vision to yield up such further tenuous meanings is evidence that Pinter has not yet solved his major problem. And that is how to fuse meaning so securely with language, gesture and setting that it cannot be extrapolated from them. The taints of the old worn-out dramatic procedures—characters who represent, action that points to something else—are still discernible in his work.

Yet, they are taints, not major infections. A struggle for the new is always more interesting than a successful appropriation of the old. *The Homecoming* is such a struggle, and nothing on Broadway in recent years comes close to matching it for the kind of excitement that our debased, ad-man's vocabulary of critical appreciation (*"The Odd Couple* is the funniest play ever!"*) has so thoroughly disillusioned us about. The play itself, Peter Hall's direction and the Royal Shakespeare Company's acting ensemble offer examples of work in a dimension beyond anything we have been accustomed to. (1967)

¶Pre-Vintage Pinter

Harold Pinter is at the height of his powers and of his fame, and the light from these spreads backwards to gather up a very early play like *The Birthday Party* in a retroactive éclat: because he is so much now he could not have been so much less then. Yet seen from a perspective of nearly ten years, since the play was first performed in London, or seven, since I first read it, *The Birthday Party* is so much manner and so little style that it is hard to see what one could have been so excited about. As someone remarked during one of the intermissions, how strange it is that Pinter should have written a parody of himself before he had written the major works which might be parodied.

The Birthday Party, for those unfamiliar with it (it has been done in this country by the San Francisco Actors Workshop and in several college productions), takes place in a shabby rooming house in a nameless seaside resort. A young man named Stanley Webber has been staying for a year as the place's only guest, doing nothing discernible except to serve, resentfully, as the frumpy landlady's substitute child. The landlady's husband announces that two men have inquired about a room. At this news, Stanley is thrown into inexplicable alarm, which increases when they arrive (although they seem never to have met). The men—Goldberg, a fiftyish pseudo-sophisticate, and McCann, a younger bullyboy—proceed to arrange a party for Stanley when the landlady tells them it's his birthday (which he denies). But before it is held, they subject him to a bizarre third-degree. "Why are you wasting everybody's time?" "Why did you leave the organization?" "Is the number 846 possible or necessary?"

During the party the landlady tries haplessly to interest the now-drunken McCann in her charms, Goldberg slowly seduces a neighbor girl, and Stanley, under further badgering, moves catatonically about until the fete ends with his attempt to strangle the landlady. The next morning the men announce to the troubled landlord that Stanley has had a mental break-down and that they are taking him to "Monty" in their big black car. Stanley is led down, dressed in morning clothes and a bowler hat and looking as though he has been em-balmed. In a climactic scene they tell him about the rich and lucky life they have planned for him, but he can only utter strangled, animal-like sounds. The play ends with the land-lady, unaware of Stanley's departure, remarking to her hus-band how she had been the belle of last night's ball.

Throughout this elaborate theatrical red herring smaller fish of that description swim through the *mise en scène*. Stanley may or may not be a pianist. McCann tears news-papers into long, even strips. Goldberg, who is called Nat by McCann, refers to himself as Simey and again as Benny in recounting his childhood. At one point Goldberg, hitherto the model of loquacity and amiable patter, breaks down at the end of a speech, saying over and over, "Because I believe that the world . . ." From moment to moment Pinter turns cor-ners, doubles back, contradicts what has just occurred, intro-duces irrelevancies, undercuts sentiment with violence and violence with sentimentality. The impression is inescapable that we are in the presence of a dramatist who, at this initial stage of his career, was in flight from the English drama as it had largely been constituted up to then: orderly, logical, discreet, sequential, rational.

The arbitrary fusion of intense domesticity and unparal-leled danger, the conversations which at times are meaning-less and at others seem to be means of exchanging exact information, the repetitions that have the effect of making grotesque emblems out of the most commonplace expressions and yet which aren't used in any but a sporadic way—all this reveals *The Birthday Party* as engaged less in constructing a new dramatic reality than in overthrowing an established one.

Moreover, the game certainly isn't allegory.

Pinter has denied any symbolic or allegorical intent in his

work, and he is to be believed. What backs him up in a play like *The Birthday Party* is the inconsequence of its most seemingly telling effects, the fact that they are nothing more than effects, the way in which the entire play stands riddled with arbitrary procedures instead of generating its own inexorable logic of illogic. But though it isn't an allegory, the play isn't an achieved dramatic vision either. Pinter has come a long way to *The Homecoming*, where nothing is arbitrary or aimed at something else, nothing is irrational for the mere sake of not being rational; the dramatic reality, fed by ten years of a growing freedom for drama to be its own reality, is secure and coherent.

The current production of *The Birthday Party* seems to resign itself to defeat from the outset. The set (by William Ritman) lacks bite; shabby enough, it is too detailed to contain Pinter's nonrepresentational meanings and yet not detailed enough, not down-at-heel enough, if the line is going to be a naturalistic one. Alan Schneider's direction suffers from the same indecision. He has asked his performers—Henderson Forsythe and Ruth White as the proprietors, James Patterson as Stanley, Ed Flanders and Edward Winter as Goldberg and McCann—for verisimilitude, but verisimilitude to what? Are they in a domestic melodrama with symbolic and poetic overtones or in a fantasy with domestic disguises? The result of nobody's knowing is that even Pinter's own tentative accomplishments, his sometimes hilarious tableturnings ("Down on your knees and confess," McCann arbitrarily orders the neighbor girl, to which Goldberg airily adds, "Go ahead, confess, what have you got to lose") are swallowed up in a pervasive mist of misguided realism. What it amounts to is a boring evening, something Pinter, even in his first inadequate constructions was never guilty of on his own. (1967)

¶Patience Rewarded

Only a handful of playwrights now at work give us an unfailing sense of the drama as potentially revolutionary, capable of discovering new forms for the imagination and thus new truths, and Harold Pinter and Samuel Beckett, for all the difference in their sizes, are indisputably among them. For this reason, even though Pinter's new one-act play, *The Lover,* falls short of his best work by a considerable distance, and Beckett's latest creation, *Play,* is scarcely fifteen minutes long, the twin bill which Richard Barr, Clinton Wilder and Edward Albee are presenting as the first offering of their *Theater 1964* is easily the most arresting evening on or off Broadway so far this year.

The Lover, to take the lesser man's work first, is a vehicle for the exploration of the relations between fantasy and actuality, the occasion here being domestic actuality and erotic fantasy. During the first scenes we see a couple married ten years, bourgeois, ritualistic, the husband in finance and the uniform of finance: bowler hat, briefcase, furled umbrella; the wife in the Home: dinner at six, here's your drink, dear, how was your day? But very quickly it is established that they are participating in an unusually sophisticated arrangement. "Is your lover coming today, darling?," the man asks before leaving for the office. "Good, well, have a nice day." And that night he pleasantly tells his wife about the whore he visits two or three times a week, no counterpart of the romantic figure she entertains but simply someone who can "express and engender lust with all lust's cunning." They agree before going to sleep that they indeed have a wonderful understanding.

It is undercutting a moment of high surprise to report what comes next, but any play that depends on twists for its life deserves to be undercut and any play that doesn't can of course survive it. Pinter's play doesn't, so I will tell you that when the lover arrives he turns out to be the husband, dressed now in suede jacket and ascot, shuffling in, picking up a set of bongo drums and then beginning to make passionate love to the woman, who is now slinky, high-heeled and hoarse-voiced. They act out a number of fantasies, including the gamekeeper-and-the-lady until their time is up and the lover has to leave so that the husband can come back.

There now sets in an increasing inability on both their parts to distinguish the fantasy life from the actual one or to keep them apart. Both become jealous and condemning, the husband insisting that the wife take the lover to a field if she has to, but "not in this house," and the wife demanding that he stop seeing the prostitute. As the walls crumble and the compartments intermingle their contents, the couple wholly lose their identities and the play ends with the husband and wife turning into the lover and whore without employing the elaborate machinery of make-believe they had used before. The image is of a breakdown of the capacity to hold reality and dream in balance, and its implications are meant to transcend the specificity of its sexual scene.

Still, *The Lover* is more suggestive than successful. It is a good deal too schematic—Pinter's periodic curse—and too un-derdeveloped to be of the first rank in his canon or that of the most significant recent drama. The fact that it was originally written as a work for television, being composed as a series of scenes divided by blackouts, is an obstacle in the way of even its most robust achievements. Yet it is almost continuously interesting, it is extremely funny for much of its length, it is bold enough to emerge from the realm of recapitulation and psychologizing of our traditional theatre of sex-and-apocalypse, and, not least in these days of performances before the mirror, it is acted with neat, arch brilliance by Hilda Brawner as the wife and Michael Lipton as the husband.

If I say very much less about Beckett's *Play* than about *The Lover*, it certainly isn't because I think the latter worth more attention. On the contrary, Beckett's piece is an extraordinary work whose relation to Pinter's is that of a discovery to an experiment. But it is precisely because it is so astonishing, a fifteen- or sixteen-minute passage through a new dimension of drama, during which Beckett goes further in the direction of pure theatre than he has ever gone before, that I find it impossible to treat it fully so soon. It is too new and too fugitive; I want to see it again and read the text if I can get hold of a copy.

For the moment all I want to say is that afterwards a friend remarked that the thing was a dream which the audience had dreamt together, and I added to myself that it was a dream from the perspective of death, which permits all incident, all event to take on essential, noncontingent existence. It was a play "about" two women and a man in funeral urns, their pale heads showing and their speech composing a reverie over the past, and telling us, as one of them says, "something about the way the mind works." In a week or two I shall have more to tell you. (1964)

◀ A Man for These Times

"I've always managed to keep everything in place," the protagonist of John Osborne's *Inadmissible Evidence* remarks at the beginning of the play. The words are actually a lament, since everything has begun to move out of place. Slipping, sliding, fading, the world is in retreat from the grasp of a man whose life is now exhibited in all its vainglory, pathos and emotional abrasion. Marred, dramatically uncertain, frequently repetitious, the play is nevertheless an extremely compelling personal statement, a dirge, a stock-taking and an outcry of protest against what cannot be helped.

Inadmissible Evidence thus marks a new phase of maturity for Osborne, since he has mostly protested up to now against what can be helped—social and political conditions—and in so doing burdened himself with narrow ideology and abstract aggression. The new play retains a good deal of Osborne's fierce invective against social stupidity and bourgeois complacency, but it subordinates them to a moral and philosophical purpose, a severe but humane sitting-in-judgment on the self.

Bill Maitland is a lawyer specializing in grimy little cases: divorces, assaults, sexual malfeasances. He is thirty-nine, frayed, exacerbated, on tranquilizers; he has a wife and two teen-age children, a permanent mistress and sporadic temporary ones; he is, by his own admission, "irredeemably mediocre." Starting with a dream sequence in which Maitland imagines himself on trial, the play compresses into two days of action the summary of an existence. Through all the revelations of Maitland's sad, compulsive eroticism and slipshod handling of his confused affairs (an editorial hand might have pared these scenes effectively), two themes assert themselves.

"With love, I succeeded in inflicting, quite certainly inflicting," Maitland confesses, "more pain than pleasure." And again, "I myself am more packed with spite and twitching with revenge than anyone I know of. I actually often, frequently, daily want to see people die for their errors. I wish to kill them myself . . . Fortunately, I've had no more opportunities than most men."

But Maitland is also, like most men, as much victim as potential executioner. As the play chronicles the gradual collapse of his world, his savage desperation, the withdrawal of all those with whom he had established those flawed, provisional connections that make do for love, sympathy goes out to him and he stands as a small, beleaguered figure, a man accepting his culpability yet unable to account for the severity of the sentence.

Dramatically, *Inadmissible Evidence* handicaps itself by starting at the center of Maitland's decline and fall. There is no ground from which to mark his descent, no perspective from which to judge its relation to an opposing possibility. Osborne's stock in trade, his great sweeping monologues, are integrated more fully than ever into a total structure, but he is still largely unable to create scenes of true confrontation, clashes of characters, themes, values. Maitland's debacle is a hermetic action, the dreamlike projection of the self to fill the universe.

Still, no audience will be bored for more than a moment. Holding the stage with an amazing overlordship is Nicol Williamson, a twenty-eight-year-old Scottish actor who plays Maitland with inexhaustible energy and overwhelming authority. On stage and relentlessly articulating nearly every minute, Williamson has had one collapse from sheer exhaustion (in London) and is replaced by James Patterson at matinées. Williamson's Maitland, besieged, muddled, at his wits' and nerves' end, incarnates Osborne's intention—to body forth a figure for the times, a man reduced not to tragedy but to that terrible condition in which tragic dignity is no longer possible. (1965)

❡ Arden's Unsteady Ground

"An object of art is artistic only insofar as it is not real," Ortega y Gasset once wrote, and meant something much broader than an attack upon naturalism. Until we are able to think of drama, for all its physical contingencies and aesthetic impurities, as existing in a different realm from the "real"—the way we are mostly able to think of poetry, painting, music—we will go on disputing over everything that is peripheral and secondary in the work of a playwright like Arden, in the effort to establish its "validity," unconscious that this validity has already been established by the play's own internal processes and conquests.

There is something dispiriting about Arden's own vacillations between apology and peevish resentment. The prefaces to his plays are full of protests against his critics, but also of weakly enunciated and what can only be called supererogatory statements of his dramatic intentions. It is rather painful to hear a playwright of his stature say, as he does in the preface to *Left-Handed Liberty*, that "I am not normally an enthusiast for didactic drama" and then proceed to explicate the play's meaning, as though we had no means of discovering it for ourselves within the work. Arden has some justification insofar as a great many critics—professional and lay—do seem to have been unable to find it, just as they were stumped by the theme of *Serjeant Musgrave's Dance* or of *Live Like Pigs*. Still, however obtuse the response to the latter play was, it needn't have led Arden to such timid, ingenuous, and wholly unnecessary comments as those he made in the preface to the published text:

> When I wrote this play I intended it to be not so much a social document as a study of differing ways of life brought sharply into conflict and both losing their particular virtues under the

stress of intolerance and misunderstanding. In other words, I was more concerned with the "poetic" than the "journalistic" structure of the play.

The temptation is to reply, "Oh," in the manner of a *New Yorker* newsbreak. The point is that Arden, like Brecht, is much more of an artist than his *obiter dicta* might suggest. Of course, one feels like saying to him, you're not really a didactic playwright, of course you're more interested in poetry than journalism. At the back of these strange tergiversations and pained, naïve avowals one senses a strand of the theatrical climate in England, a weather which is also beginning to take shape here: the need to be concerned (or to appear to be) in one way or another with socially and politically significant material, the fear of being seduced into too thoroughgoing an aesthetic stance, the embarrassment at not having, or not seeming to want to have, a clearly defined social commitment.

To describe oneself as a political or sociological playwright may very well be in this climate a ticket of admission, a way to get in out of the rain. That is to say, it seems clear from the context of Arden's remark, its surrounding clichés about man's being a social and political animal, etc., and first and foremost from the evidence of his plays, that caught between his *prédilection d'artiste* and his communal sensibilities he covers himself (without guile or hope of concrete gain, it goes without saying) by pleading both. To the ideologues who would enlist his dramas in support of programs and are baffled by their resistance, he speaks wanly of poetic structure taking precedence over the journalistic; to the formalists who might wish him to be less reportorial than he is, he points to the necessary basis in concrete events which all his plays exhibit.

Yet it should be obvious that the "events" of these plays are not simply dramatizations or, more subtly, aestheticized analogues of those other, historical happenings, and that the poetic interest he takes in them is not simply greater than his interest in reportage but of a different kind altogether. That Arden is in some sense a thoroughly political playwright has never been at issue; every one of his works is steeped in politics and is the product of an imagination for which nonpolitical reality—private myth, insular fortune, the discrete ego—would seem to have no independent standing as material for drama. No, what is at issue is the fate of political subject matter in his plays, the unpolitical uses to which he puts it, the transformations it undergoes under the action of his half-lyrical, half-civic and polemical sensibility, the sensibility, one might call it, of a passionate citizen, a brooding burgher.

What is the nature of political reality and how does the rest of the life of man (the title of his first play, a radio script) relate to it, or rather how does man's life come to know itself in the crucible of power, rule and social governance? What are the prices that political necessity exacts from the moral self and the psyche? How does one celebrate life in the midst of abstractions? Such are the chief energizing questions of Arden's plays. They are what make him something extraordinarily different from a traditionally "political" or "sociological" playwright, by which, if definitions and terminology have not already descended into chaos, we mean someone for whom the immediate data of political or social organization are paramount, for whom, too, the choices involved in public existence are more or less co-terminous with the choices involved in all existence, and for whom, finally, a play is an exemplification, subtle or gross, of the virtue of making the right choices or of the cost of failing to make them.

For Arden, however, there are no clear choices—which is what pitches him above ideology; although there is a clear necessity to act publicly—which is what keeps his plays anchored in a perception of social actuality. Again and again, in one form or another, he questions, or rather raises to the dignity and ambiguous sincerity of a question, something we might call the humanness of politics, its role and function as the process and measure of our life in common. That public life *has* to be organized, and that power *has* to be exerted, are the assumptions, with their roots in a tragic awareness, of all his plays; that the private self rebels against this inexorability, in the name of its spontaneous, wayward life, of all distinct values and of the simplicities of what it considers its natural choices, is the agency which generates the "drama" of his dramas. If there is any modern book outside the literature of the theatre which provides a clue to Arden's temperament and procedures, it is surely Freud's *Civilization and Its Discontents.*

This conflict of the self, or its spontaneous element, with the organizing, abstract, equally self-interested and therefore inherently repressive action of politics is complemented and enlarged by another encounter which runs through most of Arden's work. This is the confrontation of a deadly impulse toward purity (which may be found both within the actions of power and in all fanatic attempts to do away with it) and the impure, flawed, capricious, and uncodifiable nature of reality beneath our schemes for organizing it.

In *Left-Handed Liberty,* King John replies to Pandulph, the Papal Legate, who in his distaste for the imperfections of the palpable has called him a "dandelion": "I am partial to dandelions. Coarse in texture, I know, and the scent is undistinguished and they are far too prolific. But powdered across the slope of a green meadow, all those thousand dots of gold —who could want to be rid of them?" The King then goes on to explain why the Charter he has signed is protected against becoming the repressive instrument such abstract documents are likely to turn into: "I said: make those clauses general— lax, if you like—because by their very laxness they go some way to admit the existence of dandelions, of disobedient women and ribbons of cloth-of-gold."

Earlier in the play Pandulph has sung of the mental tyrant's dream of absolute order and purity in the organization of existence and of attitudes toward it:

> *Storm breaks in among the perfect circles,*
> *Every day a puff of wind or a rumble of thunder*
> *Declares some vain attempt to declare—what?*
> *Very busy very busy very busy!*
> *Whatever it is, it will be vain,*
> *It will be some broken blunder:*
> *But we who preserve the circles*
> *Preserve their unfaulted music . . .*

To which John, accounting for his backing and filling, his devious behavior and slippery dealings, replies: "I am delivering the antidote to all those circles with no kinks in . . ."

The pure—that which refuses to admit the exceptional, the capricious, or the contradictory—and the abstract—that which incarcerates living phenomena in reductive systems—are the enemies of the actual, and it is this enmity which, under a variety of grave and comic masks, is on exhibit throughout Arden's theatre. On one level the abstractive impulse allied with power results in men being treated as things. At its most burlesque—and most schematic—this is a chief theme of *The Happy Haven.* Here a group of people in a home for the aged are made the object of a scientific—more properly, alchemical —experiment on the part of their doctor, who has developed a formula for making them young again. That they turn the tables on him in the end, forcing him to drink his own potion and thus return to helpless infancy, is the play's farcical mainspring but not its best imaginative possibility.

If anything, this comic revenge motif obscures something much more interesting and original. For what the inmates are really trying to hold on to is their integrity, which consists—against the pretense of the state and the tastes of everyone—precisely in being old, being what they are. There can be few rivals in recent literature to Arden's intuition of what old age consists in and feels like than the song of the old woman, Mrs. Phineus, rightly quoted by John Russell Taylor in his essay on Arden as an example of his writing's "hard-won strength and sinew":

> *I'm an old lady*
> *And I don't have long to live.*
> *I am only strong enough to take*
> *Not to give. No time left to give.*
> *I want to drink, I want to eat,*
> *I want my shoes taken off my feet.*
> *I want to talk but not to walk*
> *Because if I walk, I have to know*
> *Where it is I want to go.*
> *I want to sleep but not to dream*

I want to play and win every game
To live with love but not to love
The world to move but me not move
I want I want for ever and ever.
The world to work, the world to be clever.
Leave me be, but don't leave me alone.
That's what I want. I'm a big round stone
Sitting in the middle of a thunderstorm.

Yet they are all seduced at first, as anyone would be, by the possibility of rejuvenation, until through a "game of truth" which they play they come to see that life is irreversible, that nothing would be changed by the doctor's elixir:

HARDRADER: I hope I would find a healthy humane existence.
GOLIGHTLY: No no, excuse me, no, Mr. Hardrader. You would be as lonely as ever you were. I know, because I would be, too. Isn't it terrifying?

The implication in the patients' discovery is that while power, in this case the hunger for far-reaching control of biological existence itself, will pursue its own ends, the proper resistance to it is sometimes not counter-power but the sustaining authority of the truth. When the patients get back at the doctor they accomplish an act in the realm of power, a reversal which satisfies our primitive sense of social justice, the villain getting his comeuppance; but when they slip out of the reach of power by understanding its limits and miscalculations they truly undermine it—and move the play a long notch up from didactic farce. Too confined, however, to immediate sociological considerations—his target, in addition to the doctor's arrogance and inhuman scientism, is the complacency of the institution's benefactors and trustees, the patients' "betters"— Arden settles in this play for an obvious truth and satisfaction when he had much richer ones within his grasp.

In *Live Like Pigs*, the events are much more realistic but the action is far less programmatic. The play concerns a nomadic, "uncivilized" group of people who run up against both lower-middle-class propriety—in the persons of their neighbors in a housing project to which they have been compelled to move from their previous home in an abandoned streetcar—and the leveling, hygienic processes of the welfare state, which cannot tolerate their dirt, their immorality, and, above all, their lack of ambition. Against the impersonal functioning of authority, which does have on its side, however, a clarity of purpose and a basis in reasonableness, their only weapons are an ability to side-step the rules and the heavy formless strength of their refusal to be assimilated. They are besieged by papers, forms, the instruments of civilization but also the artillery of bureaucrats:

RACHEL: He says, "Complaints relating to condition of—of aforesaid residence. And gardens appertaining." Ach, all that it is—words.
ROSIE: They send those words at us under the door all the time. It's not right. What can *we* do when we get them? They put us, it's like a dog in a box, you can stick spikes through every corner at him and he's no place to turn at all.

To their neighbors, proper, tacky, narrowly ambitious, terrified of them but also fascinated, they are invaders from a world of irrationality and brute appetite, anachronisms in an age of universal plumbing and savings accounts. In time, fear and fascination turn into rage, in a scene which Arden drew from an actual occurrence and which has its historical analogues here in the riots that have broken out in white neighborhoods when a Negro family has moved in. To this collapse of civilized restraints in the face of the unassimilated, Arden's nomads respond with an inchoate roar of blatant, perverse animality, a turning of the screw. In an action reminiscent of one in Zola's *Germinal,* where a strapping girl striker thrusts her gigantic nude bottom in the direction of a phalanx of bosses and soldiers and invites their homage to it, Big Rachel, the earthy, whorish "mother" of the clan, assails the besiegers of their house (the attackers are mostly women), her words "interspersed with sheer animal noises":

You want us out o' here? I tell you, you want more'n you know you want, you darling lovely girls! We'll come out, oh we'll come

out, you'll not forget us when we come. I tell you: we live like
bloody animals, you don't know what animals are! You hide in
your hutches in your good warm straw and you think you got
thirty-two teeth in your heads; but we carry fifty-three, ohoho-
oho—and there's blood for each of 'em between the leg and the
neck, when *we* come, when *we* come blooding . . .

But the defiance cannot be sustained. Rachel's bellow has
been into the void, into the emptiness that lies between in-
commensurate existences and contradictory codes. In the end
social order, majority values and the weight of the unexcep-
tionable prevail. As Sailor Sawney, the clan's patriarch, tells
Rachel:

You don't know this bastardy-like of folk like I do . . . Aye,
aye, they belong inside their hutches . . . And they don't fight
strong. But when they're out and calling *you* out, they don't
run home soon, neither. They're in their crowd and they'll
swarm you and you'll drown. Live and let live, I say. But that's
been broke into two by this lot . . . They're feard o' Big
Rachel, O.K. Begod they're that feard of her, they'll kill her. All
of us. Just cos we live.

They are not killed but they are indeed "drowned," swarmed
under, defeated and exiled from any life they might have in
the eyes of others. There is no place for them, Arden is saying,
in a society which roots out the indigestible and is forever trying to see to it that there are no loose ends. As their members
are dispersed all they can do is repeat, like children protesting
against rationality and authority, the last two lines of the
primitive little religious verse they had earlier sung at the
windows as a talismanic act to keep out the mob:

Window close and window true
In and out and who comes through?
Mary and Jesus and the Twelve Tall Riders
Nobody else nobody else nick nack noo!

Live Like Pigs is a robust play, humorous, touching,
scarifying by turns, but it suffers from a central opacity and

its dramatic trajectory is impeded. John Russell Taylor has ascribed the puzzled, disgruntled public response to it to Arden's refusal to take sides, to choose between the opposing ways of life represented by the anarchic Sawneys and the law-abiding Jacksons. And it is true that the former are not romanticized; their dirt is real and unpleasant, their moral ugliness is plain to see. Yet Taylor's point is an answer only to those ideologues who wanted Arden to go all the way in his defense of the outsider (or, for certain audiences, the insider), to be explicit about it, to draw conclusions and a moral. He has not done that but he has also failed, despite his clear intentions, to give the Jacksons—his representatives of the socially conventional—anything more than a thin, conventional dramatic reality.

Taylor stresses the fact that the Jacksons are not meant to be representative, that they exist as individuals. Doubtless this was what was intended, but it remains true that they lapse back into the general and representational through their lack of detail, interest, and specificity. Beyond that, there is no real clash except on the level of physical action; the cards may be stacked against the Sawneys socially but dramatically they have all the aces, so that Arden's vision of an inevitable conflict, the world as a place of incompatible entities which nevertheless have equal right to existence, has to be largely extrapolated from the play instead of finding its true and adequate form within it.

Despite the much greater acclaim it has received, *Serjeant Musgrave's Dance* is as widely misunderstood as *Live Like Pigs*, but in this case the play, although suffering from certain structural weaknesses, is perfectly well in possession of its theme and idea. Almost universally described as an "antiwar" drama, *Musgrave* is nevertheless a source of extreme bafflement precisely to those viewers who persist in seeing it that way. Its militant pacifists come to ruin, its denunciation of war seems confined to colonial aggression, it seems to throw up its hands in the face of the problem of violence. Indeed, regarded as a political exhortation, *Musgrave* is extraordinarily ineffective, a lame sermon; but it is not a political play except in the sense that Arden wishes to test certain modes of political action by more rigorous standards than that action can ever provide in itself and in so doing test something more profound than politics.

Musgrave is, once again, a play about purity, except that here the impulse and ravishment of the pure is noninstitutional, centered in the figure of a fanatic for whom the world's fire must be fought with fire. For Black Jack Musgrave, the ostensible recruiting sergeant but secret "priest" and avenging prophet, his mission is to strike a blow against violence and the cruelty of power politics, an act—the taking of twenty-five lives for the five his men were responsible for in some unnamed colony (Britain's role in the Cyprus upheaval was Arden's historical datum)—designed to teach the townspeople the horror and futility of political aggression and the exercise of military power. It is "God's dance on this earth" that he will perform, and in these words—so like Pandulph's in *Left-Handed Liberty*—the fierce, inflexible, proprietary nature of his sense of power are revealed.

What is most crucial to an understanding of the play is to center one's attention on the manner in which Musgrave shoulders aside all phenomena that may impede his straight true course to his murderously righteous objective. To the barmaid who threatens the irruption of love and desire onto the clean lines of his scheme and its philosophical framework he sets forth his "higher" values:

> Look, lassie, anarchy: now, we're soldiers. Our work isn't easy, no and it's not soft: it's got a strong name—duty. And it's drawn out straight and black for us, a clear plan. But if you come to us with what you call your life and love—*I'd* call it your indulgence—and you scribble all over that plan, you make it crooked, dirty, idle, untidy, *bad*—there's anarchy.

Much later, after his plan is revealed and has disastrously failed and he himself is awaiting death, he is still unable to comprehend where he went wrong:

MUSGRAVE: Good order and the discipline: it's the only road I know. Why can't you see it?

MRS. HITCHCOCK: All I can see is Crooked Joe Bludgeon having his dance out in the middle of fifty Dragoons! It's time you learnt your life, you big proud serjeant. Listen: last evening you told all about this anarchy and where it came from—like, scribble all over with life or love, and that makes anarchy. Right?

MUSGRAVE: Go on.

MRS. HITCHCOCK: Then *use* your Logic—if you can. Look at it this road: here we are, and we'd got life and love. Then *you* came in and you did your scribbling where nobody asked you. Aye, it's arsey-versey to what you said, but it's still an anarchy, isn't it? And it's all your work.

MUSGRAVE: Don't tell me there was life or love in this town.

MRS. HITCHCOCK: There was. There was hungry men, too—fighting for their food. But *you* brought in a different war.

MUSGRAVE: I brought it in to end it.

ATTERCLIFFE: To end it by its own rules: no bloody good. She's right, you're wrong.

On the simplest level Musgrave's crime is that of practicing homeopathic medicine: he would put a stop to killing by killing, the end justifying the means. But more profoundly the play brings into question the nature of all abstract values, when they become embodied in a passionate urgency toward social reformation. The horror such zeal can bring lies in its obliviousness of complexity, the way it cuts down the living in its pursuit of what is seen to bring death, the way its insistence on purity becomes a fulfillment not of human desires or needs but of its own internal propositions. That *Serjeant Musgrave's Dance* leaves the problem of political violence where it found it, offering no prescriptions and no programs, is exactly why it is not a "political" play; it is not real, it is an artifact of the dramatic imagination, and it leaves the problem of violence to those agencies, outside art, whose province it properly is.

If *Musgrave* is a play about the consequences of purity, *Armstrong's Last Goodnight* is one about impurity, about the brindled color of politics and the devastations brought about

by the perennial conflict between the general and the particular in society, the rival claims of authority and the individual. The clash between Johnny Armstrong of Gilnockie, a
provincial lord and freebooter, and King James of Scotland,
who is struggling to establish a centralized, secure realm, is,
the play makes clear, an inevitable one. There is no thoroughgoing villain and no unassailable hero; "Here," Sir David
Lindsay, the "very subtle practiser" who is the King's diplomatic troubleshooter, announces at the end, "may ye read the
varieties of dishonour."

It is clear that Arden's sympathies lie with Armstrong. For
Armstrong contains in himself an element of passionate life, a
simplicity and directness which seen from a certain point of
view puts the deviousness and calculated operations of the
state to shame. His virtues, however, are what constitute him
as the very principle of anarchic individualism, which brings
him into inevitable collison with the generalizing principle of
the state. The latter must seek his betrayal and death for its
own physical self-protection, but even more for the preservation of its existential nature—authority cannot be another
thing than that which strikes down whatever attempts to
thrust itself before the general welfare.

Yet nothing is clearer than that the action of authority in
bringing about Armstrong's death has only a provisional value,
a temporary effectiveness, and that in the moral realm, whose
values are different, judgment will continue to be pronounced
upon it. As Lindsay tells the King, summing up the affair:

> The man is deid, there will be nae war with England: this year.
> There will be small turbulence on the border: this year. And
> what we have done is no likely to be forgotten: this year, the
> neist year, and mony a year after that.

Still, we are witnessing the *varieties* of dishonor. Armstrong
has been no blameless victim; in his arrogance and unbridled
egotism he has treacherously killed a rival laird, and has
demonstrated a childish, overweening concern for the ap-
purtenances of power, with no sense of responsibility to go

with it. It is one of the deepest proofs of Arden's artistry that virtue is not allowed to accumulate in Armstrong's hands, just as it is not allowed to accumulate in the hands of any of his erstwhile heroes, those passionate, anarchic souls who struggle inconclusively against the realities of the structure of the world.

It is Lindsay, the keen diplomat, who understands those realities best. Yet his skepticism and sophisticated mastery of *Realpolitik* are not permitted to have the final word. For his consciousness and rationality, his wit and sense of the way the world runs, are not ultimately serious; simulacra of seriousness, they are actually the instruments of a game he plays, the game played by anyone who is too civilized, too given over, that is to say, to one side—practical, abstract, logical—of the perennial conflict that runs through man's organized life in common. Like Musgrave's instruction in the realities of his own life by Mrs. Hitchcock, Lindsay hears his truth from his secretary, McGlass:

> Ye did tak pride in your recognition of the fallibility of man. Recognize your ain, then, Lindsay; ye have ane certain weakness, ye can never accept the gravity of ane other man's violence. For you yourself hae never been grave in the hale of your life . . . your rationality and practicality has broke itself to pieces, because ye wad never muster the needful gravity to gar it stand as strang, as Gilnockie's fury.

Gilnockie's fury stands on the other side, with its own consequences in undiscipline, imbalance, and self-injury, but real, distinct, to be accounted for. On that side, too, stands his sexual passion, in Arden's work a principal agency of opposition to the rationalizing of human activity. The Lady's Song, invoking that passion and summoning it forth, is one of Arden's most splendid lyrics:

> When I stand in the full direction of your force
> Ye need nae wife nor carl to stand
> Alsweel beside ye and interpret.
> There is in me ane knowledge, potent, secret,

That I can set to rin ane sure concourse
Of bodily and ghaistly strength betwixt the blood
Of me and of the starkest man alive. My speed
Hangs twin with yours: and starts are double flood:
Will you with me initiate the deed
And saturait consequence thereof—
Crack aff with your great club
The barrel-hoops of love
And let it pour
Like the enchantit quern that boils red-herring broo
Until it gars upswim the goodman's table and his door
While all his house and yard and street
Swill reeken, greasy, het, oer-drownit sa-foot four.

With its range and sure-handed balancing of contrarieties, its supple, muscular rhetoric (the sixteenth-century Scots dialect is much easier to understand in performance than has been made out) and its fusion of lyric energy and reflective strength, *Armstrong's Last Goodnight* may well be the masterpiece among Arden's non-masterpieces. In any case, it most fully exhibits his new species of postpolitical and post-ideological drama, resisting partisanship, disclaiming solutions, neither hortatory nor tendentious yet strenuously involved in actuality.

Probably the most frequent comment that has been made about Arden is that he is unclassifiable, that he cannot be put into a category. The argument is sound up to a point, but beyond that it gets specious and is an evasion. No true artist is classifiable, if by classification we mean a reductive, imprisoning act which deprives his work of the right to conjure up unheard-of entities. But it does no service to Arden to treat his plays as though no controlling impulse and thematic concern were to be discovered in them, as though they were a series of discrete, arbitrary phenomena. What he has done, an important act for the theatre, is boundable and can be identified: it is to have taken the social and political life of man and rescued it, as a subject for drama, from didacticism on the one hand and from impressionism on the other. The new ground he occupies could scarcely be expected to be steady. (1967)

¶ Black Jack's Prayer

Nothing about John Arden's plays compels immediate acceptance or even assists the spectator toward it. Gnarled, rough, complex, inconclusive, they do not "grip," "haunt," "charm," "overwhelm" or in any way seduce an audience or reinforce its stock responses. Arden is a tough nut, a playwright outside established forms yet not within any newly legitimized revolution, a writer whose work possesses such extraordinary integrity that in a theatre of infinite accommodation and spontaneous sellout it appears as misanthropy.

Serjeant Musgrave's Dance is generally regarded in England—where Arden's reputation is polarized between acclaim and loathing—as his central work, not necessarily his best but the one which most vigorously and tautly represents his deepest concerns and attitudes. Its presentation for the first time in New York is marred by an inept production which distorts the play's values and cramps its life, but for it to be here at all is a cause for gratitude.

The play is set in the north of England in the middle of the last century. To a bleak mining town come four soldiers, ostensibly on a recruiting mission. A strike is in progress and they are at first regarded with suspicion, but manage to convince the men that they are not strikebreakers. It soon becomes evident, however, that they aren't recruiters either, but engaged on some mysterious errand whose moral fervor and mystical import are conveyed by the behavior of their leader, "Black Jack" Musgrave. Stern, cold, a martinet, he seems possessed by some overriding purpose for which everything else is a pretext.

Slowly, as Arden's dramaturgy builds its heavy, oblique, not always coherent structure, the purpose comes to light. At one point Musgrave is seen and heard praying, "God, my Lord God. Have you or have you not delivered this town into my hands? All my life as a soldier I've made you prayers . . . My regiment was my duty and I called Death honest, killing by the book. Now I have my duties different. I'm in this town to change all soldiers' duties."

In a long climactic scene of enormous power and intensity his intention is revealed. He calls a public recruiting meeting in the town square and there unveils to the crowd a box of rifles, a Gatling gun and a skeleton dressed in the shreds of a British uniform. Like a mad prophet in the hour of his apocalypse, he announces that the skeleton is that of a local boy who had been killed by a patriot in one of Britain's colonial wars, that he, Musgrave, is there to teach the wrongness of war and that the lesson will take the form of blood for blood, twenty-five townspeople to be shot for five whom his unit killed abroad. As his demented plan unfolds, his fellow soldiers (another has previously been ironically, and somewhat distractingly, killed in an accident) begin to pull away from him, and the crowd to turn. The arrival of a detachment of dragoons ends the threat and Musgrave is led away in irons to face hanging for desertion.

There is no single "point" to *Musgrave*. Read by some as a muddled pacifist tract and by others as an equally muddled anti-imperialist one, its real dramatic vision is that of the horror of single-mindedness, of ends determining means and even more crucially of abstraction in moral life. Musgrave is forever talking about "order" and "logic," especially the logic of God, whose agent he feels himself to be. He has "worked it all out," and cannot understand why his plan's purifying virtue should not be apparent to others. What makes the play not itself a tract is Arden's dense, many-sided, physically oriented imagination, his employment of vernacular speech, verse and song to compose a texture of diversity, his refusal to make his play "argue" anything. Executed rightly, *Musgrave* presents itself as a thick, reverberant, somewhat opaque but very moving dramatic experience.

The current production is far from right. Director Stuart Burge has ignored Arden's explicit instructions to "stylize" the play, to make its acting and direction "realistic" but not "naturalistic." He has failed to impose the slow, intensifying, finally explosive rhythm it demands, has made the action much too literal and busy, the backgrounds too blurred, and thoroughly scanted the musical possibilities of the songs. The cast, with one exception, is of a piece with the direction, most of the key roles being filled with actors of little talent and less understanding of the play. The exception is John Colicos as Musgrave, whose portrait of a fanatic of logic, a man for whom truth burns with an inhuman purity, is never less than compelling and at times reaches moments of great and harrowing brilliance. (1965)

¶Here We Go Round
the Albee Bush

Because "Who's Afraid of the Big Bad Wolf?" is copyrighted, the title of Edward Albee's first full-length play is sung by its characters to the tune of "Here We Go Round the Mulberry Bush," thereby establishing a pattern for the evening's procedures and the public discussion that this unsettling work has provoked. Nearly everything is a substitution or an imposture: a folk melody when Mr. Albee would clearly have preferred a tinny contemporary one; an enormous three-act play whose conception rattles around in the space; experiment clothed in conventional attire so as to be allowed to live; on our part, the acceptance, as an imaginative breakthrough, of the play's intentions instead of its accomplishment, or its out-of-hand rejection on grounds having more to do with decorum than aesthetics.

I accuse Albee of nothing. He is not a confidence man, and if some people have given him theirs it is because there is nowhere else to put it. He is the American stage's young master *faute de mieux*. He makes us feel alive and of our time, he will not let us get away with our habitual evasions and behavior. He is in fact a transcriber of those evasions and that behavior, everything he has written, culminating in *Who's Afraid of Virginia Woolf?* being less a construction of new vision than a series of split-level suburban houses in which we can see ourselves the way the neighbors only speculate. He makes Lillian Hellman seem like the recording secretary of a garden club.

But he also makes a playwright like Ionesco, from whom he used to borrow certain materials, appear more than ever a model of fullness, unity, zest and staying power. For *Virginia Woolf*, though the most interesting play of the season, a work of many compelling virtues, high seriousness and enormous verbal éclat, is an exemplary failure, a fascinating demonstration of the difficulties American playwrights face in trying to cope with all our sundered realities: the split between commerce and art, between tradition and the single voice, between surface and substance and between those aspects of the imagination we identify as form and content.

Hebbel wrote that content presents the task and forms the solution. From the moment the curtain goes up on *Virginia Woolf* and we hear Albee's central characters—a history professor at a New England college and his wife, the daughter of the school's president—tell one another: "You make me puke," and "I'm six years younger than you, always have been and always will be," and "If you existed, I'd divorce you," we are aware that there is going to be a struggle on a more consuming level than that of personal antagonism. For the ferocity of Albee's domestic scene, the feral quality of his naturalism, isn't going to be satisfied with a conventional theatrical destiny—there is going to be a mighty conflict between a dramatic task and its elusive solution.

The evening grows more and more violent. The love-hate relationship of the couple fills the stage with wounds, glancing blows, destructions of confidence and of attitudinal clichés, revulsions, weaponless and unbearable intimidations, bitter exaltations and hopeless embraces. The wife despises the husband for his lack of *cojones,* his inability to step into her father's shoes; he is revolted by her promiscuity and her intolerable sexual pressure. Another couple arrives, a young all-American biology instructor and his inane, ethereal wife, and they begin to function as audience for and participants in the marital horror story.

There is nothing "absurd" about this play. Albee has largely abandoned the specific parodic elements and dragooned whimsy of *The Sand Box* and *The American Dream* and the obliquities of *The Zoo Story* and has, if anything, returned to *The Death of Bessie Smith* for savage inspiration and neurotic prototypes. But he has advanced from that problem play. Here the action is more inward, and the rhetoric, apart from a few speeches of improbable and high-pitched lamentation, is straightforward, cocky, brutal, knowing and tremendously *au courant* . . . and very funny.

When the wife, played robustly—too robustly, perhaps—by Uta Hagen, stretches out in a chair after an abortive off-stage dalliance with the visiting biologist and huskily announces, "I'm the earth mother . . . and you're all flops," we are with Mr. Albee at his insider's best. And when the husband, whom Arthur Hill enacts crisply, but without much force, remarks, "I've been to college like everybody else," we receive confirmation about one source of Albee's appeal. He is the poet of post-Freudian, post-Riesmanian, post-intellectual, wised-up and not-to-be-had, experiential and disenchanted United States of America 1962 Man.

But poets, of course, want to sing, discover new lands of the imagination, be healers. That is Albee's self-imposed "task," and it is his downfall. The pressure in him toward the transcendence of naturalism and psychological notation had previously resulted in the painfully coerced denouement of *The Zoo Story* and the descent into incoherence of *The American Dream*. In *Virginia Woolf* the failure is on a larger scale. He has driven into the body of his scrupulously observed *Walpurgisnacht* (the title of Act II; Act I is called Fun and Games, Act III The Exorcism) a shaft of fantasy designed to point up our sad psychic aridity and fix the relationship between reality and illusion. Its effect is to break the back of the play.

We had been led to believe that the couple have a son in college, much of their mutual recrimination having concerned his upbringing and present attitude toward them. In Act III we learn—as a *coup de théâtre*—that he is imaginary; unable to have children, they had invented him, keeping him a secret and using his legendary existence as the major bond uniting them in their enmity and need. But when the wife mentions him to the visitors, she breaks their pact and the husband decides to kill him off, announcing his death in an accident and thereby ending the reign of illusion. The play ends with the wife sorrowfully accepting the necessity to live without myths while whispering that she remains "afraid of Virginia Woolf," afraid, presumably, of life, art and truth.

There is something doubly wrong with this. Structurally, it leaves the play in division from itself, the psychological realism separated by a gulf from the metaphysical data, just as in *The American Dream* the parody and fantasy lay gasping out of each other's reach. But more than this there is the question of vision, of dramatic truth and rightness, of the proper means to an end, in short, of a "task" and its solution. What Albee has done is to smuggle in an element alien to his physical procedure, asking it to carry the burden of revelation he cannot distill from his mere observation of behavior. He wants to say something profound about the human condition, and he ends, like O'Neill in *The Iceman Cometh*, offering a cliché about illusions.

The sharpest psychological observation will no longer communicate the kind of truth we need and that Albee, with acute but limited sensibility, keeps trying for. As so many developments in art have demonstrated, the psyche is only one element among others and needs to be *located,* tested against other realities, and not simply described. Naturalism gives us nothing but our reflections. However painful, bold and accurate they are, as in *Virginia Woolf,* they are not enough, we are not changed by them, as we are not ultimately changed by this play. The paradox is that human reality can best be apprehended today by indirection, by "inhuman" methods, which means a step beyond the literal, the behavioral, the natural. Our condition is extreme; old measures won't work, but neither will new half-measures, half-dramas such as Albee continues to produce. (1962)

¶ Chinese Boxes

When Sir John Gielgud, who has the leading role in Edward Albee's new play, asked during a rehearsal, "What does it mean?" Albee replied, "You can't play the meaning of the play. You have to play the reality of the characters." To puzzle, therefore, over the "meaning" of *Tiny Alice*, as New York's theatre world was agitatedly doing last week, is to miss the play's complex, self-torturing, nearly self-defeating but somehow unextinguished actuality as drama.

Yet Albee, for all his knowledge that a play should not mean but be, has laid himself wide open to the inferior game of find-the-meaning. The poor spectators, some of whom booed in bewilderment last week, do have a grievance. For *Tiny Alice* is a thoroughly confused play, and it is just its characters, not its "higher" meanings, that are the source of the confusion.

Albee has constructed the play on two levels, which he has publicly described as a "metaphysical mystery" and a "conventional, *Dial M for Murder*" one. To succeed dramatically, the two levels must interpenetrate, the characters must move logically from one dimension to another. But in *Tiny Alice* the two levels are never organically related, and the characters move murkily from one to the other. The result is that they become neither real people nor effective symbols.

For three of the characters—"the richest woman in the world," her vicious lawyer who is also her lover, and her butler, all of whom live in a castle containing an exact replica of itself—the dramaturgical weakness is especially crippling. They are revealed at the climax of the play as representatives of supernatural powers. Up to then they had seemed to be characters in a suspense story. That story has concerned the woman's offer to the Church of two billion (dollars, presumably) on the cryptic condition that the transaction be conducted by a certain cardinal's secretary, a fiftyish lay brother named Julian.

A pious man who once suffered a six-year loss of faith and reason—"My faith is my sanity," he says—he is placed at the heart of an atmosphere thick with portents, implications of perverse sexuality and hints of cosmic chicanery. (At one point the chapel in the model smokes while the actual chapel is on fire.) Eventually the satanic bargain is made known: Julian is seduced by Alice, leaves the Church, marries her, and awaits the new life of the senses. Yet there has been no real marriage and there will be no new life. Transformed fully now—or so Albee hopes—into symbolic figures, Alice, the lawyer, and the butler prepare to leave Julian after instructing him in the nature of his "test."

He has been made to see that reality and appearances are intertwined, that things are contained endlessly within things ("tiny" Alice within physical Alice within cosmological Alice, etc.), that "consciousness is pain" and that "we need what we get," not the reverse. And he has been asked to make an act of faith, an acceptance of the impossibility of straightforward existence.

In the last long scene he becomes an inverted Christ, at the center of Albee's post-Christian vision which sees God made in the image of modern, disoriented man. "Alice, why hast thou forsaken me?" Julian cries as he lies wounded by a gratuitous pistol shot from the lawyer, and then: "Alice, God, I accept thy will." The play's metaphysics are, then, not so unclear. They have to do with existential agony and blindness, with the desperate condition of man caught in the Chinese boxes of existence, wanting love, the solidity of others, yet mortally confined to his own skin and heartbeat—the play's last sound, portentously magnified.

The final effect, however, is one of strain and unclarity, an unclarity not so much of idea as of image. The detective story must carry the mind along a suspenseful surface to cajole it toward wider, more difficult truths. But Albee, caught between his desire to write a play of ideas and his capacity to write one of melodramatic action, has written neither clearly.

The suspense play is full of false starts and red herrings—the mystery impedes the metaphysics instead of establishing a base for it. We cannot accept the demonic trio's change into super-reality because their reality is so murky.

And yet in a peculiar way, *Tiny Alice* is far and away the most significant play on Broadway this year. Its acting is generally superb—Irene Worth as Alice, John Heffernan as the butler, William Hutt as the lawyer, Eric Berry as the cardinal, and John Gielgud, a bit overtaxed but with moments of intensity, as Julian. More than this, it contains scenes that break down the walls of reticence and safety that mark the commercial theatre.

Most important, it is clearly the work of a playwright who, if his ambitions exceed his capacities, still has ambitions we can respect. Albee characteristically exhibits an eventual failure of mind, an inability to infuse his action with thought, and seeks to cover that up by arbitrary fantasy and metaphysical gymnastics. Nevertheless, a deep stream of dramatic perception and committed passion flows underground in him, and when it occasionally comes to the surface it irrigates our dry theatre the way almost nothing else is doing these days. (1965)

¶ Williams as Phoenix

By now it should be clear that Tennessee Williams' real subject is the painfulness (not the tragedy) of existence, and the fate of human dignity (not of the soul) in the face of suffering. It should also be clear that however neurotic Williams himself may be and however widely neurosis enters into and affects his work, there is little point in looking for the roots of his art, and less in searching out the meaning of any particular play, on one or another categorical Freudian plot of ground; because to Williams *everything* is painful—sexuality, touch, communication, time, the bruteness of fact, the necessity to lie, the loss of innocence. And finally it should be clear that toward his material Williams has alternately been elegist, soothsayer, mythmaker, immolator, exorcist or consoler—none of the incarnations final and no one incarnation carried through to finality.

Unfortunately, nothing is clear. The state of Williams criticism is a jungle, in which every hot opinion flourishes. You may find the three or four or seven critics you most respect each sending up a different species of leaf. No American playwright, except possibly O'Neill, has been so much praised or damned for the wrong reasons, just as none has so successfully (and to the exacerbation of the problem) straddled the popular and elite camps. And no playwright has so helped to muddy his work's image by coyness, obfuscatory pronouncements, false modesty and inability to accept that when you eat the cake it is gone.

Thus Williams' new play came to us and was greeted with the familiar irrelevancies and extraneous considerations, and the familiar embarrassment. It was dismal to read his breast-beating acceptance of the Chicago critics' unfavorable notices. (The Chicago critics indeed! Can anyone imagine Brecht,

O'Casey, Giraudoux or even O'Neill deferring to Claudia Cassidy?) And now that the supreme court has reversed the verdict, what has the playwright to say? What, for that matter, does the new verdict, the New York talk, have to tell us about *The Night of the Iguana?*

The talk is that the play is Williams' best since *Cat on a Hot Tin Roof*, and the talk, for once, is right. But it seems doubtful that it is right for the best reasons or that it tells the whole story. In the general eagerness to rediscover a humane or optimistic or elegaic or non-apocalyptic Williams, the Williams of *Streetcar* and *The Glass Menagerie*, two things have mostly been ignored. The first is that *The Night of the Iguana* perpetuates nearly all of Williams' failings as a dramatist; the other is that the renewal, the moving up from the depths of *Sweet Bird* and *Period of Adjustment*, is precisely of a kind to throw light on what those weaknesses are.

Essentially, it is the never-settled dilemma of what kind of playwright to be. The problem divides here into three. The décor: a detailed, exact reproduction of a seedy Mexican hotel near Acapulco, circa 1940; realism at the zenith (flakiness of walls, lushness of vegetation, *real* rain), yet also attempts at "poetic" atmosphere, suggestions of symbolic values. The text: an amalgam of hard realism, expert and winning, and sloppy lyricism; the dialogue used conflictingly to advance the plot or create character or establish vision or as abstract self-sufficiency. The structure: two nearly separate plays, a first act of tedious naturalism filled with supererogation and subsidiary characters of strictly commercial lineage (a Nazi family, a lesbian, Mexican boys lounging darkly); and a second wherein much is stripped away and a long central anecdote with its attendant effects rests securely on a base of true feeling and dramatic rightness.

The anecdote, neither so long nor nearly so shocking as that in *Suddenly Last Summer*, but having much the same purpose, to establish and compel assent to the play's central difficult proposition, is only partly detached from the main flow of action, struggling to issue from it, correct it, illuminate it and give it permanence. It is an example of what Williams does best, as so much of the earlier business exemplifies what he does worst.

Told by a forty-year-old woman who has lived a life of celibacy while shepherding, on a nomadic, Vachel Lindsay-like existence, her aged grandfather, a minor poet who will read his work for coins and is fighting against failing powers to complete his last mysterious poem, a prayer for courage, the story constitutes a revelatory experience to set against the despair over the inexorability of erotic compulsion with which the play is otherwise largely concerned. There is a possibility that it would lose much of its splendor without the incandescent purity of Margaret Leighton's performance as the woman, but one tends to think that it would be hard to destroy.

What is so new in it, and in the play, for Williams, is the announcement of chastity as a possibility, as well as unromantic pity for the sensually driven. For the man to whom it is told, and who exists on the stage as wound for Miss Leighton's ministrations and arena for her victory (sadly, he is played unclearly and with spurious force by Patrick O'Neal), is an Episcopalian priest who has been defrocked for committing "fornication and heresy in the same week" and has become a tourist guide in Mexico, where he maintains an unbroken line of lust and self-pity.

At the play's end he is not healed, nor are his circumstances altered—his last act is in fact to accept ruefully his condition, marked out for him by the person of the female hotel owner, a woman of absolute appetite and primitive sensuality—acted with great gum-chewing, buttocks-wriggling, nasty *élan* by Bette Davis. But what has happened to him, and to the audience whose surrogate he is as Val or Brick or Chance Wayne could not be, not even Blanche or Maggie, is that there is now a sense of destiny continued under a placating star, that the painfulness of what we are and are driven to do is eased by being faced and by being given a counter-image, tenuous but lasting; and the whole thing has managed to work because for once there are no false moves, no violence seeking meaning but exhausting it, no orgasmic aspirations and no proliferation from a center without its own center.

It is almost enough to compensate for all those other things, that ephemeral, debased theatre, that Williams hasn't yet ceased to give us. Indeed, as memory pares away the inessential, it does compensate. (1962)

¶ Mistuh Williams, He Dead

Sitting among the ashes of Tennessee Williams' latest play, his erstwhile defender, the veteran sufferer who has stayed with him through the entire cycle of extinctions and resurrections, now thinks: This time it's finished, he has had it and I have had it too. There is no point looking for another rebirth, because whatever it is that gives back to consumed birds their wings, plumage and beating hearts is not going to listen to another word.

Why, rather than be banal and hysterical and absurd, doesn't he keep quiet? Why doesn't he simply stop writing, stay absolutely unproductive for a long time in Key West, or the South of Spain, or the corner of any bar, and just think? We know this is what he has been trying to do, but how is it possible in the midst of that self-created din, the clatter of the somersaults he keeps turning in front of us, like a spoiled child who needs to have his existence continually justified, indeed ascertained, by our glances, which show admiration, fear, disgust and troubled love.

How many plays in how few years? How terrifying it must be to feel that a season cannot pass, as for that child an evening cannot, without your name being on clucking tongues and your reflection in the encircling eyes. But Williams seems unable to let go; he is wedded to his fear and compulsion, which are bringing about his creative suicide because they are the very things that make a silent, fertile period in the desert, his possible salvation, so unthinkable. Unlike D. H. Lawrence, one of the sources of his sensibility, Williams cannot "shed his sicknesses in his books," because to write them has become a malady itself.

The Milk Train Doesn't Stop Here Anymore is not diseased in the way that certain detractors of Williams find the bulk of his work to be. If anything, it is in subject the "healthiest" play he has written, which establishes once again how unimportant subject in art really is. For this thrust into allegory, which speaks of renunciation and transcendence and a way of the spirit, represents so nearly complete a collapse of Williams' imaginative powers, such a massive failure of rhetoric and structure, impulse and control, that next to it a "black" play like *Suddenly Last Summer* or *Orpheus Descending* seems robust and encouraging simply because of the relative victory of the shaping imagination; it is form, in other words, that most directly answers questions of health in art.

Williams has followed *The Night of the Iguana*, last year's surprising emergence from the pit of *Period of Adjustment* and *Sweet Bird of Youth*, with another and ostensibly more radical movement of quest: for a way out of the impasse created by a belief in the redemptive nature of sexual efficacy—or, more broadly, physical love—that is in absolute conflict with a foreboding that the flesh cannot yield up deliverance. The moralist, hidden or inverted in the bulk of the Williams canon, is in these two plays increasingly on stage.

Like its predecessor, *Milk Train* is situated outside the American South, but its central figure, an aging, wealthy ex-Follies queen, is a Southerner. That provides Williams with a conduit to his past and results in nearly all the energetic and effective dialogue the play possesses. "Old swamp bitches from Georgia don't go in for hand-kissing," is certainly to be preferred, both as philosophy and as rhetoric, to "life is all memory, except for each passing moment." But the latter is the sort of thing we encounter over and over in this deeply embarrassing work.

The woman, Flora Goforth, whose name is only one of the many symbolic elements that rattle around in *Milk Train*, has rented a summer villa on the Italian *Costa Divina* below Naples, where she is dictating her memoirs—five husbands who "looked like apes," one who looked like an ostrich, countless lovers, a long blaze of fame and flamboyance—and preparing, or rather refusing to prepare, to die.

The death is the story, and Williams is, typically, at pains to let us know, in a preposterous program note which assures us of the "universality" of his theme, that it is *our* death he is talking about, the perennial pain and fear which surround the thought of dying. For the woman of his play, the knowledge that she is soon to die, of tuberculosis it seems, is a goad to a furious repudiation which takes the form of a determination to take another lover, to hold death off by throwing the body's special and inconsolable claims in front of it.

The chance comes when a handsome young man, a poet and maker of mobiles with a reputation as a gigolo, arrives at the villa in search, he announces, of someone to be useful to. For he is a *soi-disant* healer, who has learned from a Hindu mystic certain central truths bearing on the peace of renunciation and acceptance of mortality. He and Williams are a little confused, though; the old Adam breaks through, in the bronzed legs under the shorts he wears, and in his remark that "devils can be driven out of the heart by the touch of a hand on a hand or a mouth on a mouth."

The confusion spreads while the symbolism proliferates. The young man, who is named Christopher, although *Zenopher* would be more appropriate, is tempted toward the old beauty's bedroom, but refuses, while milk (for innocence) dribbles down his chin, and after she has told him a harrowing story about the death of one of her husbands, who murmured "The terror! the terror!" (out of *Heart of Darkness*) and fouled his bed, "the bed where I gave him my body," Chris, you see, is holding out for her surrender to his spiritual powers (never specified beyond that hand or mouth touch) and in the end she of course submits, throwing pride, passion and credibility to the wings.

Iguana got by, narrowly against its tendencies to self-debasement, because its symbolism was sparser and more controlled, because its central proposition—that there is a need for courage and for the acceptance of mortal frailty in ourselves and others—was sustained by an adequate structure and a frequently distinguished rhetoric, and because its characters had the dramatic existence proper to their intellectual and imaginative intentions. But *Milk Train* has almost no structure (originally a one-acter, it is agonizingly overextended), no decisive language beyond the most pretentious ("We all live in houses on fire" is a fair example) and no characters with a greater degree of existence than long residence in Williams' hothouse can confer on them.

The woman does have a certain palpability, especially in her bitchy moments, and is played by Hermione Baddeley for all the role is worth, though with a tendency to lapse into the Cockney speech and mannerisms with which we associate this English actress. But Paul Roebling, a handsome figurine, reduces the young man beneath even the incredibly low level of realization Williams places him on; he is a paler Val, a less plausible Chance Wayne, a vastly inferior Hannah Jelkes (for they have the same function) from *Iguana*. And Mildred Dunnock, while as competent as ever, has been handed a part that bears no relevance to the play but that of an extra symbol: a *really* depraved woman, in contrast to our redeemable heroine.

About Herbert Machiz's direction I have nothing to say, since the problem is that there is nothing to direct. About Williams, one more thing. Perhaps it is still too soon to write him off, since no creative death is irremediable. Yet how often can the phoenix rise, and must there not be some source of grace intact, some channel of air kept open for the bird to be summoned up into? In using the stage not to solve his dilemmas aesthetically but to exhibit them in their inchoate form, he is bringing about the permanent death of his art, intruding himself into the space it should occupy and thus drawing the sickness it is meant to heal more airlessly and irrevocably around him. (1963)

¶The Play's the Thing

Twenty years ago Stark Young, the greatest American drama critic, wrote a brilliant and prophetic review in *The New Republic* of a play by an unheralded newcomer. The playwright, he said, had "a true, rich talent," one that "New York will buy tickets for in later plays, especially if enough of the sexy is added to things, but will never quite understand." The author was Tennessee Williams, the play *The Glass Menagerie*. To see it now in a new Broadway production is to be reminded forcefully of what Williams' fate has been as America's best, most abused and self-abusing playwright.

The play, one of his earliest, holds up wonderfully well. A drama of "memory," which transforms autobiography into lucid, objective art, it is small, domestic, deeply felt, its lyricism reined in by perception, sentimentality tightened by insight, experiment anchored in sure classical techniques. All Williams' later concerns have their seeds here: neurosis as a form of stamina, the vulnerability of the spirit, the interaction of myth and reality, the body as both hope and betrayal—all displayed in guarded, oblique shapes.

This domestic, seemingly ingratiating surface is what inspires the excessive nostalgia for this play on the part of reviewers who have always been disturbed by Williams' sensuality and periodic efforts to use the stage for dangerous encounters. Of all his works it is the one which most readily satisfies that craving for the "haunting" and the "magical" which to the Broadway intellect substitutes for dramatic experience. But the play is deceptive. The tale of a Southern family's erosion by its loss of the past and incapacity for the present conceals a stern awareness: that there are no solutions or exits from necessity, that men endure despite having natures opposed to the nature of things.

It is a sad and ironic fact that Williams is constantly

praised and damned for the wrong reasons. And, caught in the Broadway apparatus (he is forever decrying it and perpetually returning to it), his plays are seldom performed with the force, subtlety, and imaginative risk-taking they require. Instead they have usually served as "star" vehicles, grossly or flabbily directed, pushed toward realism, their complex truths dealt with as so much emotional merchandise to be peddled.

True to this pattern, George Keathley does not so much direct *The Glass Menagerie;* rather, he milks it. He has staged the play with hardly any rhythmic distinction or emotional resonance. His all-star cast is therefore largely on its own, and has a hard time surviving the state of nonsupport.

Maureen Stapleton plays Amanda, the mother, who is struggling against her romantic escapism to find a husband for her crippled daughter and to keep her son from straying. She acts within a narrow range, conveying Amanda's silliness but not her underlying toughness. George Grizzard handles the son, Tom, who dreams of writing and finally breaks away from the family, without style or definition. Only Pat Hingle as the gentleman caller is easy and sure-handed; but then Hingle himself was, so to speak, written for the role, the incarnation of black-and-white-shoed, bow-tied, gum-chewing, affable American materialism.

It is in the performance of Piper Laurie as Laura, the crippled girl who lives in a world of glass animals, that the vicissitudes of the production are clearest. Miss Laurie, an immensely sensitive, lovely and intelligent actress who is still seeking self-confidence, is wise enough not to play the girl as a pitiful victim or a maimed Madonna. But though she tries to give Laura the quiet strength and embattled sensitivity Williams intended, she is hard put to find a full body of expression and gesture. It is heartening that she works as well as she does, and that the play itself is apparently indestructible.

¶Slapstick Tragedy

Whatever Tennessee Williams does is bound to be of some interest. His imaginative powers never quite desert him and his sense of the stage never wholly fails. But this axiom is severely tested in *Slapstick Tragedy*, which is composed of two one-acters. At present Williams seems in the sad position of an aging soprano who is forever straining to demonstrate that her cracked, expiring voice can still hit the high pure notes that won her fame.

The two plays are entirely dissimilar in style and mood, although not in underlying attitude. Between them they reveal Williams stretched painfully between opposing impulses: to recapitulate himself and to strike out for new dramatic forms. Both impulses collapse, the one in pallid sentimentality, the other in witless, arbitrary farce.

The Mutilated, the curtain-raiser, is the less catastrophic of the two failures. Set in New Orleans during the thirties, it exploits a vein of memory and feeling which have always been near the center of Williams' dramatic vision. The memory is of seedy surroundings, rootless people and warped yet naïvely hopeful relationships; the feeling is for the victimized of the world, whose prototype is the weak sensitive woman, drastically reduced in circumstances, who stands with a curious wrecked nobility as a reminder of how existence treats those who trust it most.

Two fortyish prostitutes engage in a half-farcical, half-bitter feud in a fleabag hotel. One is tough, aggressive, proud of her "still-firm" breasts. Her enemy, who has had a breast removed (a fact only obliquely revealed), is the obviously "mutilated," but as the play advances, the message is trumpeted that all humans are mutilated and that all they have to hope for is a miracle, a temporary surcease of pain. The miracle arrives (after being heralded by a chorus of skid-row minnesingers) in the form of a vision of the Virgin Mary which the reconciled whores have, or think they have, or want to think they have, on Christmas night.

This exercise in sweetness and light is strengthened from time to time by a flash of the old Williams fire, a moment of sardonic humor or poetic grace, and is extremely well acted by Kate Reid as the tough chippie and Margaret Leighton as the sensitive one. Miss Reid is particularly fine when she rushes through the streets in search of a pickup, furiously muttering "Jingle Bells" in a voice like a pneumatic drill. And Miss Leighton has some moments of despair and nakedness of spirit that would be touching if the play itself touched anything besides empty, adolescent, mawkish fantasy.

The second play, *The Gnadiges Fraulein,* would be a total disaster were it not for the presence of Zoe Caldwell. The play, a hapless attempt at Ionesco-like absurdity, concerns a former "artiste" (embarrassingly but gamely played by Miss Leighton, who twitches spastically about the stage in tights and an orange fright-wig) who, after a life of appearing before "crowned heads," is now reduced to competing for throwaway fish with the giant cocaloony birds which inhabit the Florida key where the action takes place. To recount the play's aimless fatuity and forced humor would serve no purpose. But Miss Caldwell deserves mentioning. As the "southernmost gossip columnist in the U.S." she displays a comic gift, a mastery of timing and of the unexpected but exactly right gesture, which are rarely found in actresses with far bigger reputations than hers. (1966)

¶ Still Falling

There is a temptation, in considering the events which compose and surround the inaugural rites of the Lincoln Center Repertory Company, to withdraw into the most absolute of silences. For how do you go about combating a nightmare, and what words are to be said over a corpse that thinks itself to be, and is so widely thought to be, a vigorous living organism? Yet the sense of obligation returns: the critic, when there is no longer any possibility of being the interpreter, the decoder or the ambassador of dramatic art, has to become its policeman, or, as in extreme cases such as this, its coroner. An inquest, then, would seem to be the only ceremony we can hold, however ludicrous it might look in the light of the dancing in the streets.

Everything inadequate, pretentious and self-serving in the life of our theatre, and indeed in that our wider culture, has converged here to raise up a monument to the false and the self-deluding. A play, heralded with trumpets, which is not even the simulacrum of a drama, a troupe of professionals whose work would shame even the rawest of amateur spirits, an audience mesmerized and confirmed in its devotion to the lowest mystique of "the theatre" to raw material in place of art and to personality instead of imaginative creation—such is Arthur Miller's *After the Fall* and its production by the company that was to effect the redemption of our stage.

Miller, sad emperor with new clothes, is more to be pitied than condemned, once it is understood that he is his own victim as well as that of the cult of success which flourishes so ferally in the jungles of the popular theatre. He is a master *faute de mieux*, a playwright whose dramatic imagination has always operated within the most stringent limitations, a narrow realist with a hopeless aspiration to poetry, and a moralist with greatly inadequate equipment for the projection of moral

complexity. Only once, in *Death of a Salesman,* did his powers
prove commensurate with his theme, so that he was able to
compose a flawed but representative image of an aspect of our
experience. One other time, in *The Crucible,* his deficient
language achieved a transcendence through its borrowing
from history. And that is all, literally everything.

After the Fall is Miller's attempt to come to terms with the
fact of his silence, the eight years since his dismal *A View from
the Bridge* announced the terrible possibility that even within
his constricted area he might no longer have anything to say.
It is his 8½, his document at the crossroads; in it he wishes to
fashion a new basis for the continued impulse toward art and,
by extension, life, to make a fecundation of what has become
sterile. But unlike Fellini, whose film broke through his personal dilemma by the highest acts of the imagination, by making its theme into its form and its terrors into its acceptances,
Miller has simply laid out the raw material and done nothing
to transform or transfigure it. And what is worse, he has engaged in a process of self-justification which at any time is re-
pellent but which becomes truly monstrous in the absence of
any intelligence, craft or art, since it is precisely in those things
that self-justification for a creator lies.

The play is so entirely autobiographical that one wonders
why Miller did not take a deep breath and go the whole way,
why he did not retain himself as a playwright instead of making himself a lawyer and keep Marilyn Monroe as an actress
instead of turning her into a singer. Had he been that straightforward the work might at least have gained in the gossip-
column interest, which is the only sort it possesses. As it is, his
life is spread before us in the manner of a confession whose
thin factual disguises only irritate us because of their pretense
at striking out for universal meaning. In his self-exposure, his
revelations of what his childhood and family were like, of why
his two marriages failed and how he came to forge the will to
try a third one, and in his speculations on these revelations, his
meditation on the nature of love and responsibility and maturity, Miller has succeeded in conveying no meaning whatsoever, but only an endless sophomoric revery about meaning,

an internal bull-session with not even the minor drama of contradiction or opposition.

For there is almost no drama at all, no true confrontation and no movement from confrontation to understanding; there are only wind, shadows and purple smoke. The very form of the play, which Miller has described, to our unbearable embarrassment for him, as revolutionary, is exactly suited to its incorporeality and adamant refusal of dramatic life. On the edge of the bare apron stage of the Lincoln Center Company's temporary theatre, with almost no props, a figure called Quentin speaks to a "Listener" theoretically seated just beyond the footlights, while the events of the play, which are described in a program note as occurring within the "mind, thought and memory" of Quentin, unfold from time to time in the areas behind him and in the interstices of his monologue.

They are not actually events but mostly unassimilated fragments of the past, and they are supposed to derive their significance and palpability from Quentin-Miller's observations about them. And this is what is so stupefying, that these observations are so unutterably pompous and flaccid, that they compose a rhetoric of such hopeless banality and adolescent mutterings, that whatever might have been palpable and actual is converted into gas. It will have to suffice here to give these illustrations, plucked from the unbroken continuity of the whole:

"Yes! To be 'good' no more! Disguised no more! Afraid no more to show what Quentin, Quentin, Quentin is!"

"That decency is murderous! Speak truth, not decency—I curse the whole high administration of fake innocence! I declare it, I am not innocent! Nor good!"

"Maybe it's not enough—to know yourself. Or maybe it's too much."

It remains to say that what Miller has given us the company and its director, Elia Kazan, have made even more atrocious. Kazan has staged the piece with the utmost fake concern, the quintessence of artiness—figures whispering in the shadows, others striking tableau vivant postures, sudden disappearances, skitterings, hoop dances and symbolic gestures everywhere. And he has made Jason Robards, Jr. (there is of course the possibility that Mr. Robards, our most complete theatrical myth, was perfectly capable of discovering the thing on his own) speak his thousands of lines in an incantatory, hieratic, incredibly inflated manner which, one does not have to be told, is for the purpose of giving "dimension" and "universality" to the proceedings and rescuing the suspected banality from its naturalistic sheathing. What it does, however, is deliver it to an absurdity which is much more deadly.

There is one performance, that of Barbara Loden as Marilyn Monroe, which does possess strength and even excitement. If a good part of this comes from our preexisting feelings about Miss Monroe, it is nevertheless to Miss Loden's credit that she is able to re-elicit even these from us through her art.

After the Fall is sold out for its entire run; the Lincoln Center Company is preparing its next production, O'Neill's *Marco Millions,* the worst play of our century by a major dramatist. Our theatrical life is a bad dream from which it is becoming more and more difficult to awake. (1964)

¶ Getting It Off His Chest,
But Is It Art?

The advantage of having Arthur Miller's new play appear in published form so soon after its opening is that it can now be examined on its own, liberated from that extraordinary atmosphere of cultural exoticism, wish-fulfillment, mystique of "theatre" and self-congratulation which has been growing steadily more dense around the Lincoln Center Repertory Company's temporary home in Greenwich Village. The liberation works for us, however, not for Miller. Which is to say that deprived of its physical existence in a theatrical milieu of utmost pretension and artiness, where audiences stir mainly to the winds of gossip, personality and empty expertise, *After the Fall* cannot live as dramatic literature.

Yet there is a place for it, and it is in the history of our self-deluding theatre, the theatre which has apotheosized Eugene O'Neill and made demigods of Paddy Chayefsky and William Gibson, which feels exalted by *J. B.* and *Luther* and is forever mistaking the sounds of emotion for the truth of passion—and the rhetoric of "significance" for significance itself. *After the Fall* is a disastrous failure but its public life is a triumph of propaganda and publicity, more deeply still of the bombastic and adolescent over the very notion of what is mature.

There are a number of ways to regard Miller's intention as a preliminary to reflections on what he has actually done. The play would seem to be a *mea culpa* and, at the same time, an exercise in self-justification, an attempt to come to terms with the past both in its moral aspect and as the field of a protracted vocational sterility, an investigation into the nature of personal responsibility and a counter-inquiry into the inadmissible claims of others. Technically, it is an endeavor to shape a form loose enough and open enough to contain so ambitious a range of material—by locating the action in the "mind, thought and memory of Quentin," the play's protagonist.

Miller has asserted that this form is a revolutionary one, but that is only the first of the embarrassments which his astonishing—yet occupationally characteristic—refusal to let the work take its chances in the world has caused us. More centrally, the pious and windy protests which he has been making in what seem like half our national magazines, to the effect that the play is universal, independent, a free object in the realm of aesthetic truth, blow inexorably against the fact that *After the Fall* is almost entirely autobiographical, and autobiographical in such a way as to be fatal to its existence as drama. The audiences which have been titillated by Marilyn Monroe's resurrection on the stage may have been seduced on other levels into thinking they were in the presence of great art, but they have had a sure instinct for the play's center of reality, its confessional impulse, its personal history offered as an accession to the history of the times.

For Miller is absurdly beside the point when he argues that autobiographical material does not invalidate a work of art. Of course it doesn't, but what does is the failure to transform such material, to deliver it from the chaos and impenetrability of event and actuality, to give it shape and definition and a coherence of its own. And these are the things which *After the Fall* so radically fails to accomplish, deficient as it is in structure, thought, language and movement, and depending so heavily on earnestness, "honesty" and the sort of judgment-freezing self-exposure, which is designed to disarm us and compel our sympathy.

Well, one does sympathize with Miller, if not with his play. He is, it should always have been clear, a master *faute de mieux,* an egregious product of our commercial theatre's hunger for gods. On the strength of one play, whose chief recommendations were not its imaginative findings or verbal éclat but its formal weight and steady contemplation of one limited sector of our national myth, we raised him to a stature he has never been able to consolidate. And what *After the Fall* so painfully reveals is Miller's desperate attempt to live up to his artificial position as a playwright of passion and ideas, with the result that his intellectual shortcomings and verbal inadequacy have never been more flagrantly exhibited.

From the opening scene, when Quentin separates himself from a mass of whispering figures and moves to the edge of the stage in order to address an invisible "Listener" in the audience, the play is almost continuously embarrassing, as much in its printed version as in performance. Structurally, it is a matter of a lack of focus and of realized encounters: almost nothing is dramatized, nothing is discovered in action. All the biography is there, thinly masked: the protagonist is a famous lawyer, but there is the collision with the Congressional investigating committee, the gradual disillusionment with radical ideologies, the childhood as an adored future redeemer, the two marriages—one to a famous "singer" who later kills herself—and the slow, mistrustful but finally joyous approach to a third.

But with the exception of part of one scene between the suicidal singer and Quentin, nothing emerges as palpability, everything is dissolved in a ruinously vague and pretentious rhetoric which is fatally reminiscent of a college bull-session or a first teen-age exercise in exploring the "meaning" of human existence.

This collapse of language manifests itself most vividly in Miller's direct assaults upon the heights; whenever he is being most ambitious, most poetic, he is invariably at the edge of absurdity and frequently over it. When he keeps to a certain modest level of common speech, the kind of thing he manages best, the play is at least endurable. But the itch is too great, so that he is constantly reaching out for splendor and finding *Strange Interlude:* "Yes! To be 'good' no more! Disguised no more! Afraid no more to show what Quentin, Quentin, Quentin . . . is!" At the same time he is capable of original nonsense: "That there is a love; limitless; a love not even of persons, but blind, blind to insult, blind to the spear in the flesh, like justice blind, like . . ."

The unfinished remark directed to the listener-audience is characteristic:

"Or is it simply that . . ."

"I'll tell her that . . ."

And it is sometimes even flown like a distress signal:

"Yes, the power, the power to . . . to . . . Wait a minute, I had it, and I lost it."

Also characteristic is a device we might call the self-answering question:

"Have I learned nothing?"

"Is it that I'm looking for some simple-minded constancy that never is and never was?"

And another device best described as the both-ways ploy:

"Maybe it's not enough—to know yourself. Or maybe it's too much."

Finally, there are the straightforward platitudes:

"I think one must finally take one's life in one's hands."

In its attempt to establish that affirmation, as a ground for both personal renewal and the continuing impulse toward art, *After the Fall* is strongly reminiscent of Fellini's film masterpiece 8½. They are both testaments at the impasse. But what separates them is the abyss between statement and image, between what is proposed and what is discovered and, finally, between the work which can only aspire to meaning and the one which embodies it.

Quentin is forever lamenting, "I don't understand what I'm supposed to be to anyone" and "I'm a stranger to my own life." But the understanding is never forthcoming and the alienation remains inviolate. Where Fellini's film, by making its agonies into its form and its theme of sterility into new instruments of imaginative conquest, broke through into a new aesthetic space, *After the Fall* stays lashed in a storeroom where the raw materials of art await intelligence and imagination to transform them. (1964)

IV/Phenomena

¶The Deputy Arrives

The arrival on Broadway of *The Deputy* has turned out to be an anticlimax, an intellectual one at least, since everything had been expended long before, all argument, partisan response, exhortation and cool theory. Yet physically the first performances were in every sense climactic. Outside the theatre the hate-groups picketed, stirring eddies of disgust but also that peculiar nostalgia we feel for periods during which hatred has clear objects and know-nothingism a face in the streets. And inside there was an atmosphere of expectation beyond anything in recent years, an edgy solemnity that curiously outran the knowledge most of us presumably had. It was as though no matter how much we had read or heard about the play, or whether we had read the text, we could not really believe in its existence until it became actual, subjecting us to its argument in the flesh. The difference might have been that between a lecture on concentration camps and a visit to the site of Buchenwald.

The expectation was never fulfilled, the demonstration was discovered to be almost wholly the lecture it was supposed to supplant. But what is so unprecedented, the reality which makes so much of the public discussion irrelevant, is the way in which Rolf Hochhuth's work manages to survive its own deficiencies and even its incorporeality, persisting in the memory as an instigation, a catalyst and an obduracy. The play as adapted and performed is very much less than the printed text, that text is in turn less than the truth of history, yet something remains that cannot be appeased, neutralized or overthrown.

We have been doing our best to accomplish one or all of these things, and not least by the insistence that despite perversions and reductiveness the play sets going a moral energy outside the framework of history and independent of its details. This is the high, or soul-supporting, interpretation. On lower levels *The Deputy* is regarded as a strict historical assertion which can only be established or disproved, or alternatively, as a no less strictly intended work of art obliging us to canonize it or deflate its pretensions. But what is so significant about Hochhuth's work is that it cuts through categories, being neither art nor history nor pure moral gesture nor autonomous call to arms. If it is anything at all it is an act of frustration in the face of categories and complexity, an attempt to give definition and location to an overwhelmingly diffuse and imprecise moral anguish.

In this sense there is a strong resemblance between *The Deputy* and the trial of Adolf Eichmann. Eichmann became the local, identifiable, graspable source of the horror, the foul consciousness which could explain all unconsciousness, the bounded agency which could account for unbounded crime. It is half the universe from Eichmann to Pope Pius XII, but we will be doing ourselves and the play a great disservice if we allow our natural indignation at the linking of the two names to prevent us from seeing what is being constructed here. As Eichmann was, for the people who tried him, the active principle, upon whom was heaped all the rage and frustration that stemmed from the fact that there was no other agent at hand and, even more, from the intolerable pressure of historical complexity, so Pope Pius, in Hochhuth's sortie against the past, is the negative principle personified, the fixed point of silence who is made to account for and bear the responsibility of silence everywhere.

Dramatically, this seizure of the late Pope for the purposes of finding a location for and giving intelligibility to the fact of silence serves Hochhuth as both a thematic center and an organizing principle. There is no tension springing from Pius' possible courses of action within the play; we know he will not denounce Hitler for the extermination of the Jews. But there is a tension which rises from the return to history, the illusion of having the agonizing events unfolding again, and another which issues from the figure of the Jesuit priest, Riccardo Fontana, who adopts an opposite course, sacrificial and circumstance-defying. He is Hochhuth's imaginative alternative to the Pope, his corrective to moral history; by his action in physically aligning himself with the victims Fontana offers the possibility of redeeming the past at the same time as he most radically indicts its failure as exemplified by Pius' inaction.

Two things go wrong, however, in Hochhuth's drama, if not in his moral vision, or at least his moral impulse. The first is contained in the enormous blunder of ascribing to the Pope's personality and human deficiencies more of the responsibility for the Church's failure to speak than rests upon the institutional nature of the Church herself. As Michael Harrington and Guenter Lewy have pointed out, by failing to take into account the nature of German Catholicism, with its pervasive anti-Semitism, and, beyond that, of the nature of the organized Church itself, perpetually risking shame by its considerations of physical survival, Hochhuth has reduced the issues to an intolerable degree.

It is true that he inserts some explanations from the realm of policy—the Vatican's desire for an independent, mediating role, its fear of Russia—but his portrait of Pius as a narrow, tight-lipped, terrifyingly abstract and unfeeling man is so unrelenting and is made so central to his thesis that the effect is to abase history to the level of personality. But what is essential to keep in mind here is that exaggerated and unfair as this portrait undoubtedly is, the real crime is not against Pius but against moral complexity, just as the real failure of imagination rests not in an ignorance of what Pius was but in an ignorance of what we all are in our relations to fact, evil, necessity and transcendence.

This imaginative deficiency is perhaps even more sharply revealed in the figure of the Jesuit, Fontana, who might have been the locus for a true examination of conscience, an arena for moral debate and illumination. But Hochhuth is unable to make more of him than a narrow agency of opposition and indictment, an emblem of revulsion from moral failure and an unchanging container for the corrective act. Dramatically, there is no growth on the part of this character; once he has learned the facts about the extermination of the Jews he simply swings into predictable motion, approaching every so often a pseudo-Dostoevskian confrontation with the anguish of faith besieged by social horror but sinking continually back into mere functionalism, a rod of indignation with which to beat Pius and a weight to throw into the scales.

All this having been said (there has been no space to describe the play's technical and structural weaknesses—its wobbly stance between a Brechtian epic mode and a portentous lyricism, nor to comment on the way in which Jerome Rothenberg's adaptation serves to reduce to the vanishing point such complexity as the text possesses) there remains the truth that *The Deputy* cannot be measured by its own dimensions. It survives in part by its very inadequacy, which is to say that its attempt to locate guilt instructs us in the supreme difficulty of the task, once the obvious man with the gun has been dealt with, and its vulnerable resurrection of history teaches us how vulnerable are our own efforts to make history transcend itself.

Pius failed to speak, and in the ultimate moral region beyond fact and physical necessity the silence is to be condemned and mourned. But we would be getting off easy if we persisted in seeing *The Deputy* as merely a reminder of his or anyone's failure, as a prick to conscience or the grounds for a reformation of spirit. Things of this sort have a way of floating like balloons above the carnage; we comfort ourselves by their presence in the empyrean. The real value of Hochhuth's play is precisely that it can force us back into history, into the intricacies of the relationship between spirit and aggrieved body, between personal responsibility and institutional indifference. If it does this inadvertently, through a passion ill-matched with its instruments, it does it in any case. *The Deputy* can be described as an accident which rides the weight of necessity, an error which can lead to truth, a failure which makes most of our successes strangely unsatisfying. (1964)

¶ Assault on the Senses

In the 1930's Antonin Artaud, the half-mad theologian and high priest of a new religion of drama, preached an incendiary manifesto: "The action of theatre, like that of the plague, is beneficial for pushing men into seeing themselves as they are, it causes the mask to fall, reveals the lie, the moral inertia, baseness and hypocrisy of our world." Artaud went on to call for a "theatre of cruelty," one that would repudiate the consolations of bourgeois drama in order to shock the spectator into new awarenesses through ritual, violence, extreme acts and the shattering of taboos.

Though his influence has been strong on contemporary drama, Artaud's central belief, that an audience's values can be reconstructed by a systematic assault on its senses, has always been more talked about than tested. But it is being tested now, most radically in a play by German-born Peter Weiss and especially in its New York production by Peter Brook and the Royal Shakespeare Company.

The play's full title is *The Persecution and Assassination of Marat as Performed by the Inmates of the Asylum of Charenton under the Direction of the Marquis de Sade,* shortened for convenience to *Marat/Sade.* Into it have gone all the elements of "total" theatre and from it rise some of the most powerful effects and most disturbing phenomena that the stage has recently seen. Through song, dance, mime, declamation and the key device of a bizarre play within a play, Weiss and Brook have sought to overthrow conventional notions of what makes a drama dramatic and what, in fact, drama is for.

It is, they are saying in *Marat/Sade,* for upheaval, perturbation, revolutionary change. In bringing together two crucial figures of the French Revolutionary era, Weiss, like Georg Büchner, whose *Danton's Death* has clearly influenced him, confronts one perennial view of history and human nature with another. But unlike Büchner, Weiss wishes to prepare the spectator for an act of choice. His Sade is the dark poet of individuality, of the extremity of personal hunger and self-validation, while Marat incarnates the social will, the desire for political regeneration. Out of their argument, as of two dreams competing for the sleeper's attention, comes the play's intellectual substance.

Weiss has drawn on the fact that Sade was allowed to stage plays at Charenton, where he was confined during his last years. The play Sade is doing now, in 1808, concerns the stabbing fifteen years before of Marat, the Jacobin leader, by Charlotte Corday. The roles have been assigned to inmates, who enact them in the context of their own madness and despair, as an act, hopefully, of psychic liberation, just as *Marat/Sade* is intended to be for its audiences.

Constructed along Brechtian lines, with scenes announced by titles like "Song and Mime of Corday's Arrival in Paris," the play moves to demented, jagged rhythms. Brook has staged it with the utmost inventiveness, stretching for absolute verisimilitude on the one hand—an inmate drools copiously throughout, blood is everywhere, a man is seen naked from the rear—and incantatory visual images on the other. Some of the set pieces are tremendously moving. As history moves inexorably to its re-creation, a herald calls: "Corday you have an appointment to keep/and there is no more time for sleep; Charlotte Corday awake and stand/Take the dagger in your hand" while the chorus murmurs "Corday, Corday, Corday." A mime of guillotined heads bodies forth all the waste and terror of violence; Marat in his tub, with an incurable skin disease, sits like the essence of stricken, powerless idealism.

The acting, too, is extraordinary. In the leading roles, Ian Richardson plays Marat with an exact fusion of abstraction and hysteria, Patrick Magee fashions a Sade of superb (if somewhat effeminate) hauteur and intellectual disdain, and Glenda Jackson is a remarkable Corday—spastic, lyrical, agonized.

Yet what is the final effect? Has Artaud's dream been

realized? Is Weiss actually a revolutionary playwright? Beneath all the business, all the violence and startling gestures, is a vacuum. Weiss, for all his pretensions, is a conventional socialist and an extremely limited philosopher. Shuttling between his two protagonists, he endows them with the speech of ideologues. "Against Nature's silence," he has Marat declare, "I use action . . . I don't watch unmoved, I intervene and say that this and this are wrong." Sade replies: "Before deciding what is wrong and what is right, first we must find out what we are . . . For me the only reality is imagination."

The irony of *Marat/Sade* is that so much of it isn't new at all, except in the sense of a new barbarism. Weiss has said that he is interested not in solutions but in posing problems, and Brook has argued that the play's strength lies in its hurling back at the spectator the burden of "meaning." But meaning isn't what's at issue. Change is, and the intellectual and moral sterility of Weiss's play defeat the possibility of change. We are left with images of violence which mount up finally to chaos, to nihilism; we are left really with violence for its own sake, and nothing for the mind to take away.

What about the senses? It is here that the limitations of Artaud's theory reveal themselves. For no matter what Brook puts on stage in the way of violent images, no matter how strenuously he tries to shake us, the play remains a play: if it works, it does so because it is art, not life, which will always exceed it in horror and pain, because its blood is real. But one of art's purposes is to transcend horror and pain by establishing the co-reality of the unreal, the imaginary. Enormously impressive as *Marat/Sade* is, it establishes only a kind of frenetic dance, a choreographed quest for the truths of the imagination. Flattering our sense of the fashionable, our desire to be at wicked, important happenings, but offering no light and no resurrection, *Marat/Sade* is to be seen but not believed. (1966)

¶ Obeying Orders

In December 1963, a trial began in Frankfurt which was to last twenty months and result in the sentencing to varying terms of seventeen former guards and officials at the Auschwitz extermination camp in World War II. From this trial Peter Weiss, the German-born author of *Marat/Sade,* has constructed a theatrical event, or at least an event that occurs in a theatre, called *The Investigation.* The cast represents thirteen of the actual accused, five prosecution witnesses (a composite of hundreds), two defense witnesses, a judge, a defense attorney, a prosecutor. The dialogue is drawn solely from the transcript and there is no "action" apart from this dialogue.

On a raked stage, with the defendants and witnesses in stalls resembling a honeycomb and the judge and lawyers at a bench with their backs to the audience, under harsh lights which dim to effect "scene" changes, the atrocious record is laid out. Four million persons, most of them Jews, are estimated to have died in the gas chambers of Auschwitz, and the play recounts a great many facts about this unprecedented slaughter. Beyond that, it describes, in pitilessly scrupulous detail, the camp's "life": the beatings and tortures, the appalling "medical" experiments, the reduction of the inmates to a sub-bestial existence.

No invented tales could be more harrowing. As the defendants—most gray-haired now, business-suited, respectable—repeatedly proclaim their innocence of the charges or reply that they were only "obeying orders," the spectator suffers from a sense of despair at history's incapacity to be redeemed, to endure its own face. Yet this pain, like the others inflicted by the evening, is somehow never converted into catharsis or, as Weiss primarily intends, a morally and politically useful confrontation with actuality. "Let these events be remembered," is the play's impulse and self-justification, implying that to remember the Nazi barbarity will help change the present and protect the future.

Yet does it work that way? The play's technical assumption is that such overbearing reality does not need the help of "art." And to the extent that these facts must move the hardest or most disinterested heart, the premise is sound. But two questions have to be asked: What is the deepest, most permanent effect of *The Investigation?* And why, if the play isn't a play at all, has it been written for and presented in the theatre?

The answers are difficult and complex. To begin with, it is doubtful that this recital of the Auschwitz infamy is capable of changing anyone. The channels of identification with the events have been blocked off—by time, familiarity, the tendency of the mind to chronologize the outrages of the world. More than that, the mind's tendency is to find culpable agencies for these outrages, dividing history into perpetrators and victims. "What terrible things *happened,* what monsters those Nazis *were*"—such was the shocked, inadequate, faintly self-congratulating yet understandable response of the audience.

Because *The Investigation* lacks any true encounter of forces, because, more crucially, it lacks any means for the spectator to incriminate himself, it becomes a doleful spectacle bound together by no principle of moral insight or aesthetic unity. Weiss is trying to outflank the "unreality" of aesthetic procedure, but this is not enough to make his play effective. Facts can outdo the products of the imagination, but their raw recapitulation cannot replace the imagination's form-giving and therefore life-giving function.

Director Ulu Grosbard must have been troubled by some such intuition. Ordinarily a gifted handler of naturalistic and psychological texts, he tries to ventilate the play's dense factuality by having his performers lay on the emotion. Catches at the throat, portentous declamations, brooding stares into the distance, shouting, table-pounding—all this undercuts the nausea and horror of the bare statements themselves. *The*

Investigation should be done like a mad, cold, sober puppet show; but that would mean doing it as a work of the imagination, something its own internal presuppositions would fiercely oppose. (1966)

¶Bad Connection

The Apple is a tremendous disappointment and a near disaster. More than that, it's a communal disaster, because we had hoped for so much from it, those of us at least who thought *The Connection* one of the two or three authentically new American dramas of the past few years. The theatre is a cruel place, and there is usually not much point in wasting tears on failure, but this time the playwright's loss is barely distinguishable from ours.

The root of the catastrophe lies in a wildly misdirected aim, for *The Apple* is nothing like the play Gelber presumably wanted it to be. The most obvious truth about the so-called Theater of the Absurd, on whose stages *The Apple* clearly wants to exist, is that its grimaces are only apparently sense- less, that they in fact make a new kind of sense which is just what this new drama is all about. But the impression *The Apple* conveys from the start is not one of nonsense releasing new meaning but of largely sterile nonsense mounting finally to chaos, and chaos, moreover, of a peculiarly aggressive and willful kind.

Perhaps an image of chaos is what Gelber intended. But, as Pirandello wrote in explanation of his own radical achieve- ments, "to present a chaos is not at all to present chaotically," and in fact *The Apple* is almost nothing but chaotic procedure; there is nothing organic, no image, of chaos or anything else —that's just what's so wrong. There is only a succession of moments that fight each other off and cancel each other out. The disorder, the parody and the destructive energy have nothing to contain them and give them outline or mass, so that they simply fly off. The effect, if you can imagine it, is of a centrifugal force operating without a center.

The Connection got by through the depth, coherence and originality of its central image, which was, as in Beckett's *Godot,* that of a "waiting." The addicts hanging around for their fix, engaged in activity and conversation of an extreme solipsism and ineffectuality, constituted a serious and poetic statement of an existential situation. The jazz helped greatly, as amplification of the image and nonverbal commentary on the play's themes. Behind everything lay bitterness and mockery, controlled however by a counterbalancing thrust toward acceptance of infirmity, solitude and metaphysical anguish. We are all addicts of one kind or another, the play said when it wasn't being a sociological broadside, and we all have a Cowboy for whom we wait.

What does *The Apple* say of us, what vision does it give of our condition? Behind the spectacle of dramaturgy gone berserk you sense the intention: to inform us that we do not want enough, or that what we do want is contemptible, that we are all hung up on one or another illusion and that life is a series of deadly mirages and our formal attempts to interpret it a set of clichés. Like *The Connection,* the play's cast is an abstract community, representing us all, but much more closely tied this time to certain prototypes: an action painter and his whoring wife, a homosexual intellectual, an embittered Negro, a beat Chinese girl, a spastic. And into the midst of this group of secessionists, whose ostensible hipness Gelber is at great pains to mock (so as to leave nobody unfingered) there irrupts the archetypal square—a barroom bigot who hates Negroes and Jews and is throbbing with megalomania, aggression and self-pity.

It is painful to have to say so, but he shares those qualities with his creator. To begin with, what else but an inflated sense of his own powers could have led Gelber to so unmanageable an *omnium gatherum* of styles and devices—mime, slapstick, grand guignol, parody, dadaist caperings, the use of insect and animal masks, the whole thing interspersed with patches of lyricism and moments of tough realism—to take from, like a kleptomaniac not an inheritor, Courteline, Jarry, Ionesco, Albee, Genet, the Marx Brothers, Henry Morgan and Pirandello, and to exacerbate things still further with shots, explosions, whistles, off-stage microphones and rough stuff in the wings?

The play, for all its energy and real though sporadic humor, comes on like a sustained assault upon the senses and has the quality of a desperate piling up of elements in an effort to keep the attack rolling. There is something cancerous about it; my companion whispered to me at one point that it wasn't ever going to end, that someone was in the wings grinding out new material which was immediately fed to the actors, and that there were relays waiting to take over.

Do I sound belligerent myself? Well, Gelber makes it clear he wants to make his hearers angry. But does he want them to get angry because they're bored, or because their values have been challenged? If he were as sophisticated as his audiences, he'd see what a losing game he's playing. *The Connection* just did survive its adolescent pretense at "really happening," and its running vendetta with the people in the seats. In *The Apple* the thing fails miserably from the start. The moment a character says, "You're going to witness and maybe be part of some destructive scenes," hostility sets in of a very different order from what Gelber intends. And all that selling of coffee that's brewed on stage and the nightly auctioning off of the painter's work made the embarrassment soar.

"It could be you up there." I'm afraid not. You either work your alchemical changes on illusion and reality entirely on the stage, like Pirandello, or you implicate the audience with the actors at a far deeper level of the former's consciousness than Gelber ever reaches, at the level of dream and erotic fantasy, as in Genet. It simply won't work on anything but a ritualistic or obsessional plane; the conscious mind of any audience, even the squarest, is perfectly able to distinguish between reality and the aesthetic artifact, and the will of any audience can be bent to a transformation of life, an enhancement, an escape or a glossing, but not to the acceptance of something purporting to *be* life.

What makes Gelber, so evidently talented, persist in being a gadfly *manqué?* For one thing, I think he envies the position of France's playwrights, who do have influence, and imagines that he can singlehandedly create the conditions for such influence here. But more important, he seems to me to be in despair about his own situation, or vocation—he doesn't really know whether he's cut out for a policeman, a political-science instructor, a hophead, a labor organizer, a stand-up comedian or an impresario of neurotic dancing. And finally, the way he deals with his disturbance is, I think, to try to beat us down. In this, he represents the latest manifestation of Yeats' cautionary figure: the man who instead of making poetry out of his quarrel with himself, makes rhetoric out of his quarrel with others. (1961)

¶ The Passion of Paddy C.

Between acts of Paddy Chayefsky's *The Passion of Josef D.* a friend of mine remarked that he had known a great deal more about the Russian Revolution before the curtain went up than he did now. The man is no scholar, but there is a pool of basic information about that tremendous historical event in which all literate persons share—all, that is to say, but Mr. Chayefsky, who has his own ideas on the subject.

It is his contention that men make history and that certain kinds of men made the Russian Revolution, which is an unexceptional thesis as long as you remember that history in turn makes men and that the upheaval in Russia was a cataclysmic coming together of immense social tides, crumbling power structures and decaying social institutions on the one hand, and violent temperaments, ambitions, idealisms, forceful intellects and messianic wills on the other. But Mr. Chayefsky has very little interest in all that.

What he is interested in and has written a play about is "character," the kind that is examined in such depth in television drama, the school of aesthetic truth where he has studied for so long without ever having been able to be graduated.

Stalin, whatever history might say, is in Chayefsky's vision a deflected religious fanatic whose unrequited passion for the Lord came to settle upon Lenin as an earthly surrogate, after having built up a ferocity along the way which simply had to express itself in mindless acts of mass murder. Lenin, for his part, was a tender, subtle, wise old man much given to rueful philosophizing on man's follies and pretensions in general and on the failure of the attempt to refashion Russian man in particular. And Trotsky, the third of the "three who made a revolution," well Trotsky, as we all know, was a fop and a vaudevillian, the Noel Coward of far-Left politics.

There is an imaginative justification for almost any crime

against the record—art has its laws which are not those of history—but you can be sure that Chayefsky is not covered by it. For besides writing a perversion of both historical event and spirit, he has written a dreadful play, so that art and the annals go down together. Which is a saving grace: the play is so bad that any danger of its corrupting the historical sense of its audience is entirely non-existent.

The Passion of Josef D. proceeds like the work of a man who has read about Brecht, or, more accurately, has heard about him. *Epic theatre*—that means lots of crowd scenes and hurlyburly. *Alienation principle*—that calls for didactic speeches and asides and winks to the audience. *Music-hall ambience*—that requires your company to break into song without preamble, the way it used to happen in those old M-G-M musicals. *Tough contemporaneity of speech*—that needs a line like "To hell with you, Siberia," as an expression of *au courant* revolutionary fervor. And as though pseudo-Brecht were not enough, there is also pseudo-Dostoevsky, pseudo-Chekhov, pseudo-Gorky, pseudo-Mayakovsky and pseudo-Stanislavski. But of Chayefsky, there is, alas, only the straight, unadulterated essence.

At least two members of the large cast struggle manfully with their atrocious assignments. As Stalin, Peter Falk never quite decides what accent to stick with and sometimes resembles a Russian bear in an uncomfortably non-symbolic sense, but he does have energy and presence. To the hopeless task of re-creating Chayefsky's Trotsky, Alvin Epstein brings all the resources of his craft and manages to be entertaining in a vacuum. But for the rest *The Passion of Josef D.* has assembled a company guaranteed to keep the idea of amateur theatrics from dying out, and Mr. Chayefsky, who has served as his own director, makes certain that they stay loyal to that concept.

For an example of the proper uses of history on the stage I recommend *In White America*, which if it doesn't transfigure the past at least preserves it and makes it animate. The offering is in the form of dramatic readings and dramatized incidents from the record of Negro-white relationships in this country, and while its author, Martin B. Duberman, is no playwright, he is a sensitive and scrupulously accurate historian. Three Negro and three white actors perform in the twenty-eight scenes, not all of which, it must be said, are effective. They range from excerpts from a Scottish doctor's harrowing account of life on a slave ship in 1788 to an episode from the events at Little Rock in 1957. The latter scene is the highlight of the evening, a tremendously moving piece of work on the part of a remarkable actress named Gloria Foster. The only spectators whom I can imagine being impervious to the suffering and terror of a fifteen-year-old Negro girl trying to enter Central High are Klansmen and the more dedicated sort of Birchites. (1964)

¶ Paddy's Big Daddy

What exactly are we to say about *Gideon*, Paddy Chayefsky's canticle for the middle classes? It is a play of such furious determination to succeed in the arena of spiritual travail and at the same time to be charming, clever, the kind of work to which we can take our aged pious grandfather and our young iconoclastic nephew on the same night; a play, in short, of such breathtakingly suave exploitation of every possibility of theatrical blandishment, and every inch-deep theological lure, that you simply look on in wonder and admiration of the sort usually given to the most genial and talented of confidence men. Would saying that *Gideon* is this season's *J.B.* be a starting-point?

That would be a little unfair to Archibald MacLeish, who after all has never permitted winsomeness to lighten the prophetic burden; but the two plays do hang together, taking their impulse and receiving their overblown response from our hardy popular appetite for "meaningful" dramas about our spiritual condition. The theatre doesn't live by adultery or the sound of music alone. We all need periodically to be put in touch with the sources, with the things that count. We need to be reminded that there is a Man Upstairs and that he's available for consultation; or, in case nobody's there, we require the occasional representation of the absence.

Unlike Mr. MacLeish's, there is nothing symbolic about Mr. Chayefsky's imagination. He has brought the Man down to our floor, in flowing robes and Sistine Chapel beard; he has given him lines to speak, gestures to make, everything of a kind that will keep us comfortable; and he has put him into relationship with one of his creatures—who is our surrogate—and led the two of them through a drama that has all the appearance of being a significant statement about man and the supernatural.

"I can't love you, God, because it makes a meaningless thing of me."

"This is the law of the universe: don't make a cult of man."

Between these two thematic poles—man's pride and God's primacy—*Gideon* moves with all the easy domestic assurance of a biblicized *Marty*. The Lord has raised up a hero in Israel. Gideon has put down the Midianites, but he was merely an instrument and now he wishes to be a king. The Lord plucks at him, fulminates, cajoles, works alternately on his pity, his gratitude and his fear. Gideon trembles, resists, succumbs, recovers and in the end turns away. But his back is to a God who, smiling winningly to the audience at the curtain, makes it clear that in fact "no divorce" is possible.

It is to the credit of most of the daily reviewers that, seduced as they ultimately were, they resisted more strongly during *Gideon*'s second act than during its first. For as long as Chayefsky is being colloquial, mildly ironic and wistful in his best Bronx vein, we do not mind so much that God grimaces, acts petulant and whistles with relief; we have seen him do these things on our stages before and it is not an impossible convention to go along with. But, oh, the serious matters, the second act of portentousness and apocalypse, the philosophy, the metaphysics, the theology! Oh my, the wisdom pouring over us, the orotund, bright-as-a-penny wisdom!

You pay a price for withstanding the pressure. Surrounded by an audience being steadily uplifted, you come to feel like a grounded plane, or perhaps more disturbingly like the Charles Addams' character who sits grinning at the unseen screen while everyone else around him is in tears. Still, you are saved from complete neurosis by Mr. Chayefsky's generosity in sometimes being so absolutely incomprehensible that not even the most ardent advocate of adult education—of whose theatrical department Paddy is getting close to becoming chairman—can fix you with his reproachful eye. I offer this remark of the Lord's in evidence: "if fear is all the love you have for me . . ."

And yet I don't think that the playwright is entirely to blame for the bemused embarrassment which is the final condition that *Gideon* imposes. Had his conversation with the deity been left to conduct itself upon a comparatively bare scene, that is to say, one reduced to the proper dimensions and vesture of a parable, it might have been endurable; we might have filled in its interstices with our own imaginings and converted its inadequacies into forgivably misguided suggestions.

But Chayefsky, to his aesthetic ruin and financial gain, has linked up with Tyrone Guthrie, and that, as we all know, means an end to innocence. Nothing has been left to chance. From the set with its inclined floor (to suggest spiritual effort and aspiration, I suppose), tents, goatskins and rocky eminences for the Lord, to revivalist chanting, authentic weapons, a belly dancer, a snake to scare the ladies, and a cast whose hairy legs, goatish expressions and ape-like movements suggest the old comic-strip about cave men, Alley-Oop, far more than they do the Bible—it is all excruciatingly physical, active, aggressive. Every possible space where one might have found the opportunity to think is inexorably plugged up.

A word about the acting. It is mostly good, at least Douglas Campbell, as Gideon, is good, and he is about sixty percent of the show. The other forty percent, however, the segment entrusted to Fredric March as the Lord, is sadly disappointing. All around me people were thrilling to the *distinguished actor's* performance, but apart from simply being unable to hear many of his words through the screen of his bird's-nest beard, I found him perfunctory, tired and unimaginative. I suppose that's understandable, however, since to play a *machina ex deus* is a lot harder than the more traditional role. (1961)

¶ With Harlow in Hell

The Beard is a difficult play to review. Apart from its internal opacities and constrictions, this short, purportedly scandalous work by the San Francisco poet, Michael McClure, has the further handicaps, as far as I am concerned, of having been called by Kenneth Tynan "a milestone in the history of heterosexual art" and of having been inserted by its New York sponsor, Grove Press (advanced publisher and now advanced theatre owner), into a "total event" where media mingle and proper hip responses are expected to everything that goes on. The club that such total cultural happenings holds over our heads, of course, is the threat of disqualification for making choices and distinctions, but at the risk of cutting myself off forever from the Underground I'm going to make a few.

On entering the theatre you are plunged into a multi-media bath. The seats have one-word messages on them (mine was "liberty"), the walls of the room, which has been given a grotto-like appearance, carry a succession of projected images—lions, owls, eagles, flowers, abstract shapes, human eyes, the faces of Jean Harlow and others—and the place is filled with a steady aural bedlam: animal roars, bird shrieks, theme music from various movies, human voices, among which I thought I could detect those of Lyndon Johnson, Lenny Bruce and Eleanor Roosevelt. After about twenty minutes of this not wholly unenjoyable sensory circus a trio of hippie-ish musicians strolls in and plays and sings indifferent Bob Dylan-like songs for another quarter of an hour before taking its casual way by candlelight through the audience and out. A moment or so after that the stage lights go up on the play.

This attempt to construct at the same time an entry into and an environment for the play seemed to me to be pretty much of a failure. In the first place, once the drama proper gets under way it goes along like any other; all the preliminary sights and sounds are gone and you might just as well be sitting in the darkness of a staid old traditional theatre which has never been brought into the era of McLuhan. Beyond that, no mood or atmosphere has been created which is more than inferentially coherent with the play itself, since the latter is very much a monochromatic and single-leveled piece of work, although there are signs throughout of its aspiring to be much more. It is just this losing struggle to reach complexity of texture and motif that gives *The Beard,* for all its occasional flashes of high interest and originality, a peculiarly sluggish and static quality, as of something working against itself. For a play which, as everyone knows by now, is supposed to be greatly shocking in its sexual excitations, McClure's work is surprisingly tedious for a good percentage of its moments.

The basic dramatic proposition is arresting enough: to bring Jean Harlow and Billy the Kid together in eternity, face to face in the sort of other-worldly middle-class room which Sartre employed for very different purposes in *No Exit,* and have them go at one another. When the lights go up they are seen sitting there stiff as studio portraits. Billy (Richard Bright) has nearly shoulder-length bobbed hair, a frilled shirt, hard black suit and gleaming boots. Harlow (Billie Dixon), with extravagant cotton-candy hair, shimmers in a seedy silver evening gown and has an enormous ratty feather-boa draped around her shoulders. Both wear little paper beards to suggest, I would imagine, immortality. They stare at the audience for a moment, then Harlow, still looking straight ahead, says in a sing-song, Mae West–tinted voice, "Before you can pry any secrets from me, you must first find the real me. Which one will you pursue?"

This ritual phrase runs throughout the play, often to good effect, and is the verbal mode and talisman of one plane of its operations. The other verbal procedure may be conveyed, in what is literally its minor key, by Harlow's snarling remark a little later on: "You're a sack of shit!" This vocabulary is undeniably as "dirty" as anything the American stage has ever known (which may have something to do with Tynan's extraordinary "milestone" remark) yet it is in no real sense shocking, which is to say morally disconcerting, nor is it in any way arbitrary in the manner of the obscenities in an ersatz work like Bruce Friedman's *Scuba Duba*. For it is there to release and embody most of the action between the pair, to *be* their central encounter in all but a few respects (crucial ones however), and as such it has to be judged for its dramatic value and effectiveness.

The ferocious lewdness is, in other words, never prurient but structural, one constituent of the play's attempted life as drama. For these two American legends, the cinema queen and the outlaw, are engaging in a duel to a certain kind of death and possible resurrection, a knock-down ballet of sexual thrust and parry, of desire and defense, come-on and come-down, with Billy's hard rapist's momentum running up against Harlow's satiny, wised-up, hands-off, daydream sensuality, her fixed and legendary position as shiny unavailable temptress. Or rather, as we shall see, such mythic-sexual-sociological dimensions are what McClure is trying, with only partial success, to fill.

The two exchange ripostes which continue to center on Billy's attempt to get her to sit on his lap and "play" with him in the sex-manual meaning of the word, and her sometimes arch, sometimes urban-savage fending him off. "You want to be as beautiful as I am," she nasally tells him, to which in a fury he replies, "You're nothing but a bag of meat!" "You creepy bastard!" she yells, upon which he informs her: "YOU'RE A REAL BLONDE!" After a time this purely verbal sparring becomes interspersed with circumscribed physical actions: he bites her toe ("Oh my God, there's going to be blood!" she wails) and tears up her panties after having persuaded her to sullenly take them off. The play ends with its only major physical event, the notorious scene in which he kneels before her and performs—in what must be said is a recognizable but extremely fuzzy and directorially diffident manner (the stage is almost dark)—an act of oral sex while she screams over and over in ecstasy, "STAR! STAR! STAR! STAR! STAR! . . ."

As sexual clash and combat, and as an exhibition of voluptuous fantasy being released into theatrical actuality, the play is obviously mostly untrammeled and hard-driving. But, as I have said, it aspires to much more than this, and it is the failure of this aspiration which keeps it from being more than fitfully engrossing even on that *Who's Afraid of Virginia Woolf* level. McClure is continually trying to move past psycho-sexual boundaries into realms of metaphysical and cultural-philosophical recognition. The whole point of the couple's being dead and legendary is that they may now serve as exemplary figures of the American confusion between orders of being, of our perpetual conversion of sexuality into one kind of art—the popular mythology of archetypal surrogates, the blond bombshell, the steely outlaw—and the consequent depletion of the sexual by being turned into emblem and shady metaphor. The hard insistent urge, beyond good and evil and beyond social "value," which sexuality continues to be at bottom is what McClure is attempting to liberate from its prison inside *culture*.

To this end Billy is given the task of trying to convince Harlow that they are both "divine," "immortal," and that this means they are free to do what they want to do, if anyone is free. "There's nobody *here!*" he keeps insisting; no one is watching them, they are beyond the social order, which has to fit sex in among other considerations and repress its amoral ambitions while exploiting it for purposes of civic and economic morale. Yet this theme is never more than stated, never made an integral element of the dramatic movement, a source of transformation for its explicit harshness and ponderable assaults against what we already know. And this is mostly because Billy is its sole proprietor; while between scatological expletives he goes on reminding her of their wonderful status, she stays on the ground of her portrait as a dumb, foul-mouthed blonde, with the result that her naturalism pulls away from his half-incantatory and poetic task. And that poetry is never acute or interesting enough to work as a kind of yeast bringing the rest of the material to a rise despite itself.

This canceling out of the play's major possibility—to be

more than a fierce sexual vignette with philosophical overtones—is exemplified throughout in the performance of Bright
and Miss Dixon. At home in their roles after months of the
play's troubled existence in San Francisco, they are nevertheless unsure of what they are ultimately supposed to be. Ritualistic and matter-of-fact by turns, really clawing at each other
at moments and turning away to reach for deeper implications
at others, rather limited in voice and range of expressive gesture, they end as murky figures halfway between the implacable clarity and self-sufficiency of the new, non-naturalistic
dramatic imagination and the familiarities and easy recogni-
tions of the school of art as linguistic and sexual freedom. The
direction, by Rip Torn (that's correct), has much the same
irresoluteness, astutely ceremonial and uninspiredly casual
in turn. Everything therefore mounts up to a perspective on
The Beard as occupying that foggy ground of contemporary
culture where new energy hasn't yet found a distinct shape
and revolutionary sounds outstrip the creation of revolutionary substance. (1967)

¶Anatomy of a Hit

Bruce Jay Friedman's *Scuba Duba* is a nearly perfect product of the new pseudo-sophistication, being a compendium of varieties of dishonesty, an icon of simulated seriousness and fake wit, a gross indulgence masquerading as a work. And it has been taken up overnight by an audience which constitutes the complement of the exploiters, their target and body politic, an audience wised up to Broadway and avid for what it considers —or has been told to consider—"real," au courant, hit-'em-where-they-live drama, absurd, cocky and daring as hell. When I saw the play on its second night, there was a long line at the box office (which was selling tickets through next April), the first time I have ever seen one at an Off-Broadway theatre in my seven years of reviewing.

This line had formed almost wholly in response to a rave review in that morning's *New York Times,* whose new critic, Clive Barnes—capable enough up until then—had gone down for the count in his first real challenge from the apparently avant-garde and the seemingly gutsy. His panegyric had included praise for the text and the production on every count, for the play's intelligence and humor, its plot, the way it was directed and performed. It was the kind of review which, whether you saw the play before or after reading it, went to deepen your sense of living in a culture of absolute unreality.

The way Friedman's own contribution to unreality masks itself as actual is twofold. Thematically he seems to be dealing with some exceedingly pertinent contemporary social and psychological material, and dramaturgically he appears to be in the full recent tradition of what we might call the scatological-absurd. In the stage's new climate, where anything goes and everything is bound to come, it is nevertheless an impressive feat of exploitive playwriting to fuse two such disparate elements of audience appeal—hip sociology and advanced bawdry—into the simulacrum of a dramatic experience. Negroes and tits, together with a dash of Jewish mother-fixation, all of it served up with what has come to be known as "irreverence" or "if cultural rape is inevitable, lie back and enjoy it": such is *Scuba Duba,* whose very title conveys that distinctive lilt of the current imagination as it sets off to appropriate the games other people play.

In not much more than five minutes after the curtain goes up, we are aware that in his first play novelist Friedman is presenting us once again with Stern and the protagonist of *A Mother's Kisses,* those archetypes of brash Jewish male exteriors which cover victims' souls. He has been diluted and transplanted to the French Riviera in the guise of a vacationing copywriter for outdoor advertising who thinks his wife has run off with a Negro frogman. It is early evening and he must somehow get through the night. He manages this flaccid movement (which is what has been praised as the "plot") with the help of an assortment of characters of the kind that are popularly known now as "zany," until the morning brings showdown, a sort of interracial, Borscht-belt *High Noon.*

The wife returns with the frogman, a caricature of hipsterism cum Black Power, and another Negro, a genteel, poetry-writing fellow, who turns out to be the actual lover. Her husband, as we have been made intolerably aware all evening, is terrified of losing her and moves through a rapid series of last-ditch ploys designed to get her back, which range from frontal assaults on the Negroes to appeals to her pity, culminating in an abject announcement that he will be willing for the man to stay in the house as her lover if she will remain there as his wife. Throughout this final scene the play, which has hitherto been trying to be funny, is making a stab at seriousness, at what we have to call the new realism, and in keeping with this impulse *Scuba Duba* ends with the wife *really* going off with the Negro, a smashing triumph over the formulas and pallid sociology of the Broadway stage.

It is as entirely unconvincing as if she had stayed. The point in fact is that nothing is going to bring conviction, comic or otherwise, to a play that has been existing all along as a fraud, an exercise in self-indulgence, and one whose chief interest in social phenomena lies in literally getting back at their seriousness through japes, fashionable wit and the most vulgar kind of mockery. For Friedman's comic impulse, whenever it isn't simply drilling down into that exhausted mine of neurotic Jewishness (mothers, psychiatrists, hypochondria, self-pity) is capitalizing on the tensions and terrors of the interracial situation by letting us hear, in that liberating communal atmosphere the theatre is supposed to provide, the "things we haven't yet dared say" about it. "We" are the Jewish liberal and anybody who has been passing as one. And what we haven't said, at least publicly, is "coon," "spade," "coal-dusting nigger," "monkey," "chocolate shithead" and a good deal more in a progressive action of getting it off our chests through Friedman's heroism, a high point of which may lie in calling a Negro girl in an anecdote "Urethra."

This vocabulary of insult and invective runs through the play as its verbal leitmotif and functions as that kind of sterile catharsis which is obtained whenever something previously forbidden is allowed a temporary and revocable release. It is hermetic, cut off from true feeling and thought, not part of any dramatic action or purpose, sent up into the air in the interests of coarse therapy, of "acting-out." And yet in the play's most cowardly procedure it is all made safe, legitimized by the playwright's having seen to it that we are made aware of our inferiority, that the Negroes come off better, that they get the girl while we, poor schnooks who have been suffering with the hero all along, get the bird. That masochism has long been a mainstay of American commercial theatre, Broadway audiences having reveled in the exposure of their middle-class deficiencies and delusions, is a commonplace observation; the bright new fact is that masochism has spread to the outlying precincts where an audience purportedly hungry for truth and art has really been waiting for its chance at homeotherapy.

If I turn now from substance to craft, it isn't because I see them as separate but because reviews have their own order of business. The fact is that if Friedman had written a true play, if he had a dramatic imagination (as *Stern* clearly showed he has a novelistic one), his substance would have altered under its pressure, even while his "subject" remained the same. But lacking a dramatic imagination, not knowing how to set people or faculties in confrontation or how to force a histrionic reality out of raw experience, he is left with that experience at its level of deprivation of meaning and form. What he seems to have done to compensate for this is to have picked up information on how other writers have gotten by with their nonplays in this era of formlessness and the cash value of gratuitous outrage.

The chief asset, of course, is that battalion of zany characters whom you can shuttle on and off the stage as purveyors of fresh *schticks,* new routines to vary your central one. They include here a zany American tourist fresh from *Babbitt* and the Elks Wednesday meeting; a zany landlady who thinks everyone's a celebrity ("Oh, Sidney!" she mistakes the frogman for the movie star); a zany gendarme straight out of a perfume ad who says "everyzing" and "nozzing," a zany effete psychiatrist who simply can't *help* our hero any longer; a zany neighbor girl in a bikini who tells "absurd" anecdotes and helps him sexually through the ordeal; a zany anarchist who runs through the set shouting that all men are "teefs"; and a zany Englishwoman named Cheyenne who walks around in thigh-length boots, a merry-widow and bare bulbous breasts, asks if there's "a crapper in the house," announces that she's trying to cut down to five climaxes a night and is hung up, culturally, on Bernie [sic] Malamud.

With such elements to compose the production it follows a predictable course. Jacques Levy is a director of evident talent who did a splendid job with *America Hurrah,* but his work is constantly threatened by a streak of tastelessness announcing itself as verve and by a predilection for stage business that would recommend itself to Olson and Johnson. The result of the release here of these two elements of his *élan* is to graft on the play's inherent obnoxiousness a hateful immediacy, a pressing, elbowing presence of arbitrary gesture and ugly, up-to-the-minute theatricality. Tastelessness may be more accurately defined as pointlessness in aesthetic matters, and pointlessness is what distinguishes Levy's direction almost throughout. There is no conceivable dramatic reason for those breasts to be exposed, for example, nor for a great many other vulgar bits of business, which are vulgar not because they are immoral but precisely because they are pointless. For the rest, Levy sends the zany characters hurtling through the action like runaway figures from other so-called absurd plays, giving them tattoos, pots for hats, and scythes (for nothing), and employs in the most gratuitous fashion a number of devices—slides, booming tape-recorded phone conversations, life-size cardboard cutouts which slide on stage and then slide off again—whose desultory use seems largely intended to assure the audience that theatrical wizardry is near, if not fully exploited.

Most of the time the actors are left to perform in a style of frenetic naturalism, what we might call domestic-absurd. Cut off from each other by Friedman's failure to achieve any kind of dramatic structure, they occupy their islands of speech and gesture to the best of their abilities, which in most cases are extraordinarily small. The exceptions are Conrad Bain as the zany tourist and Rudy Challenger as the frogman; true pros, they at least give the illusion of believing in what they are doing. In the major role of the husband Jerry Orbach starts promisingly, drawing on his gift for stand-up patter and musical-comedy projection of personality, but he rapidly grows vocally monotonous and, more damagingly still, begins to play Milton Berle in earnest. The damage is to the pretense that we are witnessing something more than a situation comedy. A black comedy if you will, but one whose darkness seemed to me to lie in its revelations of what is likely to be esteemed for some time to come in certain quarters as wit, imagination, theatrical zest and social sophistication. (1967)

¶Che!

A friend of mine, a brilliant, sophisticated anthropologist in his early thirties, told me that he knew for the first time that there was a present culture which he found thoroughly mysterious, which seemed to him remote and unfathomable as a secret Persian society, when he saw *Che!* He and I are among the handful of theatregoers who are likely to have this experience. Having got through a few previews (at a $10 admission charge and to considerable word-of-mouth publicity) the play was closed down by the police after the opening night, and its participants and a half-dozen other persons associated with it arrested and charged with "public lewdness, consensual sodomy and disseminating indecent material to minors." There will be a hearing in Criminal Court in New York on April 30.

Che! is an emanation from the world of recent rebellion and disaffection, from hippiedom, the new anarchism, the new sexual iconoclasm. It rises in all its baffling authenticity, its dogged air of knowing itself, from phenomena such as the drug scene, the rejection of the past, the theory of the world as implicitly sexual, the loss of egos and their replacement by bodies. The one thing it doesn't rise from is drama as an art form, although the stage as an arena for acting out is centrally in the calculations. And yet, sad and awful as it is, a memory with which one will doubtless cope unavailingly for a long time to come, it isn't an aberration but a solid, representative, indigenous artifact, as real as a carved polar bear's tooth, something we have been waiting for since everything announced its preparation.

On the makeshift stage of a seedy little place called the Free Store Theater on Cooper Square, four performers (and a fifth in a monkey mask) enact a ritual charade in the form of a play about sex as politics and politics as sex, about the world seen as an orgasm, power as a phallus and utopia as a wet dream. The chief "characters" are Che Guevara and a president of the United States (not specifically Lyndon Johnson) who engage in complicated philosophical and erotic colloquies and finally in (simulated) sex itself, with each other and with two women. One of these is a creature with a tommy gun, a silver jump suit, breasts covered with clear plastic cups, and the name of Mr. Fong—for which I can give no explanation. The other is a nun and at the same time, in some obscure gesture to actuality, the woman who led to Che's capture and death in Bolivia.

The actor playing the President, a tall, sallow, puffy-faced, melancholy young fellow with hair to his shoulders and the pitted back of a one-time acne sufferer, is nude throughout, except for an Uncle Sam hat. The one playing Che, a short, long-haired and long-bearded, sallow young man, is dressed, except for a number of occasions when he takes his penis out, as part of the action or of the philosophy. Mr. Fong is clothed except for her see-through brassiere, while the nun is mostly naked. What they do is this: they touch each other's parts, refer to each other's parts and to various erotic activities in no-nonsense language, and pretend to perform on the stage intercourse, sodomy, cunnilingus, fellatio and auto-fellatio. One of them also pretends to defecate into a large urn that up until then had been purely decorative.

The point about the simulation of the sexual and scatological acts is a crucial one. The troupe was arrested, as far as one could determine from the language in the *Times*, for *doing* these things. But they don't do them, they merely pretend, entirely unconvincingly, to do them; in the scenes of fellatio, for example, two whole fists are between one man's mouth and the other's genitals; in the one of heterosexual intercourse, anyone not caught up in an avid dream can see that nothing is being penetrated, no consummation is even approached. There is never the slightest hint in this most anaphrodisiac of events that anyone is being aroused; nothing rises or flows, nothing leaps or trembles. The sad, unlovely, unbelievably inept performers, young persons reeling up to the frontier, wander

zombie-like through all the proceedings, zonked, most probably, on acid as real persons, and, as performers, flattened by
the sheer improbability of what they are being called upon
to do.

I refer now not to the sexual illusions (which after all
should be the easiest thing in the world to bring off; bodies
squashing bodies can be doing *anything*) but to the occasion,
the work, the drama if you will. The thing is by Lennox
Raphael, a twenty-nine-year-old West Indian who has lived
most of his adult life in New York. In composing his play
(whose theme or point, I suppose I ought to mention, is that
revolutionaries and capitalists are all involved in trying to
make it sexually, that power is a question of who literally—
symbolically if geography and such things interfere—screws
whom) he has employed a rhetoric of such staggering unreality, so amazing a literary falseness and pretentiousness, as
to make you suspect for a moment a sensational satiric tour
de force. But there is nothing satiric; it is all straightforward
dialogue, or rather hundreds of one-liners thrown out into the
air, of which I offer a few examples, with the warranty that
they are wholly representative.

> To dream is to hunger for reality.
>
> You are my psychic indifference.
>
> My identity will resort to violence.
>
> Revolution is pink negative.
>
> Responsibilization is futile.
>
> I am inherently attuned to my chaos.
>
> My loins are aflame with terror and caution.

The effect of such language, absolutely without existence and
constituting an activity from some acquired dim sense of what
verbal beauty might be, is to eradicate the possibility of any
human life at all, let alone sexual, being present on the stage.
Rigorously cut off from one another by the hermetic and self-
sealing language, the actors go about in a trance and move

into the required eroticisms like pure exemplifications, proofs that it is possible to show such things. And that is precisely what one sees: something being proved, something else surpassed, extended and *placed in the record.*

The event's reality, which I referred to before, its evidence of a new and impenetrable culture, lies in its having incarnated the desire to do what it does. Not to have sex in public, not yet anyway, but to *make* sex public. This is what accounts for the particularly joyless and dispiriting quality of what goes on, its sense of being nothing like a liberation but instead a new and pathological unfreedom; nothing is being experienced, imagined or felt, everything is being promulgated, demonstrated and forced out as evidence. The strangely negative atmosphere of the evening stems from the sight of young men and women without talent or personality or the remotest physical beauty lending themselves to the repudiation of their private beings, their mystery, their unreported and previously unreportable actuality, and offering what is left to us.

Had they really done the acts, it would have been better. At least the sex wouldn't have functioned as a replacement for self, but as one of its actions. Whether or not to see it then seems to me to be a matter for the individual taste and conscience—I am against censorship of any kind—and whether or not it will ever be possible to see it on the stage a matter of the development of the theatre and of our culture in general. I doubt that true actors will ever be able to perform sexually in public, unless some dramatist comes along with a power of imagination so great as to be able to overcome the inherent contradiction: that sex, the most personal and autochthonous of all our acts, would in a drama have to be performed by people impersonating others.

Of course it can be performed publicly by people whose business is to do just that, people such as you used to be able to see in the Chinese Theater in Havana. They can always be hired by the theatre. But then we would have not drama but stag shows for the public. Another possibility is quasi-religious public orgies. But that is carrying theatre past its foreseeable future and changing its modern definition.

The authorities didn't close down *Che!* because it puzzled them or made them feel estranged from a culture, but because they were acting out of their own: the normative tradition of a limitation on public sexual expression which has been under such siege and strain these days. "How far will it go?" everybody has been asking. To which the answer is, this far and farther, the unfortunate thing being that this kind of linear answer to a linear question has nothing much to do with what is at stake. (1968)

¶ A Hit and a Success

Neil Simon's new comedy, *Barefoot in the Park,* is the kind of popular stage piece Broadway is always feverishly searching for, without any clear notion of what its elements are or any ability to analyze them even when the work has made one of its annual or biennial appearances. It is enough to know that success is in the air. To be a hit means, on Broadway, to not be a flop; to be good means to not be thought bad; to be intelligent means to not be thought stupid. In this negative fashion the commercial theatre organizes the life of its products and distributes its praise and blame. Thus *Mary, Mary,* which has almost no intelligence or humor or originality, rests on the same eminence with *Barefoot in the Park,* which possesses those qualities to a reasonable degree. Since both have been acclaimed, they share the same existence, having been given their being by the fact of being a hit.

Mr. Simon's little endeavor, it should scarcely be necessary to say, is as ephemeral as a theatrical offering is possible to be (how perpetually astonishing it is, thirty seconds after the last curtain call, not to be able to remember a single thing that has happened). But there is nothing wrong with this, once you adjust your values. If Broadway presented only plays of this kind—inoffensive, rather charming, adroitly directed and performed, corrupting nothing—there would be no reason to complain, since the Street would then be doing exclusively what it does best and we would be entirely free to look elsewhere, as we now do fretfully in any case, for solid, permanent, light-spreading works of dramatic art. But of course a comedy like *Barefoot in the Park* is extremely rare, and perhaps the chief reason for its being rare is that it is indistinguishable in the Broadway mind from *The Marriage-Go-Round* and *Mary, Mary.*

Mr. Simon's chief virtue is his ease. He has a minor comic

imagination and is wise enough—or has been helped to be
wise enough—not to force it too far, with the result that he
lets his inconsequential fable about life among the newly
married take itself casually into moderately amusing, because
relatively free and unprepared, situations, instead of tamping
it all down into one central, dragooned situation where
comedy becomes the self-congratulating recognition of the
familiar. He allows his young couple to inhabit their sixth-floor
post-honeymoon walkup with some unpredictability and personal edge; he brings in auxiliary characters not in order to
advance a spurious narrative but to extend the area of humorous surprise and spontaneous invention; he throws away
a great many lines which a more mechanical contriver of
entertainments would hang onto for dear life.

And he is immeasurably assisted by his director, Mike
Nichols, who has resisted all but one temptation to try to get
laughs from something which is guaranteed to be innately
funny—his one lapse concerns the putative drolleries of having
to climb six flights of stairs—and by his cast, which is, with
one exception, almost brilliant in its deftness and ability to fill
out comic lines with exactly illuminating contributory movement. The delinquent is Elizabeth Ashley, whose pointy
little beauty, like that of a Pepsi-Cola siren, mannered delivery
in which every sentence ends on an interrogatory, and habit
of scrambling over the furniture like the incarnation of young
Mademoiselle womanhood, nearly spoiled my moments of
delight. But Kurt Kasznar, a ham but an engaging one, Mildred Natwick, a cool, unhurried, adroit matron's matron, and,
especially, Robert Redford, an amazingly talented young nat-
uralist, kept those moments safe.

But there is one more crucial thing to say about *Barefoot
in the Park*. It concerns the response that has been made to
it. In the way that Jean Kerr's ersatz piece and Mr. Simon's
largely genuine one have been awarded the same medal, the
various parts of Mr. Simon's work have been admired indiscriminately, both the daily reviewers and the audience on the
night I attended (and on other nights, I have been informed)
reacting to everything with equal pleasure. Yet there are a

good many conventional and simply unfunny lines in *Barefoot in the Park:*

"Did you miss me today?" "No." "Why?" "Because you called me eight times."

"Stand still—the both of you." (Spoken of course by a drunk.)

"When you were a little girl you said you wanted to live on the moon. I thought you were joking." (The reference is to the sky-lighted sixth-floor apartment.)

The audience roared with precisely the same degree of happiness at these and similar inadequacies as it did when it was informed that the inhabitant of another apartment in the building had never been seen, the only clue being six empty tuna-fish cans left in the hall each morning, which elicited the guess that it was a big cat with a can opener; or when it was told about the hazards of elderly women traveling alone, there having been a recent case of such an adventurer falling off a cruise ship and going entirely unmissed. But a hit is a hit is a hit, and in the atmosphere of one, discriminations and comparative judgments are as out of place as objections at a wedding. (1963)

◀ When Words Fail

Nothing is more revealing of a lack of sophisticated knowledge of the nature of drama than the habit of regarding a play's language or insights as separable from its form. We hear a great deal about gifted young writers, blessed with sympathy and *élan*, who have not yet learned to construct properly, whose words lack "tension," who aren't "dramatic" or, on the ticket-broker level, "theatrical" enough. On the other hand, we know of playwrights like O'Neill whose language frequently dismays us but whose "vision" or "sense of theatre" is supposed to carry us over the difficulty.

Now the idea that a play's language can somehow be admirable while the work as a whole is not, and the corollary which argues the reverse, are as destructive of understanding in drama as their counterparts are of understanding in the other arts. To say, for example, that a painting succeeds in color while its shapes fail, or that a poem possesses great verbal felicity within an unpleasant structure, is to say, really, that you have not confronted the object in its own being; you have performed an act of dissection and reduction, a kind of murder, such as we commit on a human face among whose features we pick and choose.

Plays which succeed verbally, or in the totality of their gestures—their tacit language—succeed; I know of no dramatic work whose language or movement excites me but which I condemn for a failure of "construction." This is of course not to say that there may not be imbalances or incomplete fusions in such works, but only that if a play possesses an adequate language it must by that fact possess an adequate structure, since speech in drama is nothing other than speech structured along dramatic lines. And this means that to speak of a play's "writing" as being remarkable while damning its dramatic procedures is simply to cling to a notion of stage art that is responsible for most everything dispiriting in our theatre: the notion of the well-made play, the belief in, or superstition of, tension, development, the caginess of suspense, the ambush of factual surprise, secrets revealed and climaxes attained.

The twin bill now at the Cherry Lane exemplifies perfectly the ineptitude of a criticism that keeps language and dramatic techniques in isolation from one another. William Hanley has been joyfully greeted for his "fine writing," his verbal and human gifts, at the same time as he has been scolded for not yet being a "real" playwright because he is not theatrical, his plays don't *happen well*. The truth is that he is indeed not a true playwright, but this is precisely due to his writing, which is flat, obvious, banal and jejune. There is nothing wrong with Mr. Hanley's situations or physical procedures, limited as they are; there is simply nothing dramatic in his words.

The evening's first one-acter, *Whisper into My Good Ear*, concerns two old men who have arranged a suicide pact in order to end their bleak hollow lives. There are no events, except the negative one of the suicides' not taking place. But Mr. Hanley has put his two characters through a long conversation in which they comment on existence, expose their secrets and grope for one another's reality. One man is straightforward, tough, practical and, as it turns out, not eager to die; the other is oblique, gentle, philosophical and entirely bent on death. His greater horror of life stems, we are made to know— it is the play's point, I suppose—from his having nobody in the world, while his companion at least has an insane wife who sometimes recognizes him on his visits.

What they say to each other is, then, what the play is "about." And they say almost nothing that is not predictable, sentimental, unrevelatory and deficient in wit, subtlety or beauty. Everything is explicit (a fake air of mystery being contrived by the withholding of certain facts and the erratic behavior of the more suicidal man), every interchange results in the reduction of dramatic edge and pressure. When one man says, "The trouble with you is I never know when you're kidding and when you're serious," we have one kind of verbal failure—the substitution of statement for implication. When he says, "You're nutty as a fruitcake," we have simple cliché. And when, while talking about "secrets," the reflective man says, "Once I found a bluebird's egg," to which the other sneers "That's a secret?" we have an abysmal inability to let even one's own rare breakthroughs into authentic vision carry themselves in peace.

The second play, *Mrs. Dally Has a Lover,* exhibits the same relentless progress along a shelf of banal expression, the unseized opportunities stretching away like mountains on every side. Its subject, the affair between an unhappily married woman of thirty-eight and a boy half her age, is nothing—or everything—in itself. But the limpness and crudity of what passes between them, the woman's suffering under her superior sensitivity and humaneness (she reads Donne's love poems and urges the boy to go see a Cellini cup in the museum) and her final exhortation, as she senses the inevitable desertion, to listen to "the sweet music [of human communication] and pass it on"—is exemplary proof that situation is indeed nothing and that ripeness is all.

The acting at the Cherry Lane has also been praised, but apart from Estelle Parsons, who plays Mrs. Dally, I found it on a level with the work. Roberts Blossom, as the harder character of *Whisper,* does at least maintain an honest line, while his partner Boris Tumarin is engaging in all sorts of fey movements, portentous spacings of his delivery and quasi-mystical breathings and twitches. But Miss Parsons, an actress of abundant vitality and great charm, almost lends her play an interest, which Blossom doesn't lend to his. How unfortunate that her co-worker, Robert Drivas, an echo of Paul Newman and Brando, does his best to deprive her of every chance to come or stay alive. I should like to see her in a worthier play. Or rather I should like to see her in a play, not an exercise in unexamined "compassion" or a recorded session of eavesdropping on the neighbors. (1962)

¶ When the Real Thing Comes Along

The impulse toward satire has always had both civic and psychological roots. At the same time as it moves to break up the public mass of congealed untruths, illusions and ritualistic perversions of experience that is the result of a society's refusal to encounter itself, it also tries to effect a psychic freedom, to detach, through the bestowing of ironic consciousness, the personal destiny from the communal one. The process is a reversal of that of tragic art, where the endeavor is to unite the two. All great satire, even its local and ephemeral manifestations, has the quality of rupture and repudiation: we are all in prison, but some of us may refuse to act or think like prisoners.

Whether or not life in Great Britain is really so much more suffocating and circumscribed than it is here, the evidence is clear that English satirists, in the theatre at any rate, are currently more active and more talented than our own. Their response to the ponderous continuity and mendacious self-expression of their own Establishment has been multiple, vivid and of increasing velocity. They are having fun, using the exercise yard for subversive capers, sometimes nearly vaulting over the wall. Next to them we are the most docile and pusillanimous of license-plate makers.

Of the two examples of British satire-making now on exhibit in New York (there are really three, but *The Affair* is of course unconscious satire) *Stop the World, I Want to Get Off* doesn't do very much to advance the claim that has just been made for our insular cousins. But that is because it is not essentially satiric: a *soi-disant* "new-style musical," it goes beyond that to try to be a new art form, a fusion of musical comedy elements, mime, myth and mockery, and it falls considerably short of its goal.

But it nevertheless does a great deal more to break up the monolith of public deceit and communal cliché, the prison atmosphere in which we communicate with one another, than almost any of our own musical contrivances. Created by Leslie Bricusse and Anthony Newley, it stars the latter as Mr. Littlechap, the Everyman of Harold MacMillan's England, and puts him through a series of primarily pantomimic and musical escapades which mount up to a confrontation of the naked simple soul with the contemporary juggernaut. You can either throw yourself under that or dance on top of it, and the latter is what Mr. Newley, who is a lesser Marcel Marceau, chooses to do. Abetted by a rather wonderful performer named Anna Quayle, who is red-headed, seven feet tall and as limitlessly energetic as the comic principle itself, and by a chorus of tights-encased nymphs whose function is the opposite of its Broadway counterpart—that is to say, it has an ironic instead of a corroborative one—Newley extracts a good amount of charm and witty commentary from his successive adventures with the *Zeitgeist.* There are some tedious stretches and a central slackness of the bow that shoots mortal arrows, but if you think you can do better with the native genre, try *No Strings,* or *Carnival* or that newly risen monument to the *unsatiric* impulse, *Mr. President.*

The other import is *Beyond the Fringe,* and there is no point in even shopping for comparisons; we have been left abysmally behind—*Second City, Premise* and the rest. In London, this four-man revue seems to have functioned as a vicarious prison-break, and even though its wit, inventiveness, brilliance of execution and elation at simply having been turned loose all operate as a specific liberation for the oppressed British, we Americans can profit almost as much. Bureaucracy, religious cant, academic nonexistence, pretentiousness in the arts, the atrocious way in which we publicly discuss nuclear warfare—these are not, after all, local matters.

A pipe-smoking tweedy vicar offers his solution to the problem of juvenile delinquency: "I want to get all this violence off the streets and into the churches . . ." An ex-theatregoer complains: "I go to the theatre to be taken out of myself. I don't want to see lust and rape and incest. I can get all that at home." A political commentator remarks that "Bertrand Russell ought to go back to thinking—and stay out of politics." (A number of reviewers missed the joke; it is politics that is being satirized, not old Bertie.) And a member of the non-Establishment reflects that "I'd rather live in great luxury than great squalor. I've been after the trappings of wealth but I have the trappings of poverty. Must have got hold of the wrong load of trappings."

But it is as an ensemble that the four men, all in their twenties, who wrote and act in *Beyond the Fringe* are at their most magnificent. Under a sign that reads "What about the Hundreds of Survivors?" the Civil Defense Commission lectures to the public: "The important thing is to be out of the area where the Bomb drops. Just get out of that area. If you're out you're well out, and if you're in you're very in." And when a pale citizen inquires as to the resumption of normal public services after the nuclear holocaust, he is told they will be quickly resumed, though of course on a skeletal basis.

There is a brilliant if a little overdrawn re-creation of the last war—"1939. Walt Disney had done it again with *Snow White!*" And there is the most splendidly antic parody of Shakespeare productions, culminating in a duel and death scene of epical comic proportions, the final turn of the screw being the lament over the fallen lord, "Oh Saucy Worcester!"

But almost everything about *Beyond the Fringe* takes us a long way from what we have been used to. To these four young men—Allen Bennett, Peter Cook, Dudley Moore (a masterful comic musician) and Jonathan Miller, who is, if one can be singled out, the richest presence of the evening, we owe an enormous debt of gratitude. Unless we owe it first to that stifling social reality of contemporary England which has, by reaction, produced them. (1962)

¶ Die? I Thought I'd Laugh!

Although it's much too soon to be feeling any degree of confidence, there are signs that the Broadway musical comedy may be preparing to bring about its own death and dissolution before we do the job ourselves. The motive may not be all that self-sacrificial—showmen are great believers in metempsychosis and when one body isn't bringing home the bacon there is always the possibility of new incarnations—but even so the general welfare can't help benefiting. How can it be anything but a gain for pleasure, sanity and the future of civilized behavior, if skill, wit and vigor are released from their servitude to formulas and aging bodies?

What has led me to harbor a modest upsurge of hope is the evidence recently provided by *A Funny Thing Happened on the Way to the Forum,* a musical comedy which clearly feels uncomfortable about being one and therefore tries rather strenuously at times to be something else. And what it tries to be, without wholly succeeding is something so refreshing and wonderfully elemental, that many of us found ourselves shaking our heads with relief tempered by a residue of suspicion, (like a starving man being assured that there really is food in the world and that he can have some): it tries to be funny.

If it isn't as funny as it might have been, this is due to the fact that its comic spirit is continually prevented from taking off on a really mad dance by the stern hand of the master of the traditional revels—the musical comedy generalissimo who, even though he senses the war is lost, is so tied to habit and the fear of peace that he persists in sending his forces on those absurd and wearying formulary sorties that go on nightly on all the other fronts along the Street. But even though *A Funny Thing* could have been a funnier thing, it still manages to be the best and freshest and most diverting piece of entertainment you can get to see this year.

There is actually nothing more original about the show's strategy than that it bases itself upon the farces of Plautus, nor anything more inventive about its tactics than that they are drawn mostly from burlesque and knockabout comedy of the kind we associate with the early vehicles of Bert Lahr, Ed Wynn, Bobbie Clarke and, on a level none of us should despise, Eddie Cantor in his cinema days. In fact, *A Funny Thing* kept reminding me of a movie like *Roman Scandals,* (the presence of performers like John Carradine and Raymond Walburn didn't hurt that) when it wasn't reminding me of *The Boys from Syracuse.* But in any case I was grateful to Burt Shevelove and Larry Gelbart for writing a book that is largely pure stampede, give-away nonsense of the kind that doesn't track down its best moments and shake them to death, the way it most often happens on Broadway.

Not that those moments aren't given a hard time. From the moment the first ballad is due, one becomes aware of the internecine warfare that is going to go on all evening: the sky turns pink and the romantic lead sings the most excruciatingly incongruous and pace-stopping love song while gazing up at the window of a flesh-peddler's house where his inamorata, a virgin destined for some senior citizen's *dolce vita,* has been infamously incarcerated. And from that point, the romp is spasmodic and half earthbound, kept in check by the exigencies of the musical-comedy formula, which requires that whenever you are feeling your way into some area of lightness and believable gesture, into something really amusing, you have to remember what the old folks expect and cut your impulse short.

But *A Funny Thing* possesses one asset besides its intermittently amusing book which no amount of by-the-numbers showmanship and no awe of the tutelary gods of the benefit matinée can fully squander: it possesses Zero Mostel, to a very large extent *is* Zero Mostel, and I should like to see the Richard Rodgers who can put that in a box. I don't want to slight the other members of the cast, especially people like Carradine, Jack Gilford, David Burns and Ruth Kobart. They do superlatively well by their uneven material, but the point is that

Mostel, as he does with everything he touches, transfigures it.

What a pleasure it is to look on at that triumph of the spirit over the body's grossness which he continually celebrates—when he isn't celebrating the body's sly revenges on the spirit's ambition toward impossible independence. What an amazing delight to be present at repeated instances of timing which put us in possession of the most hidden truths about relationships (there is simply nobody around who can deliver a line like "You, sir, are a gentleman . . . and a procurer" with half the majestic rightness of Mostel). And how regenerating it is to be put back in touch with sex, after the endless suburban bedrooms and Norman Krasna's juveniles, in a mode of straightforward bawdy whose secret of not offending us lies in its power to suggest that high spirits have a way of redeeming low desires.

I could only have wished that Mostel had been allowed to have his head more often. In one sense, the civil war I've referred to was between him and the musical-comedy format that periodically cramped his style, so that you could almost see him fretting, as the rest of the cast also did, whenever those sterile injunctions had to be obeyed. There was one moment, though, when the full, glorious possibilities of *A Funny Thing* were marvelously present. "Hide the girl on the roof," Zero tells someone, who replies, "Why?" "Why not?" Mostel answers, tiny hands trilling in the air, foot kicking backwards in that gesture whose only rivals are some of Chaplin's. Why not throw away the plot, the logic, the surrenders to expectation, and really have a ball? Whose approval do we have to have? (1962)

¶A Love Letter

A recent *feuilleton* devoted to Zero Mostel informed us that the great comic actor openly aspires to the weightiest and most distinguished roles (Lear was mentioned) and that in the opinion of many qualified observers he could do a magnificent job with them. I don't think it necessary for us to wait until he is literally gotten up in beard and scepter before we can accept the enormous range and high suppleness of his talent; he has demonstrated, like Chaplin before him, that the supreme clown is the alter ego of the supreme tragedian. The Greeks after all, had two *masks* for comedy and tragedy, not two separate figures.

If today, in America especially, we tend to keep two distinct shapes before our eyes, they are actually those of the comic and the *serious*, tragedy having long since passed beyond our capacity for creation—although we may and do re-create it—and therefore not being a real alternative. As far as the theatre goes, the dichotomy may affect the playwright more than the performer, but the latter suffers, too. I remember not liking Bert Lahr's performance in *Waiting for Godot* but being happy that the stereotype had been broken, that the clown had been asked to try a different dance.

But the real point isn't whether a clown may play a Gogo or a king—if Mostel wants to act Lear or Macbeth, by all means, somebody, arrange it—but whether we will continue to regard his comic art as inferior to someone else's serious one, whether, as a larger matter, we will continue to regard comedy itself as inferior in the light of our aspirations toward seriousness. We want so much to be serious that we sometimes fail to notice that for a long time now much of the best work being done, in fiction as well as in the theatre and a good many other arts, has been, by all the old standards, comic—and that such comedy is quite possibly the highest form of seriousness we can hope to achieve for a long time to come.

It is a new kind of comedy, and its spirit unites, whatever else separates them, Bellow, Roth, Salinger and even Flannery O'Connor in fiction, Albee, Kenneth Koch and the Absurdists in drama, the neo-dadaists and the junk-sculptors, John Cage, Lenny Bruce, and Zero Mostel. It is one of the spirits of the age, a spirit composed of some or all of these elements: irony, parody, irreverence in search of reverence, innocence obtained provisionally and by an act of will, mockery designed to bring down false gods, extremity reached or sought for by trampling, with greater or lesser harshness, on all the stiff, lifeless forms and genres that still satisfy certain imaginations—those for whom Broadway is the Mirror on the Wall and who keep our literary taxidermists busy.

The thing that has been trampled on most heavily of all is the very notion of what constitutes the comic and the serious. Whether we laugh or not is no longer the criterion. Ionesco, let us remember, describes his various works as a "pseudo-drama," an "anti-play," a "comic drama" and a "tragic farce," thoroughly confusing the traditional categories, as indeed the works themselves are made up of inextricably matted elements, so that we are brought into the presence of realms of experience and response for which the old divisions—tears or laughter, hope or despair, fantasy or reality—have not prepared us.

The serious is, in the end, whatever changes or replenishes us. And the "new comedy," operating in the space left by almost all our previous seriousness, our sanctified cultural values and humanistic schemata for interpreting and dealing with experience, whose emptiness and irrelevance astound us continually, presents us with the paradox of the humorous being more effective and more fecund than the sober. It also presents us with the invitation to throw out all classifications whatsoever, including its own name. If we insist in retaining them, we shall at least have to set up a nomenclature in which appear "new comedy," "bad old comedy"—for Billy Wilder and

Norman Krasna—and "good old comedy"—for clowns, un-mechanized wits and bird imitators. And probably something along the same lines for drama.

I have set down these observations because the season has come to a whimpering end and I find that when I think back on it the occasions I remember are comic ones—whether of the new or good old variety. N. F. Simpson's *One-Way Pendulum*, with its masterful destruction of logic; Beckett's *Happy Days*, in which the most painful laughter arises from the confrontation of our absolute condition of loneliness; Kenneth Koch's *George Washington Crossing the Delaware*, where fantastic innocence exists alongside the sharpest parody.

The old comedy provided moments of pleasure, too. But only when it was *really* old, when it was farce or physical humor or simple high spirits and not the attenuated *au courant* witticisms of Gore Vidal or Herb Gardner of the prurient yet anaphrodisiac tics of Krasna or of most musicals. I cite here the scene with the bellhop in Greene's otherwise flat and crimped *Complaisant Lover*, certain antics of Bobby Morse in *How to Succeed in Business*, a splendid bit by Gabriel Dell as a cowardly and inept duelist in the City Center's woebegone revival of *Can-Can*, and a good part of *A Funny Thing Happened on the Way to the Forum*, the latter a mixed blessing which offered us so much of Zero Mostel and held back so much more.

Even so, I remember Zero best. And that is to say I remember a man in whose ambience all the categories fail, the performer who is the equivalent of the plays I admire, a phenomenon beyond pigeonholes, an untrammeled (or only locally and temporarily trammeled) minister of grace, a firebird, a spa, a principle of health, a man who has more to say of mortal things than all our preachers and more to say of the immortal than all but a few of them. Must I continue to call him a comedian? Isn't that what we call Milton Berle and Red Buttons? (1962)

¶ Bert Lahr:
The Cavalry Arrives

If we needed more evidence that there is almost nothing personal and serious that Broadway permits itself to do these days except comedy, *The Beauty Part* has come along to provide it. For the past several years it has been the comic endeavors to which have accrued nearly all power to rouse us from our apathy or cure our distaste: embattled comedy like *A Funny Thing* or *How to Succeed in Business,* which thrusts against a wall of formula; strategic comedy, such as that of *Virginia Woolf,* deployed for the purpose of softening our defenses against the technically "serious" but ending as the serious itself; untrammeled comedy, of which *Beyond the Fringe* is the current custodian and which is almost inevitably satiric in its nature.

The Beauty Part is cartoon comedy, which means among other things that its satiric velocity is curtailed and its virtues of personal statement and unbeholden spirit are considerably weakened by professional hi-jinks and a broadness of platform. But cartoons, like certain acrobats, are sometimes able to invest themselves with singularity and victorious *élan*—how many more revelatory, inspiriting commentators of any kind do we have than Steinberg?—and become unchallengeable works of the imagination. If *The Beauty Part* is by no means on that level, it still remains authentic, vivifying and, for the most part and within its limitations, secure.

Its limitations are largely those of its creator, S. J. Perelman, who is a superior cartoonist, but not a dramadist and especially not a visual one. That is to say, he sketches, intensifies and leaves out—the cartoonist's work—but his strength is verbal, he is a master of the hunt for cliché and pretentiousness of utterance, mocking our language in its windier reaches and our mores in their journalistic aspects, and holding up to us the broad mirror of our foolishness, our comic quest for seriousness. He has done little that has been effective in the theatre, and the screen miracles in which he once played a part depended greatly for their radiance upon their execution by masters of another, more properly physical comic mode, the Marx Brothers.

But Perelman is once again given life by a clown who is capable of taking a deficient though honorable text and transmogrifying its essentially literary humor into something that can be seen, into a *performance*. Even more solidly and effulgently than *A Funny Thing* has existence around Zero Mostel, *The Beauty Part* takes its life from Bert Lahr.

Without him we would be left with a humor toward which we might feel grateful for its not being that of George Axelrod or Garson Kanin, for getting out of suburban bedrooms and into some insolence and bite, but it would be a case of making do. We aren't likely to be more than momentarily amused by a fable of our national hunger for self-expression, a parody of both fake High- and genuine-Middle Culture, whose characters gravely pronounce words like "empathize" and "sublimate" and "therapy," make collages out of "seaweed and graham crackers," do soap sculpture on a "Procter and Gamble fellowship," speak nostalgically of "halcyon days in the groves of academe," and when asked "How can you tell if you have the creative spark?" retort: "If it sets fire to your pants."

Yet there stands Lahr, filling in the spaces between the gags, turning the radio humor toward the purposes of the stage, a preposterous seal whose colored ball never rolls away, a buffoon of absolute unconscious sureness, whose measureless brow is furrowed with unanswerable perplexity, whose eyes roll whitely toward the far corners of our absurd dilemma, from whose thick burlesque lips the indictment, "You're a matzoh ball" emerges with inexorable and overwhelming justice.

In this loosely strung-together series of skits, he plays a half-dozen roles, from a garbage-disposal tycoon named Milo Leotard Allardyce DuPlessis Weatherwax (Perelman's penchant for parodic names—among others in *The Beauty Part* are

Rob Roy Fruitwell, Vernon Equinox and April Monkshood—
are fine for the printed page but not much help on the stage,
since we cannot keep referring to our programs) to a lady
pulp-magazine editor called Hyacinth Beddoes Laffoon and a
magnificently unscrupulous Hollywood agent named Harry
Hubris.

In each case he lifts the material above its sketchy ambitions, bestowing upon it the unexpected and undomesticated,
infusing it with antic palpability and kinetic force. But he is
at his most unopposable as a judge who has become a television personality and whose smile into the camera is the
hilarious epitome of all self-seeking pomposity everywhere,
and even more impregnable as a chair-ridden, crotchety old
millionaire with violent leanings toward John Birch. The episode is a masterpiece of timing and comic invention, and may
profitably be compared with a very similar bit in *Little Me*,
one in which Sid Caesar's conscious, crafty, *comedian's* work
looks even smaller than it really is next to Lahr's bottomless
wide pool of clown's inspiration.

It remains to be said that he is not entirely alone, being
supported by a generally good cast, whose outstanding members include Charlotte Rae and Alice Ghostly, but also that
both he and Perelman are badly served by a director, Noel
Willman, who doesn't seem to have grasped the fact that a
cartoon is a cartoon, something all of a piece, something big
and blown-up and full of light feet and unfinished gestures.
Willman has kept the action under a heavy hand and nearly
brought it to ruin in the interests of orderly "theatricality," but
dear old Bert, a professional with an amateur's soul, keeps res-
urrecting it every time. (1963)

¶ King Lahr

Among the few solid pleasures which our theatre continues to afford is that of being in the presence from time to time of a performer like Zero Mostel or Bert Lahr. Lahr may lack Mostel's complexity and sorcerer's intelligence, but he shares with him a miraculous sense of timing, a mystery of movement and the great comic actor's openness to the absurd. But, what is more decisive, the transfiguration that places Lahr and Mostel so far above "comedians" such as Bob Hope or Red Skelton, is their existence as cosmoses, total worlds in which every gesture coheres with every other, all speech composes a single and inevitable language and nothing takes place without a history and a future.

Chaplin was of course such a world; Buster Keaton and W. C. Fields were others. They, along with Lahr and Mostel, are the great clowns, who in our time have replaced the great tragedians as the primary sources of wisdom and replenishment. It need no longer be a matter of astonishment that one's sense of existence and courage to continue to wrestle with experience are better served by comic art when it reaches this plane than by a pseudo-tragedy empty of everything but ambition.

This is why it is possible to recommend *Foxy*, which is an atrocious musical comedy whenever Lahr is not at the center of things, but no sort of problem when he is. That is to say, as soon as he comes on stage the mechanical and the superfluous (the pretext, really; why not simply *An Evening with Bert Lahr?*) fall away—the sub-cretinal Klondike-based version of Jonson's *Volpone* (why not *Volpone* straight, with Bert Lahr?), the unbelievably dreary songs by Robert Emmett Dolan and Johnny Mercer, the choreography by Jack Cole that would have seemed derivative at the time of *Oklahoma*.

When all that is mercifully dispensed with and Lahr stands

forth in the circle of his own being, we can begin to live again and better. The eyes roll up toward heaven or the house dick, the great moose-calls shake the furniture, the miracle of lust wedded to innocence and appetite to ineptness is once more effected. "Play me like a harp!" the temptress challenges him. An exquisitely fractional silence, a baring of the teeth, and an 'I can't, I got a sore pinky." You will not find a more cogent comment on our human predicament than that. (1964)

¶High-Level Acting

Cultural time in some ways is like time in the unconscious which, as Freud pointed out, has no tenses, makes no distinctions among past, present and future. The theatre, of all arts the one most subject to the temptation to hang on to what has been accomplished, lives for the most part in an unconsciousness concerning time; new gestures, practices, aesthetic ideologies exist without affecting the main usages of the stage, which goes on according to an arrested calendar, stiff with repetition.

This is partly a sociological phenomenon, partly a matter of the theatre's impure nature. The main audiences for the stage are caught, by spiritual disposition and the placid gentilities of their education, in a desire for repetition, for re-experiencing what they have already been taken through. And the theatre itself, because it is so burdened with economic reality and so often pieced together as if by a committee, finds it immensely difficult to ascertain what its own soul and proper movements might be at any time, and so settles for what they have been.

Nowhere is this more evident than in the question of acting. That acting, that central pillar of the stage, should even be in question doesn't of course occur to most theatre persons, who are, by and large, perpetuators, at best revisors or would-be reformers, of the values that rule the theatre's sad, timeless career. And yet acting *is* in question, in all those areas where the theatre is attempting to overcome that deadly kind of timelessness, which is to say the kind that doesn't know what the present is like or where the past has left off or what the future is asking for. Whatever its present quality, all theatre of epic, abstract or nonnarrative impulse, of audience "participation" or physical involvement, of nontextual emphasis, and so on, is repudiating or putting to a heavy test the traditional notions of acting: as impersonation, role-playing, the skillful miming of reality.

These reflections are occasioned by the presence on Broadway right now of a number of performances whose authority and éclat would seem to demonstrate the opposite of what I have just argued. Acting, a look from a certain vantage point might indicate, is flourishing, indeed is in far better health than drama itself. Dustin Hoffman, in Murray Schisgal's *Jimmy Shine,* is wholly supporting a woefully deficient play. Alec McCowen is converting a run-of-the-mill melodrama, Peter Luke's *Hadrian VII,* into a smash hit, and James Earl Jones is rescuing Howard Sackler's *The Great White Hope* from the fate of being merely interesting.

I have talked about the latter performance (Oct. 26) and want now to talk about the other two and about the place of acting—acting at a very high level, you understand—in the theatre at this moment. To begin with, I don't believe that acting can truly "flourish" in a moribund theatre, one in which the dramatic impulse is suffering from a great many disabilities: the steady grip of convention, the erosion of a "dramatic" way of conceiving of experience, the shift of the best imaginations to other forms.

An art of many elements, theatre swings from time to time among them; there have been periods when directing or stage design was the revolutionary thrust and others in which texts, language, carried the main impetus toward aesthetic vitality and relevance. Acting, too, had at one time to be regenerated, but it is significant that when the Moscow Art Theatre, for example, set about its transformation of acting methods, it had Chekhov's splendid new texts to work with and would have been unlikely to triumph had it lacked them.

The point is that imaginations outside acting are always needed for its resurrection, which is inseparable from that of the theatre as a whole. John Osborne's *Look Back in Anger* helped change the nature of British acting, which had been awaiting the arrival of just such a new task and opportunity to shed its tight breeding, and would not have been able to propose them by itself. All acting can do in the traditional theatre when drama is in a low state is repeat and refine itself, holding the fort, which is now defending a narrow and more or less barren territory.

Or it can fall back on its perennial temptation to put itself forward in place of what it is supposed to serve, in which case the play is not the thing and an isolate, self-generating and self-justifying activity of personality or "character-building" is. (Which is not at all the same thing as the abandonment of texts by actors attempting to create new forms of occupation of the stage.) This is what I felt was happening in the performances of Hoffman and McCowen. Watching them do their histrionic thing, taking account of the difference in their styles—the one broad, personal, casual; the other intricate, subtle, formal—I felt I was witnessing something disconsolate, rootless, work done in a void.

Good work, in McCowen's case brilliant work; had it been bad there would have been no sense of such disjunction or of such sterile enterprise. A bad play badly acted is a whole, a kind of fitness, the clear consistent outlines of what not to do. But a bad or substanceless play well acted is a murk, an aching contradiction, a vision of the flying apart of the coherence and integral purpose that the theatre, if it is to be an art, has always had to struggle for and whose absence is one cause of the revolts we see.

Schisgal's *Jimmy Shine* would not have lasted a week on Broadway—which does have a certain thin commercial sophistication—despite its author's inflated reputation, had not Hoffman agreed to star in it. The play has been described by one reviewer as telling us "what youth is thinking today," and this is true—if by today we mean the thirties and by youth Henry Aldrich. An incredibly naïve work, lacking wit, insight, language, force and any kind of revelation, it tells the story of a young man who sets out to be a painter and has then to resist the pressures of a conforming and commercial world. The only way I can find to convey the work's absolute failure of imagination is to say that in it Greenwich Village functions as a shining, mysterious lure, and to quote a nymphomaniac character: "I can't stop, it's like eating peanuts."

Against this painful nonexistence Hoffman exerts the force of his own existence as an actor, an actor, moreover, who has going for him a newly won status as a culture-hero. Though the script calls for nothing except a generalized and coy "sensitivity" and a species of romantic, outdated disaffection, he manages to place before us his own much more contemporary, tough and original qualities of dissidence and nonconformity, the kind that made his performance in *The Graduate* so affecting. But the work continually closes in on him, and though he holds our interest to the end (he is one of those American actors, like Brando, to whom one is riveted by the possibility of unexpected, exactly right moves), he holds it in this case like a juggler at a funeral or a broncobuster at a pet show: we wonder what he is doing there and what to do with the thing he has performed.

Though *Hadrian VII* is a much more substantial play than *Jimmy Shine*, its substance is that of a nice, well-made, entirely conventional British melodrama with spiritual and humanist pretensions. Based on the book by the turn-of-the-century English eccentric Frederick Rolfe, who sometimes called himself Baron Corvo, the play concerns a Catholic who after having been expelled from a seminary has spent twenty bitter years trying to become a priest. He is suddenly made one and soon afterward, as the result of political machinations, is made pope. As the fantasy proceeds, the new pontiff, a radical of the stripe of John XXIII (though he lacks that great man's serenity and sweetness; the character in the novel lacked them even more), shakes the Vatican out of complacency and privilege and is finally martyred by an angry Irish Protestant. The play, if one can move aside its dominating elements of spectacle and melodrama, is presumably "about" the way in which goodness can coexist with neurosis, faith and the faithful can be at cross-purposes, and other such unremarkable truths.

McCowen's performance deserves all the praise it's been given. Small, sandy-haired, fierce and flexible, he is one of those actors who energetically fashion their domination over the stage instead of bringing it with them in the form of fame, physique or vocal splendor. He squints, scurries, ducks and dodges, breaks into small petulances and towering rages, shows his contempt as well as his agony, his generosity as well as his resentment; the portrait he fashions vividly recommends itself to us.

But as what? A picture without a frame, a floating image; what we see is an immense amount of skill devoted to the creation of a phantom. For the "character" McCowen has so painstakingly created has no milieu, no "place" for the exhibition and unfolding of its fictive life. *Hadrian VII*, having thinned out all complex reality from the novel it bases itself on, and having established nothing new except predictable melodramatic events, is not an imaginative milieu for its leading character but a set of machinery to make him *work*. And seeing him work, admiring his adroitness and inventiveness and sangfroid, is like seeing the man in the rope trick; he has been working in air, his passion is in the service of a useless illusion, the world is exactly the same. (1967)

¶Murky Soup and Trivialized Actuality

The political realm has always fed the theatre, in gross or subtle ways, as material or incentive, and the theatre has sometimes returned to politics its own reality in the shape of legend, reflection or question. The "theatre of commitment" is on many tongues these days; the "theatre of revolution," radical beyond aesthetic avant-gardism and designed for upheaval—Artaud's plague to overthrow the established order—is more prominent than in a generation. And then there is a theatre of commercialized politics, politics adapted to the conventions of the stage, politics as melodrama, or "meaningful" narrative or fable for the cultured and concerned. That kind of theatre is always around.

The events of the world in a cast of characters; ideology, issues and public history in three acts: the political play, as distinguished from the drama or theatrical act whose instigation is the political order, shapes itself most often as lesson, anecdote, exhortation, and almost never as alternative to what exists *out there*, what the imagination balks at in the organization of the world, or sees through or would dispose differently.

Two new plays for which public events suggest a lesson or a fable contribute, or try to, to this species of theatre. One, Jack Gelber's *The Cuban Thing*, has been rejected by its prospective donee, Broadway, while the other, Robert Shaw's *The Man in the Glass Booth*, seems to be something of a hit. By the standards and values of the commercial stage this is just and proper.

Gelber's play, which closed after one performance, should never have been allowed by its author to publicly embarrass him the way it did. The blindness that afflicts so many theatrical enterprises once they are under way, the simple inability to see how bad something is, was especially powerful here,

I should think. For Gelber, who did after all write *The Connection,* an "anti-drama" in a fecund new sense, has now written an anti-drama in the oldest sense, a weak, largely incoherent, boring and foolish play with literally no redeeming elements.

In tracing the vicissitudes of an upper-middle-class Cuban family from 1958 to 1964, Gelber seems to want to say, first, that Castro was necessary and in the beginning therapeutic, second, that *plus ça change plus c'est la même chose,* and third, that, despite the second, hope remains and promises may yet be redeemed. His stage family and their friends constitute a gallery of familiar political or apolitical types—the fervently revolutionary daughter; the intellectual, somewhat aloof son; the light-headed, frivolous mother; the businessman father with liberal instincts—and to these he adds a homosexual, a proletarian, a couple of prostitutes and an American CIA agent, all of whom help stir the pot and make the soup murkier.

Everyone survives with faith more or less intact—in the face of the Castro revolution's bureaucracy, puritanism and insensitivity—but nothing happens, not imaginatively, not dramatically, not even physically, as something for the eye to light on. All that occurs is that people say lines like "We must restore the constitutional guarantees," and "Wisdom is not the special province of the poor" and "Pimping has invaded every sector of Cuban life," and try through various gestures and grimaces and in Hollywood-Latin accents to make such utterances plausible. And the direction, by Gelber himself, is a hapless mélange of the old and new, nineteenth-century groupings and blockings together with up-to-the-minute film projections that are occasionally interesting in themselves but never contribute anything relevant to the stage action.

All the excitement of that opening and closing night was projected from outside, the street being filled with shouting wild-eyed anti-Castro pickets who tried to drown out the actors with their screams and to throw themselves on us as we came out. The police protected us from what would have been an addition of injury to insult. What I couldn't understand was why the pickets hadn't learned that the play was so minimally pro-Castro and that, in any case, it couldn't possibly have convinced anybody.

Had anyone been alert, *The Man in the Glass Booth* might also have had pickets outside the theatre, in this case the kind of people who hated Hannah Arendt's book about Eichmann or, more rationally, people for whom the play's subject is nothing to play around with. For Robert Shaw's drama about a Jewish businessman who is exposed as a former SS colonel, a member of Eichmann's *Einsatzgruppen,* and then exposed again as a real Jewish businessman posing as a Nazi is, at bottom (and the way down isn't very far) at the very least insulting to the reality of Jewish suffering at the hands of Hitler. And this isn't because Shaw, a very good actor and a mediocre novelist whose first play this is, says anything openly calumniatory about the Jews but because he trivializes terrible actuality, plays with it and turns it into "entertainment."

But nobody seems to have noticed or cared, with the exception of Jack Kroll, whose *Newsweek* review touches with fine perceptiveness on all the play's strange perversions and ambitions. Shaw's chief ambition is to construct a hip moral drama, one informed by our contemporary awareness of how the oppressor and the victim may be united, how the sufferer may be a secret, powerless Nazi, dreaming of his torturer's jackboots. But crowding that ambition and muddying up the play is another motif: the Jew poses as a Nazi in order to say in the dock "what no German has said," that is, the world will now hear the voice of Hitlerism, strident, unashamed and brutally clear.

Well, as Kroll remarks, it would take a Dostoevsky to do justice to the first notion (although a recent story by Irvin Faust, *Jake Bluffstein and Adolf Hitler,* isn't a bad try at it; but Faust is controlled, clear-headed and unpretentious, as Shaw is not), while the second strikes me as at best supererogatory and at worst dramaturgically thin. At any rate, those are the play's premises, and Shaw proceeds to build on them a confused melodrama whose air of significance comes more from the raw subject matter than from any internal accomplishment.

It comes even more from Donald Pleasence's performance in the title role. Pleasence is certainly one of our most effective actors in certain parts, a master at communicating neurosis, alienation, the kind of lucid dementia so characteristic of our deracinated times. And he is at the top of his form here, if anything a bit over the top, since the performance is of such violence and intensity as to ask for occasional toning down, a breather or two. But it holds you, especially in the first act, where the businessman, a real-estate tycoon, is exhibited in megalomanic splendor, surrounded by flunkies, with the ashes of his wife (a gentile, he lets us know) in a gold urn, and the louvered windows of his office opening to reveal all of New York.

With an accent that is half-Yiddish, half-something else, with his mad glittering eye and the intricate body English he puts on every movement, Pleasence shapes the portrait of a quintessential arriviste, cocky but coy, relishing his power but at the same time shrouding it in mystery and "humanizing" it with jokes. The characterization isn't too far from the one he's called on to do next, the SS colonel, and he manages the transition without a hitch. But the play's second act, which takes place in a prison and courtroom in Israel, steadily collapses under the weight of its misconceived impulses, so that Pleasence's virtuoso acting becomes more and more estranged from its ground, more and more a matter of brazening it through.

The Man in the Glass Booth has been directed by Harold Pinter (in whose *Caretaker* both Shaw and Pleasence did memorable work), and I suppose he has done all he can to disguise the play's melodramatic ethos, its fundamental subservience to a stage convention of pedagogy with a couple of emotional shocks. From time to time a Pinter-like mysteriousness and ambiguity begin to steal over the proceedings, but it doesn't last long; the text keeps reasserting itself, and there the mystery is mostly fog and the ambiguity irresolution. One leaves feeling that this gravest of events in the political order hasn't been newly imagined but exploited, and rather ineptly at that. But exploitation is what the theatre of commercialized politics is of course about. (1968)

¶ Growing Big

The skit called *Ma and the Kids* takes place on a stage bare except for a table and chairs made from paper cartons. The kids are adult actors dressed in vast, shapeless, striped sweaters and paper wigs; the mother is a male actor in apron and similar wig. The children sit down to dinner. "Ma, we're out of ketchup," one says, pouring it furiously, and the mother brings another bottle. "Ma, we're out of salt," a second demands, and she rushes to bring it. "Ma, I want more water," "Ma, more ketchup," "Ma, more water," "More salt," "More water," "More ketchup," "Water, salt, water, ketchup, salt . . ." Within moments the cardboard table overflows with ketchup bottles, water glasses, and salt shakers. It is like a scene out of an Ionesco play, an absurd epiphany of objects proliferating dementedly. And the audience, composed mainly of children from four to ten, roars in delighted appreciation.

The skit is part of a revue called *Fortunately,* the work of New York's Paper Bag Players, probably the best, certainly the most original children's theatre group in the country. Using almost no props apart from cartons and the large paper bags from which their name derives, improvising their costumes after raids on dime stores and old-clothes men, the Paper Bags in six years have built a following—among children, their parents and, for that matter, childless adults—whose enthusiasm might well be envied by our leading regional repertory companies. Such groups might profitably ponder the fact that the Paper Bags have succeeded without fanfare or physical resources—by being themselves, refusing to kowtow to tradition and paying more than lip service to originality. Honest, witty, adventurous, unsentimental, they have opened up an imaginative realm accepted and enjoyed by both the most wide-eyed child and the most sophisticated grownup.

For the Paper Bag Players the task is to introduce children into the very essence of drama, not by reproducing classic tales or bringing adult theatre down to a juvenile level, but by creating, as Judith Martin, one of its members, says, "another kind of form, geared to our audience . . . an adult outlook for children. Our audiences, surprising as it may seem, *think*. And we feel we have something to say to them. It doesn't deal with the everyday world but with projected fantasies, with the things children are really involved with. For example, growing big, as when we show a caterpillar turning into a butterfly. Or changing from one kind of person into another, like our cupcake that becomes a wedding cake. Or a cup that grows up to be a bathtub. In a fantasy a child thinks he can do it himself, he sees he can imitate adults."

The Paper Bags were organized in 1958 by Miss Martin, a modern dancer, actress Sudi Bond (no longer with the company), painter Shirley Kaplan, composer Daniel Jahn, and author-illustrator Remy Charlip. Today the group includes Irving Burton and Betty Osgood, and is run along totally communal and democratic lines. "We all have a different emphasis," Miss Martin says. "I'm movement-oriented, someone else is visually geared. Dan's base is music. The talents merge and build on one another and things happen."

Homeless for their first four years, the Paper Bags toured with their productions until in 1962 the Henry Street Settlement Playhouse was made available to them for Saturday performances. Admission is far lower than prevailing children's theatre rates—20 cents for children, 60 cents for adults—and even though the group gets some support from the New York State Council on the Arts, its members must have other jobs to eke out a living. So popular have they become that they are swamped with requests from schools and community centers, but they lack the funds to fulfill the demand. "We feel that children's theatre needs support from the big foundations," Charlip says. "We'd like to give daily performances, all the time. But every time we've approached a large foundation they say there's money for a survey to see if children's theatre is needed but none for an actual theatre."

The foundations might have a different view if they became acquainted with the response of children to the theatre. Naïve yet penetratingly aware, unself-conscious, lending themselves to the experience as adult audiences have long since become unable to do, children enter the heart of action openly and generously. The Paper Bag Players are fond of recalling the description a ten-year-old gave of one show to a classmate: "It's a riot. A man plays an old lady. And an old lady plays a little kid." Nothing simpler yet more accurate has been uttered about the eternal fascination of the stage, where man can be many more things than himself, the capacity he once, indeed, had—as a child. (1964)

¶Evasive Action

LeRoi Jones's *Dutchman* earned him a reputation as the Negro scourge of white complacency, an angry, knowing, ultracontemporary playwright. But his two new short plays, *The Toilet* and *The Slave*, reveal him as an archsentimentalist, a dramatist who uses obscenities and wrath to mask a poverty of ideas and a painfully immature emotional structure.

The Toilet takes place in the boys' room of a high school. There, before a row of gleaming urinals and a graffiti-marked wall, a group of Negro youths have gathered for a fight between their leader and a white boy who has sent him a homosexual love letter. After some preliminary gymnastics by the first arrivals, the participants enter and the fight takes place. The white boy is severely beaten by the others, who then leave. But his opponent reenters the bathroom, cradles the hurt youth's head, and weeps. The point could not be more obvious: social pressure, the need for a show of toughness, is what keeps us from displaying the love we feel.

But it is entirely unconvincing. There has merely been an undramatized assertion that out of perversion can come love, a sentimental broad jump over all the intervening difficulties. Beyond this, the presence of a second white character who functions as a voyeur is an infuriatingly juvenile note introduced so that Jones can have it both ways. For the white boy speaks up against the brutality but at the same time is a fairy who clearly doesn't "belong there," where *real* life is going on.

The two plays are united by Jones's adolescent need to have his cake and eat it, to seem to be arguing for peace and reconciliation while flaying whites with every weapon his limited arsenal contains. *The Slave* is a "fable" set at some future time when a Negro insurrection is devastating the country. It is a *pas de trois* among a white liberal couple and the woman's first husband, a Negro who is now the leader of the rebellion. He breaks into their house and holds them at gunpoint, his purpose being to take away the two daughters he had by the woman. Jones's purpose presumably is to have the three engage in denunciation and counterdenunciation, giving both sides of the racial question.

But on one level Jones writes like nothing so much as a lesser Edna St. Vincent Millay pontificating on the state of world and soul—"I have killed for all times any creative impulses I will ever have by the depravity of my murderous philosophies," the Negro says. On another level Jones employs frequent obscenities exactly the way people in real life do—to preclude the possibility, and danger, of thought. And though Jones allows the white man to call the Negro a maniacal, destructive racist, he stacks the cards ferociously against him. Once more the white is effete, incapable of satisfying the woman as the Negro did, and a liberal whose values pale before the apocalyptic vision of Negro power and healing violence.

In the end the Negro shoots the white man, after which a bomb flattens the house. "The children," moans the fatally injured wife. "They're dead," replies the Negro. Whatever tragic insight resides in these words comes too late. Jones has simply bypassed a terrain mined with all the explosive truths about human conflict. To traverse this dangerous ground he will need more resources—and more courage. (1964)

¶ Win, Place and Show

David Ross's revival of *Ghosts* isn't something to make an Ibsenite bring votive offerings to Fourth Street. If it comes through, it's by a narrow margin, the triumph of an indestructible core over a shredded surface, Mrs. Alving managing her heartbreak against a flood of distractions and misdirections.

To begin with, what aberration led to Ross's choice of the R. Farquharson Sharpe translation, which surpasses poor old Archer's in vitality and sense by about the same margin by which Kennedy beat Nixon? He must have suspected something, for he had Carmel Ross, his wife, jazz up some of the lines, the result being rather like a soiree in which Queen Victoria and Prince Albert converse animatedly with Jack Kerouac and Harry Golden. "Humbug," "hussy," "filial sentiments" and the like ricocheting off contemporary slang brings you about as far from Ibsen's poetry as it's possible to get.

Then there are the performances. The acting in *Ghosts* is not so much bad as wrong. Perhaps only Chekhov requires of actors a greater sacrifice of the part to the whole than Ibsen, but in Ross's production we have a collection of wayward personalities instead of a five-figured body. Leueen MacGrath is an accomplished actress, with force and outline, but she is pitched too high above the play, on too aristocratic a plane; she takes a long time coming down to the gutty realities that are her pressure toward awareness and the site of the tragedy.

Of the rest, Staats Cotsworth plays Manders in much too parodic a vein—he is not meant to be so obtuse; Carrie Nye as Regina is impossibly breathy and wild-eyed; Joseph Marino as Oswald is simply a young handsome actor without an inch of range; and only John McQuade as Engstrand comes close to what must have been Ibsen's intention.

If after this I nevertheless recommend your seeing *Ghosts*

you will, I hope, take it as a tribute to Ibsen who, it may be my special derangement to believe, is worth more in theatrical extremis than any number of other playwrights in the best of health. (1961)

After the first act of N. F. Simpson's *One Way Pendulum* the audience can be forgiven for thinking it's witnessing a British version of *You Can't Take It With You*. Among a number of transients, there's a crippled aunt who mutters about locomotion, a son who is training speak-your-weight machines to sing the Hallelujah Chorus and a father who is building a replica of the Old Bailey courthouse in the living room. It is all extravagant and not very amusing.

But to leave at this point would be a serious mistake, for the second act blossoms into an extraordinarily comic bit of theatre, an exercise in precise absurdity that owes a little to Ionesco but perhaps even more to Kafka, whose legends of disconnection and the simulacra of meaning were, it will be remembered, read aloud by him with gusts of laughter. What happens in *One Way Pendulum* is that in a mock trial scene both the logic of the law and our penchant for dovetailing systems of values are subjected to merciless scrutiny, full of exactitude, acerbity and painful jest. It seems impossible to convey the true quality of Mr. Simpson's metaphysical humor, but I suspect I shall be back one day soon to try. (1961)

I want to say a word about *The Red Eye of Love,* Arnold Weinstein's antic fable about the American experience. The play has been running for some months, but hasn't yet been mentioned in these pages, and for all its occasional gaucheries and its unevenness of tone it deserves to be known as widely as possible. *Red Eye* is a hoarse romp between certain fixed poles of our national ambition and mythology—our desire for the "key to existence" and our equally strong craving for cash—and as it moves like a slalom race down an exceedingly gnarled mountain it tosses off successive minor miracles of language, gesture and sheer visual éclat. I should add that its cast, almost uniformly up to the job, is headed by the wondrous Jane Romano, who has all of Ethel Merman's brassiness without any of her tin. (1961)

I had been hearing good things about The Judson Poets' Theater, which operates in a far-seeing and socially responsible Baptist church in the Village, but I had not seen any of their work until I finally succumbed to the insistence of friends who had. Well, the Judson production of Miss Stein's tiny play, *What Happened,* was without any question a minor masterpiece, more inventive, more high-spirited and more animate than anything I have seen recently at the higher levels of professionalism. Under Lawrence Kornfeld's astute direction, and with splendid music by Al Carmines, the church's assistant rector, the work employs three male singers, a pianist and five female dancers who are called upon for a combination of dance, mime, speech, song and capers, and the best way to describe it is that it has found perfect musical and visual equivalents for Miss Stein's incantatory cliché-overturning language. A triumph of total theater, *What Happened* was the most hopeful event this increasingly desperate pilgrim of the theatrical apocalypse has witnessed in many a week, month and even year. (1963)

¶ George Washington
Crossing the Delaware

I was not in New York when *3 x 3*—subtitled *An Evening of Comedy*—opened, and it closed before I returned, having been deemed by the dailies, unanimously, I gathered, not to have been an evening of comedy. I cannot say what Arnold Weinstein's *The Twenty-five-Cent White Cap* or Elaine May's *Not Enough Rope* were like, but *George Washington Crossing the Delaware,* by Kenneth Koch, which I saw at a special performance was, or is, the funniest play I have seen this year.

I have a feeling it's the funniest play by an American in a lot longer than that. Oh, and a very indigenous play, one about which Birchers and beats can agree, or at least break bread at. For while it is a parody, or set of interlocking parodies, the purest kind of fantastic innocence—such as probably prevailed at the birth of our nation and such as still prevails on the level of presentation at high-school patriotic pageants—continually warms the scene, that décor of cut-out boats, horses and guns and those costumes of splendid sashiness, tri-corned *élan* and big-buttoned spirit-of-'76 which Alex Katz has designed so brilliantly.

You see, Koch really loves George Washington, the way we are supposed to but can't until all the parodiable elements are worked through and burned away. The play is the recovery of a childlike vision of American origins and one strain of our persisting reality, the child having been helped to see freshly through the sharp wits and memory for eras of language of the adult looking over his shoulder, the one who prompts the actors to mock Shakespeare, the diction of masques, melodrama, Barbara Frietchie, cigarette ads, Max Lerner and Fulton Lewis, Jr. And the distortion that emerges, the verbal and visual minor miracle, is of the order of Picasso's women, truer than the mirror, or of Kafka or Beckett when their language moves into the most uncomplicated yet primally mysterious play.

So then, if you want to hear Cornwallis say wonderingly of the father of our country that "he walks as he rides!" or of the British cause that "love makes it right," if you want to hear the Redcoats pray "If only we could win him over to our side!" and hear George himself declare that "We have nothing to fear but death" and then settle back for a nap with a murmured "Goodnight America," if you want to see "democracy in action . . . actuality exemplified in a military situation"—I strongly urge you to cross the Delaware, or whatever river separates you from the play, if, as I hope, the current attempt to bring it back (coupled with a Saroyan play, I hear) succeeds. No better investment around at any price. (1962)

¶Novelists in the Theatre

One of the persistent complaints against the American drama has been that it lacks language, that it possesses a native idiom but no true speech, a vocabulary but not a heightened system of expression. O'Neill is our Shakespeare and this perfectly reveals how deficient we are in verbal resources. The most painful moments in his plays—Hickey's monologue in *The Iceman Cometh* is a most egregious example—are precisely those when rhetoric is called on to move into a new dimension, to lift the play's action into purpose and permanence, but settles instead for mere earnestness, recapitulation, bravado, a straining after significance that ends in the grandiose or a reliance upon the colloquial that ends in sentimentality. I am not the only one who feels that the literary insufficiency of our drama is acutely summed up in Hickey's use of the word "pipedreams" when he means illusions.

The Ford Foundation has been trying to remedy this condition by giving grants to established poets, novelists and short-story writers who are interested in writing for the theatre. The grants enable the recipients to work with theatre groups, study stagecraft and see their own works through production, thus making the transition from poetry or fiction to the stage very much less arbitrary, theoretical and clumsy. At least that is the way it is hoped things will turn out. As a critic I have been asked to nominate two persons for the program, and the request, coming immediately after my having seen two plays of a high literary intention, one by an important novelist and the other adapted from a work by an even more important author, has set me wondering about the possibilities of a theatrical resurrection arising in this quarter.

J. P. Donleavy is the author of an esteemed novel, *The Ginger Man,* which recounts the bizarre and bawdy adventures of a young American in Ireland and is distinguished by an exuberance and comic inventiveness that are quite out of the ordinary. His first play, *Fairy Tales of New York,* was recently given its American premiere by the Columbia Players at the University's Wollman Auditorium, and I went to see it with advanced expectations. To say that I was disappointed is to be milder than milk; I was left wondering what calamity this was, what strange process of denaturing and shrinkage had come over the imagination responsible for *The Ginger Man*'s originality and gusto.

To learn from the program that the central character was named Cornelius Christian sounded a minatory note. But with a rush the full-scale disaster was upon us; trapped by anticipation and incredulity we were never able to break loose from the dismal sequence of inorganically related episodes that took this allegorical figure through the stages of his education in the perversions and inhumanities of the metropolis. Four scenes after a prologue, one flat and strained, another impossibly chaotic, a third entirely clichéd and only one making an approach to freshness and coherent vision although failing to attain them—such was Donleavy's *Fairy Tales.*

Christian is an American about thirty who has come home after some years in Europe, bringing the body of his wife who has died on shipboard, apparently through the indirect effect of his failure properly to love her. His wanderings through the city in search of an identity and a vocation are also a spiritual quest of some kind, although it is difficult to know what Mr. Donleavy had in mind. At any rate, Christian goes to work for the insidious and caricatured undertaker who has buried the dead wife, tries to get a job as idea man for a manufacturer (the play's one scene with enough wit and singularity to make it endurable), engages in a boxing match with a brutal politician, and teaches a young girl a lesson in the snobbishness of headwaiters.

If this sounds terribly scant and unprepossessing, I assure you that I have racked my memory for anything I might have missed, any symbolic levels or epiphanies of beauty, and have not found any. I do want to say, however, that the Columbia Players being a preternaturally inept troupe of thespians and

William Driver, from this specimen of his work at least, an extraordinarily heavy-handed director, there is a possibility that the play was murdered in production. Not a large possibility, though; it was just its language, seldom anything but flat, predictable or faintly modish, almost never rising to the opportunities provided by even the limited *mise en scène*, that insured its death even before it had its chance for immortality. The production was only a bullet fired into a corpse.

Saul Bellow is a novelist of far greater stature than Donleavy, but this of course is no guarantee that any play of his will be better. And that the one I saw was in fact immeasurably superior to *Fairy Tales of New York* doesn't constitute a real proof of Bellow's capacity for the theatre, since the work was an adaptation, by Mary Otis, of the short novel *Seize the Day*, and was, moreover, presented in the form of a reading; finally, for all its incidental virtues, it was not truly successful as a drama.

Yet there was much to enjoy in it, most notably, in our present connection, a sense of language doing its job, a literateness and bold verbal intelligence, speech enhanced to the dimensions of minor revelation, sad, ironic, lyrical and painfully shrewd by turns. Miss Otis stayed almost entirely faithful to Bellow's superb story of a man of forty-four beleaguered by debts, failure, a condemning wife and an unsympathetic father and, even more, the feeling we all have of oppression by an opaque, unrelenting, unappeasable destiny that insanely misconstrues our needs and wants. Her failure to bring the thing off dramatically (a reading allows you to stage the work in your own mental theatre and mine saw a slow, stately, elegiac urban processional without true conflict or development) wasn't due to anything perverse or inadequate in what she did but simply to the fact that the novel is tightly bound to its own proper form and could not be fully transposed; the device of narrator, for instance, is cumbersome and reductive.

Still, blessings, blessings however small, these days especially. Herbert Berghof did a capable job of direction and the cast was for the most part a splendid one, Kurt Kasznar and

Alvin Epstein shining most steadily. The one failure lay with Mike Nichols, who played the central figure in an extremely old, offhand, side-of-mouth, buried way, thoroughly missing the "large, shaky, patient dignity" of the original.

Seize the Day was presented by The Theater for Ideas, a group with some promising notions about what we need for a theatrical rejuvenation. This play wasn't quite the answer but it was worth doing. It left me with a renewed desire to see Bellow's own play when he finishes it (a section has appeared in *Partisan Review*) and a strengthened determination to help the Ford people find other writers who can raise the melancholy level of our dramatic literature. Words fail us; by words we may yet be reprieved. (1963)

¶Bellow on Broadway

In one of the three playlets by Saul Bellow which rest uneasily beneath the collective title *Under the Weather,* a woman delivers a complicated speech and then asks her listener, "Do you follow me?" to which the reply is "I wish I could say no." One follows Bellow well enough through this evening of farce and sociology, but it would be much more comfortable if one didn't. To know what he is trying to do is to see how painfully short he falls, to see the greater part of his literacy going to waste and his special kind of shrewdness about contemporary manners and mores displaying itself in a thoroughly misconceived framework.

Bellow on Broadway is an anomaly, as his earlier play, *The Last Analysis,* demonstrated. He is far too intelligent and original to write standardized comedies like the widely acclaimed works of Neil Simon and Murray Schisgal. But his intelligence and originality—as a dramatist, at any rate—lack the strength and precision to push through an alternative to such melancholy comic "masterpieces." He is a triple victim: of the novelist's craving for instant success on the stage, of the commercial theatre's befuddlement in the face of any departure from its notions of what is comic and of his own architectural weaknesses as a playwright. Whatever is memorable in *Under the Weather* has to survive all three sieges.

The "weather" of Bellow's title is the weather of the modern psyche—exacerbated, put upon, put down, and struggling to right itself, to come up for air. In one playlet a harassed suburban widower works out a bizarre scheme to escape having to marry his recently divorced high-school sweetheart, a garrulous take-charge sort. In another a Nobel Prize-winning atomic scientist tracks down a woman with whom, thirty years before, he had played a game called "Show" and had conceived a mystical appreciation for a birthmark in her most private regions. In the third a Polish prostitute tries unavailingly to interest her only customer, a dour eighty-eight-year-old tycoon, in her household skills and social graces.

All three exude something of the atmosphere of *Herzog* and Bellow's earlier and better novel, *Seize the Day*. But only the second approaches any realization of its impulse. Inflamed, frantic, the scientist craves a sight of his erstwhile playmate's strategically placed wen, as a relief, evidently, from his life of cerebral abstraction. He skitters feverishly around the stage on his ridiculous quest, acceding finally, in a moment of inspired political satire, to the woman's request for a government secret in exchange for what he wants. At this point the skit deteriorates into a clumsy, vulgar piece of business, as the longed-for vision is granted behind a sofa, but until then it has been bright and amusing.

The amusement in the rest of the bill is fitful, to say the least. Bellow is fine on the minutiae of social ego—there is the chiropodist who "gets very angry if you call him mister"—and on the absurdities of the struggle against man's fate—"Why am I so afraid of slavery?" the widower asks, magnificently, as he contemplates his impending marriage. Such wit emerges only in isolated flashes. Bellow wants to stand modern man on his head and shake him until his perversities fall out, but much of the time he gets only hollow thumps and small change.

And yet *Under the Weather* might have made a reasonably pleasant evening if someone other than Shelley Winters had matched Harry Towb's stylish and witty performances as the widower, the scientist and the tycoon. As the divorcee, the woman with the wen and the whore with the heart of gold, Miss Winters is confined to one or two gestures—an open mouth to indicate both suffering and bewilderment, a shrug to indicate weary sophistication—and a single verbal timbre. Her shrill naturalistic mannerisms blur much of the work's satiric values. And in Arthur Storch's staging, everything, including an actual soufflé cooking in an oven, is done as if the show were a nice, folksy glimpse at what the neighbors are doing these days. Produced Off-Broadway, with few props and no attempt to please the suburban audience, Bellow's plays might have come into the restricted but genuine life they possess. (1966)

¶Ginger Without Bite

There are any number of ways to fail in the theatre, but the central one is not to have life. Most of the time there is no problem of recognition; we know what a corpse looks like. But a play like *The Ginger Man* is a much more difficult business. A simulacrum of robust existence, a trap without teeth, a promise without fulfillment and a daunted act which is perpetually throwing out hints that it is about to burst into bravery, the play can never be wholly resisted nor fully received. To be kept on the hook in this way is what one finally resents about *The Ginger Man*, after having made, God knows, every effort to jump up into the boat.

What is especially surprising about the play is that its author should have been so incapable of seeing where its true life and potency might have been obtained. For J. P. Donleavy has adapted his own novel, that lusty, lyrical, extraordinarily funny and vision-inducing book, and thrown it nearly away. It is possible that for an onlooker who has not read the book the events on stage will seem lively, wry and revelatory; but this is to be more starved for authenticity and pleasure than even our long dismal search for excitement in the theatre would seem to warrant. No, the play doesn't fail only when it is measured against the novel, but as an independent work of dramatic imagination, although it is true that one can easily conceive of a production which would serve it better and perhaps release it into a minor life of its own.

Still, it is essential to consider the novel because the drama explicitly and doggedly refuses the materials and virtues that are at hand there. Donleavy's book is a fable of the self, particularly the self of appetite and corporeality, lusting for fruition against the world of fact, of duty, order, claims, responsibilities and imposed expectations, the world of civilization in its role as oppressor and breaker of the individual will. Freud wrote a gloomy book on this subject, but Donleavy's is a comic song. Here the self is conceived of as pleasure-seeker, instinctual, full of wayward music and untrammeled possibility, its demands pitched in the teeth of necessity. That is exactly the novel's special grace and force, that necessity is daringly treated the way the imagination, in one of its perennial activities, has to treat it—as the direst enemy there is.

For Sebastian Dangerfield, Donleavy's American who lives in Dublin and battles the Irish for their poetry and poverty, their ugliness, unaccepted beauty and deflected instincts, existence is a strategic problem: how to preserve the green island of the self from the waves of necessity that are always lapping higher on its shores. He will let nothing hold him, neither marriage, fatherhood, vocation or friendship, although every claim is rooted in his flesh. He is the comic and lyrical counterpart of John Updike's Rabbit Angstrom, and like that fugitive from necessity and responsible choice he runs a course beyond morality and judgment, tracing one arc of the imagination in its desire to establish a counterforce to fact.

He is childish, brawling, spontaneous, a liar of heroic proportions, an irresistible lover, an innocent yet the most cunning of tacticians, a dreamer who cannot distinguish the streets of his dream from real thoroughfares. And he sings. "God's mercy on the wild ginger man," he sings when his saga is over, when everything is exposed and awaits mercy, which is here—as everywhere else—the acceptance that it is all wrong but all true, that it has all been and will be again, since man is what he is.

Why Donleavy should have turned this splendid creation into the figure we encounter on the stage is a mystery and a reinforcement of our fears that there is something about the stage today that inhibits even the boldest talents. For the Dangerfield of the play is small, winsome, charming, sly, tired and fragile, an eccentric instead of an inimitable, and a manipulator instead of a power. And his story is told domestically between walls, not merely the physical walls of the two tiny interiors in which the action takes place (the novel ranges all over Dublin in the manner of *Ulysses* and with a good deal of its mock-epic vivacity) but the walls of a basically naturalistic form, a circumscribed set of encounters which have the effect of putting us in the presence of a *character,* an oddball, but not an essential truth. Being traditional in this way enables Donleavy to distill from his bizarre material an odd charm, a hint of poetry, a relief from earnestness and a slight fever of expectation, but not a vision or the kind of music he must surely have wanted to hear played.

The hint is there. To have conceived the play musically, as a set of orchestrations, a fugue, and even more literally, a sound, a ballet, releasing the spirit of Dangerfield (field of Danger—a war, a tournament) from the incidental and anecdotal into the ceremonious and incantatory—might have carried it past its debilitating verisimilitude. Something such as was done by Jean Erdman in her adaptation of *Finnegans Wake, The Coach With the Six Insides,* is what *The Ginger Man* desperately requires: song, dance, lyrical fragments, voices from nowhere, shapes, apparitions, unexplainable gestures.

Had Leo Garen's direction been less amateurish, less cute and arch, even the existing intimidated script might have gone a degree or two beyond itself. Even more pressingly, had the performances been better, or rather had they been more in the spirit of Donleavy's original, the production might have worked tolerably if not with exuberance. But Patrick O'Neal, an actor of talent who cannot seem to forget that he is an actor, does everything possible to make Dangerfield still more repressed, coy, languorous and mildly picturesque than the text insists on, and only Marian Seldes among the three other performers is able to transcend it and enter a region of poetry and vigor.

But to go back to the center. One of our most respected critics has written about *The Ginger Man* that it should not be faulted because it fails to obey some of the chief canons of the popular drama, because, that is, it has no steadily building action and no clear denouement. Of course it should not be attacked for lacking these things: they are what we have been trying to get past in all our experiments and plunges.

But that is just it; *The Ginger Man* doesn't experiment and doesn't plunge, it simply sits on the edge, its back turned to some of the major theatrical conventions and its face to a dramatic possibility it isn't willing to enter. (1964)

¶Mixture Almost as Before

No writer of our time makes more of a point of labeling his works than Graham Greene, so that if he carefully calls his new play a comedy we can be sure that he very much wants us to think of it as one. There would be nothing wrong with that if it weren't for the fact that *The Complaisant Lover,* while unfolding a basically humorous surface, continually mutters in another language which, if it isn't actually tragic, is not really the true voice of comedy either. It is the familiar voice of Graham Greene in one of his moods of romantic despair, this time ringing more dulcetly, as if he had sent a child to relate, disarmingly he hoped, the same tale of duality and dilemma with which he has been seducing us for so many years.

Until we are well along in the first act everything about *The Complaisant Lover* suggests a traditional exercise. Here is the London drawing room almost entirely filled with its triangle: the husband in his late forties, comfortable and foolish and without passion; the wife ten years younger and still full of desire; and the lover of her own age and inclinations. And here are the tactics and strategies of adultery—the introduction of the lover into the home as a casual friend, the schemes for clandestine meetings, and finally the master plan for getting away for a few days together.

But when we hear the wife tell the lover that "There are different kinds of love," we are alerted to the possibilities of something more original than domestic farce. And indeed what takes shape after that is unconventional enough, a play about adultery in which the central energy is directed toward the setting forth and resolution of a moral and philosophical dilemma and not to the tying and eventual unloosening of a merely physical knot. It is a play, moreover, wherein the element of choice, so basic to the genre, becomes painful rather than liberating, the very intolerability of the necessity to choose constituting the substance and tension of the drama.

"I don't know. I don't want to choose," the wife tells her husband after he has finally been made aware of what is going on. "I don't want to leave you and the children. I don't want to leave him. Victor, why can't we sometimes, just once, have our cake and eat it?"

And so *The Complaisant Lover* proceeds to establish a mode of action in which having one's cake and eating it becomes possible, mythically possible, beyond the reach of psychology or of morals, or, for that matter, of practical impediments. To make it work, the lover is the one who has to become "complaisant," rather than the husband, as in traditional bedroom farce. That is to say, it is he who has to make the sacrifice, to accept the fact of "different kinds of love" and be willing therefore to share the woman with her husband, in a *pas de trois* that they will dance to a hitherto unheard-of melody.

A motif such as this is of course an aspect of Greene's perennial position at the center of what appear to be certain immutably opposed pairs of truths: supernatural and fleshly love, pity and love, marriage and passion. It is this fundamental seriousness—in Greene's case an obsessive and anguished seriousness—that threatens constantly to tip *The Complaisant Lover* toward pathos, if not tragedy. The anguish does, it's true, remain mostly in check; the solution proposed has the quality of a daydream, of something offered to our good nature and secret hungers, like an impossibly charming and bold and unwearable costume; and there is enough sophisticated wit and humor along the way to preserve an illusion of artifice, so that our demurrers are forestalled. Nevertheless, smuggling is a crime for which there are known penalties.

What has been smuggled in is, as I have said, a potentially tragic and actually pathetic situation in the guise of a lighthearted one. But it is not enough to treat a subject lightly in order for true comedy to result; what has to be there is an attitude toward the subject that sees it as detached from fatality, set free to lead its own life beyond the laws, beyond any law but the one it itself enacts, so that it becomes a paradigm of a new kind of imaginative existence as well as an instruction, by exposure and derision, in the insufficiencies and lies of our actual stances and beliefs.

The Complaisant Lover doesn't succeed in this. Its lightness is a mask. It is too heavily anchored in abstract pain and pity, too full of the kind of statement that we have come to mistrust in Greene because of its half-truth and fundamentally evasive quality—remarks like "The good are horribly hard to leave," or "What liars and cheats love makes of us." Beyond that, it doesn't work well because its nourishing life is so thin, its dentist-husband so much a figure from Greene's universe of sad ineffectuality and quiet despair, its lovers so lacking in vitality and real passion. And on still another level, the penalty Greene pays for his attempt to combine genres is that the mechanics of amorous comedy give him so much trouble that he has to spend an inordinate amount of time simply getting the thing in motion.

Still, the play does have a certain *visibility* and richness of presence. Almost all of this is imparted to it by its cast, who stand before us as the latest proof of the dictum that an inadequate play can sometimes be rescued by its players. You find yourself watching Googie Withers as the wife, Richard Johnson as the lover, and most of all Michael Redgrave as the husband spinning a texture of complex and precisely delineated behavior that almost compensates for the wanness of the dramatic vision lying behind it all. You even find yourself wanting the whole implausible thing to work, if only as recompense for such civilized and generous gifts of the self. (1961)

¶ Sows' Ears Out of Silk Purses

It might seem at first that the entrepreneurs of *A Passage to India* and *The Aspern Papers* have undertaken an act of cultural heroism, the drawing power on Broadway of E. M. Forster and Henry James being what it is. But you always have to look twice in these days of advancing cultural breakdown, one of whose symptoms is that collapse of the capacity to make distinctions which leads to Herman Wouk, Arnold Bennett and Dostoevsky all being novelists together, Sophocles, Pinero and Dore Schary all being playwrights; and which further results in the existence of a great grab-bag of art and entertainment wherein classics and best sellers, plays, novels, travelogues, circuses, epic poems, opera and concentration-camp memoirs mingle indiscriminately, change skins and merge with each other, the whole bag being tied together with the legend "Everything here has worked!"

With the loss of originality comes the itch to make what has worked in one form work in another. And indeed it is possible to make good plays, let us say, from great novels, though it is easier to make them from bad ones. But it won't work if you proceed on the assumption that a property is a property, a success a success; if, in other words, you hope to effect a translation merely, something good in French promising felicity in English, a novel's wealth of dialogue and confrontation auguring its successful reconstitution as a drama.

Naturally, it is not so simple; you will have to telescope, rearrange, perhaps fill in spaces. But where the aim remains to *reproduce* a work of fiction on the stage, which inevitably means to reproduce its story, the thing that presumably made it successful in the first place ("from the pen of the master storyteller"), the ironical result is that you will produce either a travesty or a shadow. For it is not the plots of great novels than can be learned from or transposed to a new medium, but their language, their vision, their inner relationships and pressures.

The question is therefore not at all one of fidelity to the original, except in the sense that you have to be faithful to something in it—its sensibility, the imaginative area it stakes out, perhaps only the thematic clue it offers. An adaptation clearly deserves to be judged in its own right, though for the initiated the prototype will inescapably be present in the mind. No, the matter is one of fidelity to the art of drama, which means almost inescapably infidelity to the art of fiction. Are *A Passage to India* and *The Aspern Papers* good plays, whatever their relations to the originals? Would someone familiar with the novels find in them some new quality to justify their transmogrification, and would a newcomer respond to them as authentic works without reference to anything else?

In fact the two plays are bad, although not equally so; one is a travesty of its original, the other a shadow. And in both cases the trouble arises precisely from an attempt to stay as close as possible to the story of the novel, its plot, thereby missing its spirit, the only thing really exportable. What speeds the destruction is, ironically, the very recognition that a play has different procedures and strategies from a novel; since both Mr. Redgrave and Miss Rama Rau are interested in art *and* success they do employ dramatic techniques—the tested, superficial ones of Broadway.

Miss Rama Rau is far guiltier than Mr. Redgrave, on every count. *A Passage to India* is actually so inept a play that only the tinniest of ears could find pleasure in it, and of course the tin ears have been reverberating all over town. It is really three plays, horribly jarring in tone and intention—one which attempts to weave a texture of cultural differences (the "East-West" misunderstanding of the novel), another which aims for broad effects of suspense and violence, and a third whose wish is to evoke mystery of a metaphysical kind.

In the novel these are the three main elements. But on the

stage nothing works since nothing is integrated. The jarring is incessant; one feels a desperate effort to make the complexity and subtle values of the novel come across without departing from the principles of the well-made play. To do this, a story is told, the tale of Miss Quested's false accusation of Dr. Aziz, which provides for the central actions, including the climactic and vulgarly handled trial scene; and around the story cluster unassimilated fragments of meaning: the ruminations of Mrs. Moore, to whom Forster had entrusted an integumentary role; the relationship between Aziz and Fielding; the neuroticism of Miss Quested. And the story itself amounts in the end to little more than an anecdote of humanist and liberal sentiment—the "timely theme" to which there has been such a predictable response.

Mr. Redgrave's *Aspern Papers,* on the other hand, is not unendurable; it simply hasn't much weight or resonance. It is the ghost of James's novel, faithful in outline and lineaments, but lacking the book's thematic fullness, its rich investigation of the relationship between art and life and between innocence and passion. Because it lacks this and has no new properly dramatic reality to offer, it has to depend heavily on the detective-story atmosphere which in James served as lure toward a more complex trap. And Mr. Redgrave, for greater insurance, cannot resist having his characters utter such imaginatively reductive and Madison Avenue-inspired lines as "This discovery will rock the whole world of literature."

But Mr. Redgrave does have something Miss Rama Rau might envy. He has Wendy Hiller. It is true that *A Passage to India* is blessed with Gladys Cooper, who gives to the role of Mrs. Moore all the exactness and finely arrived-at ambiguity of which she is capable, and it also has Eric Portman and Zia Mohyeddan, a young Pakistani actor who does as well as he can with Aziz. But *The Aspern Papers* can counter with Maurice Evans, whose professional éclat of speech matches Portman's professional briskness of manner (both being a trifle dead at the center), and with Françoise Rosay, whose foreignness is as exotic as Mr. Mohyeddan's.

But who can counter Miss Hiller? Not Miss Cooper, because *Passage* doesn't give her much to do and keeps her isolated in any case. The role of Miss Tina in *The Aspern Papers,* is, however, a central one, and Miss Hiller achieves with it a performance that almost makes the play come off. That is a miracle we frequently see, the hermetic marvels of a job of acting in a play we might otherwise scorn. An unparalleled delicacy, a grace, a lightness, a spirit coupled with an intelligence, for lack of a better word, a radiance—such are Miss Hiller's possessions, and she puts them all in the service of this ghost. She nearly brings it to corporeality. (1962)

V/Theatres

¶Epitaph for Lincoln Center

"Although they naturally will as one man deny it," George Jean Nathan once wrote, "the majority of drama critics, unlike the majority of literary critics, are always prejudiced in favor of reputations." This bias has never been more apparent than in the journalistic response to the events at Lincoln Center's temporary theatre. To a disaster of absolute proportions there has been a response of nearly absolute evasion, double-talk and special pleading. There are doubtless reviewers who really do believe that Arthur Miller's *After the Fall* is a masterpiece, but there are more who have clearly felt trapped between the heavy counterpressures of truth and reputation. And with the addition to the repertoire of the final two plays of the company's first season, the twisting and squirming have reached the level of St. Vitus dance.

Even the dullest reviewer has found it difficult to remain unaware that *Marco Millions* is considered one of O'Neill's worst plays. But with that knowledge as a floor, the comment has mainly consisted in making out some kind of case, any kind, for the work's nevertheless being put on, or in dwelling on some presumed glories of the production. The truth, which is to be found of course at the exact point where the reputations involved in this scandal leave off, is that there is no conceivable case for reviving a work of such radical ineptitude, and that the production is, if anything, more incomprehensible still.

O'Neill wrote *Marco Millions* in the twenties as an antidote to that era's hunger for expansion and its economic idolatry. His was an effort to compose a fable that would do for the imagination what Sinclair Lewis' *Babbitt* and *Dodsworth* were doing for the straightforward sociological eye. Materialism was crowding out the spirit, and O'Neill's Marco Polo, a man of consummately naïve appetite and acquisitiveness, a sharp dealer with the bloom of innocence, was intended as a cautionary figure. If you lust after progress and the piling up of profit, the play informed its audience, you will leave behind you a broken-hearted Princess Kukachin and a disillusioned Kublai Khan, or their equivalents, and you will also confirm all wise men in their conviction that the East has its finger on spiritual treasures our Western grossness will not even let us come near.

It is all incredibly banal, dreary and forced, when it is not being damply lyrical or shudderingly romantic. O'Neill had a hard time *knowing* anything (in his last plays he did come to know himself partially and was thus able to write true dramas), but in *Marco Millions* his understanding, of the East, the West, the self, love and the relations between ego and appetite, was at its barest. When this intellectual failure is coupled with a failure of language matched in the O'Neill canon only by that of *Lazarus Laughed* and *Dynamo*, the rout is complete.

But for the Lincoln Center Repertory Company no play simply routs itself; it can always be pushed toward absolute debacle by a production which seizes on its worst elements. "A Chinese fashion-show," someone in the audience said of what José Quintero has mounted, and the term is as good as any. As for the acting, there is only one source of nonembarrassment, David Wayne in a wry, capable performance as the Khan, and one source of amusement, Joseph Wiseman doing his demented sleepwalker's act at the imperial court. But they are isolated in a sea of imbecility whose main tides are Zohra Lampert's Princess Kukachin at Sarah Lawrence and Hal Holbrook's Marco Polo in Illinois.

The third nail in the Lincoln Center coffin was driven in by S. N. Behrman with a major assist from Elia Kazan. Behrman, who in his heyday was an accomplished light artificer is now, in his seventies, a man who hears things wrong. His new play, *But for Whom, Charlie*, is about integrity, as it is threatened and defended within the walls of a foundation whose purpose is to help deserving but noncommercial authors. Radiating out from this nucleus are strands of thematic material having to do with sex, love and manners. And it is all sadly wrong; people do not speak the way Behrman thinks they do (a woman does not say, "Just a moment while I slip into my coat"); sophistication has passed beyond this representative exchange: "You're a lecherous old man." "Course. Why should the young have it all?"

If the surface is deficient, the structure is nonexistent, a string of encounters perpetually dissolving through lack of pressure and organic connection. The reviewers were mostly aware of this architectonic disability, but they protected their stake in reputations by going on at length about Behrman's incidental virtues, his mellow wisdom and vivacious *obiter dicta* upon experience. The latter may be measured quite fairly, I think, by these examples: "Life is monotonous," "Everything is funny to me because everything is funny."

As for Kazan's direction, it seems accurate to say that it is no worse than his work on *After the Fall*. He either has no more ideas or he has suffered such a depletion of spirit that he is allowing his performers to handle their jobs the best way they can. Without compass or helmsman Jason Robards, Jr., Salome Jens and Ralph Meeker drift all over the stage indulging in their special vices—Robards turning ever closer to petrifaction, Miss Jens to emotive elephantiasis and Meeker to complete illegibility.

But perhaps the most telling revelation of what has been going on at Lincoln Center is the set for *But for Whom, Charlie*. The open stage clearly will not lend itself to a domestic drama of this kind, but Jo Mielziner, as superannuated in his art as Behrman is in his, has bucked the odds. A two-leveled affair, with furniture out of a Castro Convertible showroom, blue and yellow floors with green scatter rugs and doors opening on the void, the set is a masterpiece of ugliness, the quintessence of physical miscalculation and aesthetic perversion. That of course makes it consonant with the larger perversion which the Lincoln Center company has now placed in its entirety before our eyes. (1964)

¶Marred Masterpiece

"A man's worst difficulties begin when he is able to do as he likes," Thomas Huxley once wrote. When Herbert Blau and Jules Irving, who founded San Francisco's Actors' Workshop and nursed it through thirteen difficult years, were named last year to direct Lincoln Center's faltering repertory theatre, they were assured of "artistic freedom." They were also given a superb new theatre and unparalleled facilities. Last week, at the official opening of both the Vivian Beaumont Theater and the Blau-Irving regime, the first product of that freedom and those resources went on display.

It was a big disappointment. Blau and Irving had chosen Georg Büchner's *Danton's Death* as their first production; and, while the play is one of the greatest in all drama, it requires the most supple directorial imagination and the finest ensemble playing to succeed on the stage. Neither was forthcoming: the direction, by Blau, was banal and confused; still worse, it betrayed a misconception of the play; and the acting, with one or two exceptions, was bad.

Büchner is one of the most astounding phenomena in literary history. Born in Germany in 1813, he died at twenty-three, leaving behind some prose fragments and three plays, two of which, *Danton's Death* and *Woyzeck,* were to influence twentieth-century drama beyond any other works. A revolutionary who combined ideological fervor with deep philosophic pessimism, Büchner foreshadowed some of the most central contemporary moods. *Danton's Death* is a play which, in a deceptively loose and episodic form, pits against each other public and private vision, lyricism and logic, sensuality and abstraction. This last dualism is at the drama's heart: in the confrontation, during the French Revolution's Reign of Terror, between Robespierre's murderously abstract political values and Danton's flexible, open humanity, Büchner saw the perennial tragedy of history, the anguish of love versus power, the private against the political.

Beginning with his translation and adaptation, Blau proceeds to render Büchner unintelligible. There are at least two English versions of *Danton* which are far superior to Blau's stiff, archaic one; and the cuts he has made come mostly at the wrong places. Their effect is to destroy the play's balance, to turn it toward ideology, making it a document of protest against power (in a program note, later removed, Blau linked Mao Tse-tung, Castro, Hendrik Verwoerd and President Johnson as terrorists), whereas *Danton's* profound truth lies in its awareness of the inevitability and tragic nature of power.

Even this misconception need not have meant total failure. But Blau's direction is so insensitive that the evening becomes an ordeal. The production has no rhythm, no unity. Scene follows scene like a series of skits. For the long speeches, which contain Büchner's always ironically held ideas, Blau has his actors rant, declaim, exhort, instead of exhibiting the subtle contradiction between speaker and idea that Büchner intended. For the private moments of sorrow, love or sensuality, he has them emote as though they were doing Paddy Chayefsky. And for the crowd scenes, he sends hordes of *sans-culottes* hurtling about the stage in a babel of shouts, screams, gesticulations, fist-shaking and hair-pulling, for all the world as though he were mounting *A Tale of Two Cities*.

The company does not reveal even a rudimentary capacity for ensemble work. There are individual performances that manage to be skillful and interesting, such as those of James Earl Jones and Robert Stattel as revolutionists condemned to death, along with Danton, by Robespierre; but mostly there is a pervading sense of amateurism. As Danton, for instance, Alan Bergmann is a figure of strapping masculinity without the slightest vocal equipment, grace or emotional power. The spectator can only leave the theatre with the hope that it is all a mistake, that the repertory company's true opening is sometime in the future. (1965)

¶ The Sorrows
of Lincoln Center

In December of 1964 I reviewed Herbert Blau's book, *The Impossible Theater,* for the New York *Times.* After remarking on its opaque, occasionally undecipherable style, I went on to say that it was nevertheless "in some ways the most important, certainly the most passionate statement of what it means to try to fuse art and theatre in America." The next day I was told that the board of the Lincoln Center Repertory Theater, which was at that moment in mortal crisis, had ordered half a dozen copies of the book, apparently on the strength of my review.

A few days later I was asked to lunch by an executive of Lincoln Center who first wanted plaintively to know why my published comments on the Repertory Theater had been so harsh and then, moving from a condition of injured feeling to one of abject inquiry, whom I might recommend to take over its troubled destiny. After a moment's hesitation I mentioned Blau and Jules Irving. They were co-directors of the San Francisco Actors' Workshop, which had a reputation as one of the best repertory theatres in the country—a reputation I took mainly on faith, it was true, since I had seen only one minor production of theirs. But Blau's and Irving's ideas had impressed me, and so had the fact that their repertoire over the years had been built around the truest notions of what was best in contemporary drama. They had consistently done plays scarcely anyone else would touch: Brecht's *The Caucasian Chalk Circle* and *Mother Courage;* John Arden's *Serjeant Musgrave's Dance;* Pinter before he became fashionable; almost all of Beckett; Strindberg's corrosive *Dance of Death.*

The man from Lincoln Center replied, "Oh, yes, we've heard about them," and a little while later we said good-bye. A month or so after that, I read with astonishment verging on disbelief that Blau and Irving had been named to replace Robert Whitehead and Elia Kazan as directors of the Repertory Theater and would take over within a few weeks.

I had never before been remotely capable of kingmaking, in any sphere. Now I felt pleased, alarmed, shadowed by responsibility, even though my recommendation could scarcely have been the only or decisive one. At first the pleasure—in the appointment and what it might mean for the American theatre, not in my presumptive role in it—was uppermost, and it was shared by almost everyone seriously concerned with the fate of drama as an art. In replacing Kazan and Whitehead with Blau and Irving, Lincoln Center seemed to have recognized the sterility of the Broadway establishment and to have taken the risk, unprecedented for bankers and similar types, of reaching out to the avant-garde for comfort, energy and deliverance from exhausted modes of accomplishment.

They had been driven to it by a saga of ineptitude, opportunism, egomania, atrocious lack of taste and thoroughgoing betrayal of everybody's hopes. When Kazan and Whitehead mounted the Repertory Theater's first production, in the fall of 1963, they could not have started with greater physical or spiritual resources nor in an atmosphere more refulgent with good will. What they had going for them were an attractive temporary theatre at Washington Square, a large, reportedly enthusiastic company, ample facilities for training, rehearsal, and so on, and above all a widespread public craving for New York to have at last an alternative to Broadway's economy of boom and bust and its lugubrious standards of dramatic art.

What happened then constitutes one of the more painful chapters of recent American cultural history. Kazan and Whitehead opened with Arthur Miller's *After the Fall,* which, on the wings of rumor and scandal, was to prove a box-office success, but which could not have been a more disgraceful work, both morally and technically. It was followed by O'Neill's *Marco Millions,* a Chinese fashion show that had been accurately described years before by Bernard De Voto as "surely the worst play ever written by a dramatist with a reputation," and by *But for Whom, Charlie,* by S. N. Behrman, who at seventy retained no shred of his one-time talent for light philosophical comedy and had developed nothing to take its place.

The enterprise was tottering, and the second season brought it to its knees. The company did Miller's *Incident at Vichy,* a windy, dated sermon about guilt and responsibility, and a version of *Tartuffe* that was tolerable mainly because the management had in desperation brought in William Ball to direct and Michael O'Sullivan to play the lead. But the death blow had been administered earlier by Kazan's production of *The Changeling;* the first play by a dead dramatist he had ever directed, the great Jacobean drama by Rowley and Middleton received such a ludicrous, uncomprehending, fearfully amateurish staging at his hands and was executed by such patently ill-trained and ill-equipped actors that scorn and ridicule of the Repertory Theater, previously most heated among intellectual critics, now spread widely among the lower echelons of reviewers.

There followed a grotesque administrative flap during which every division of Lincoln Center was at the others' throats, the cancellation of the Theater's fourth scheduled production, and the resignations—among the least convincing in the history of face-saving—of Whitehead and Kazan. Then came the bombshell—the announcement that Blau and Irving had been signed to three-and-a-half-year contracts as co-directors of the Repertory Theater. "We have been assured absolute artistic freedom," Blau declared.

The appointment was greeted, as I have said, with enthusiasm by all of us who felt that the catastrophe of the Theater had stemmed from its having been entrusted to the most egregiously commercial minds, to men who had once been in some form of avant-garde themselves but who for years had been practicing counterrevolutionaries to whom changes in dramaturgy and new philosophies of dramatic art were anathema when they were not simply enormous puzzles. There had been bad plays badly done and good plays badly done; there had been no sign of an ensemble sense in the company (which was in fact sprinkled with star names), and no indication that its members were getting any sort of training. There had, finally, been no evidence that the idea of repertory theatre—a permanent body of significant works linked to one another by an articulated aesthetic of drama—had in any way taken hold.

The new regime promised to remedy all these deficiencies. Repertory theatre consisted, Blau remarked during the interregnum before he and Irving moved East, "not just in a lot of plays but in a certain relationship among plays over a sustained period of time." He also spoke of their intention to "perpetuate what we call the ensemble-acting approach" and promised that New Yorkers would see in their work "an ever-evolving style, growing from within, never predictable in direction."

Blau and Irving were themselves New Yorkers who had migrated to California after the war, become teachers at San Francisco State College and founded the Workshop in 1952. But when they finally made it back to New York in March 1965, it was as though the provinces had sent two of their toughest lone-wolf sheriffs to show the big city how to handle its aesthetic crime wave. When they announced the repertoire for the season that was to open in October, any doubts were dispelled that they might start off cautiously, with their big guns in reserve. They were going to do Georg Büchner's *Danton's Death,* Wycherley's *The Country Wife, The Condemned of Altona* by Sartre and Brecht's *The Caucasian Chalk Circle*. It seemed to me a splendid program, balanced, challenging and full of substance.

As the summer wore on and rehearsals started for *Danton's Death,* I began to hear disquieting rumors of difficulties at the Repertory Theater, problems in casting and staging that were afflicting the first production. The new directors had brought with them a dozen or so of their San Francisco actors and had signed a number of New York performers, most of whom had struck me as exceedingly problematic choices. I waited, trying to reserve judgment but feeling the first twinges of anxiety. In a thickening atmosphere of storm warnings and disaster signals, opening night arrived. It was to be a double debut, for the resplendent Vivian Beaumont Theater—$10,000,000 in turntables, cycloramas, projection screens and 1,100 red-plush seats—was ready for the public.

As I look back I think my feeling of shame and embarrassment was greater that night than it had been at the opening of Kazan's *The Changeling*. *Danton's Death* is one of the masterpieces of dramatic literature, a dark, fevered, beautiful work so fertile in ideas and theatrical invention that it took the stage a hundred years to catch up with it. Büchner's theme was the tragedy of history, the anguish of love versus power, of the self against political necessity, particularity against abstraction. In the confrontation of Robespierre's murderously theoretical political values and Danton's skeptical, concrete humanity he saw and rendered, in amazingly accurate and resonant alternations of lyricism and oratory, a cosmos we have been exploring and struggling in ever since.

Yet as Blau directed it and the company performed it, the play was a travesty, resembling nothing so much as a bad movie version of *A Tale of Two Cities*. Inflicting a heavy political hand on the proceedings (a few days before opening he had caused an uproar by linking as "terrorists," in a program note hastily removed, President Johnson with Mao Tse-tung, Robespierre, Hendrik Verwoerd, Fidel Castro), Blau tipped the play toward liberal ideology, a radical misconception. What was worse, the production had no rhythm or unity, was ridden with arty clichés and dreadfully performed by a cast that seemed at times to share the audience's awareness that it was miserably over its head.

So complete was the debacle, so indefensible the choices Blau had made—from his crowd scenes, which were like Union Square gatherings blown through a wind tunnel, to his employment of Alan Bergmann, an actor of absolute deadness and technical deprivation, in the role of Danton—that I found it impossible to take comfort in the thought that Büchner's play was, after all, extraordinarily difficult to stage well. To tell the truth, I gave up then, along with most of my colleagues; from then on it was up to Blau and Irving to demonstrate not that they deserved our trust and expectation but that they did not deserve our contempt.

The next production was *The Country Wife*. This time I felt neither outrage nor despair, merely boredom and a sense of waste. Wycherley's play is savage, witty and turbulent, well beyond the popular notions of Restoration comedy as all elegant phrase-making and amorous complicity. Under Robert Symonds' direction nothing went blatantly wrong—but nothing went vivifyingly right. You could not have expected any American company to have the polish and security necessary for such a play, but what was surprising was the production's failure to maintain even a surface of rough liveliness; everything was daunted, obvious and tame.

Everything was even more daunted and obvious in Sartre's *The Condemned of Altona*. Admittedly a far from perfect drama whose theme of human sequestration, of man's isolation along a whole range of moral complicity in evil, never quite finds its proper form or structure, the play nevertheless wonderfully exhibits Sartre's extraordinary intelligence and unerring eye for what is crucial in human affairs. Done heavily, naturalistically, with issues spelled out and movement mechanically faithful to the text, it can be tedious and utterly incomprehensible. Yet that was just how Blau directed it. Beyond that, the brooding *Buddenbrooks*-like interior overwhelmed the performers, who, perhaps because the small cast and the circumscribed arena focused every degree of attention on each one, seemed more than ever inadequate to the Theater's ambitions.

The final offering of the season was *The Caucasian Chalk Circle*. Again aspiration outstripped capacity. The company was handsomely decked out in imaginative costumes and masks for Brecht's parable of the ironic triumph of justice in a world of power, but these were the only imaginative elements of the production. Jules Irving's direction lacked both decisiveness and risk; it was both arty and artless, as though opposing voices had competed for the director's ear: Brecht is important, so you must be heavy and sober, but he is also entertaining, so there has to be lots of business. At no point did Irving apply the visual and kinetic pressure by which Brecht's superb and crucial sense of irony can be released—pressure on one's actors to walk a delicate balance between straightforward performing and detached, witty, surprised comment on that performing. But then the actors hadn't shown that they were capable of responding to directorial firmness of any kind.

I said that I had given up after *Danton's Death*. Everything that followed served to deepen my rejection of the new administration, although it was true that the last three productions were in no sense the nightmare the first was. Yet nightmares may be only especially intense and concentrated expressions of a prevailing malaise; when the work had not been flagrantly wrong-headed and profoundly disturbing, it had been flat, tasteless and unskilled. Everything that had seemed to be on the verge of happening at Lincoln Center—the birth of a repertory company of daring enterprises and the equipment to sustain them, the use of physical resources for purposes beyond themselves, the driving of a wedge of purposeful dramatic art into the mindless, stultifying activities of the commercial theatre—had been painfully aborted.

That Blau and Irving had been overrated was obvious, but no sort of illumination. For they were as much victims as agents. They had been operating far from the center of taste and judgment, so that their standards and procedures could not be tested against others, which is after all what being provincial means; and in our rush to repudiate New York, or rather Broadway, as the arbiter of dramatic art, we had forgotten that the country has no other. The real tragedy of the theatre in this country is that skill and technical capacity are concentrated in New York, where for the most part they are crowded into the service of commercial practice, the soul-killing popularity hunt of Broadway, while ideas, new visions of dramatic art, can be found anywhere but are usually found unarmed, without means of implementation. The situation is changing with the growth of theatres outside New York, but we have a long way to go.

But the matter goes beyond this. Like certain other theatre

intellectuals, Blau's and Irving's ideas (which I still admire, except for a potentially deadly politicizing tendency in Blau) are ideas *about* the theatre, about its place in society, its torments and triumphs, the value it can have once it becomes free from the need to be popular, from the madness of "hits." They are not useful ideas about dramatic values and their means of being made palpable; they aren't visions of theatrical art. Or when they are, they are inferior ideas, just as the new directors' taste, as it exhibited itself during this first season, is inferior taste.

In all their work, in their direction and staging, in their choices of actors, they seem to lack sight and hearing, to be deaf and blind to the ways things sound and look on the stage. It is the kind of deficiency that no amount of enthusiasm and dedication can atone for, and what makes its revelation now so painful is that for years people who care about drama and despise the commercial theatre have been pinning their hopes on just such spirit and dedication. It would seem that perhaps those crafty "practical" theatre men who deride the hopes of the intellectuals for an alternative to Broadway, who equate professionalism with commercial éclat and amateurism with failure, are right. One discouraging result of the year's events has been just this half-secret, half-open sneering: OK, the boys have had their shot, now let's get back to business.

I don't think this is what we have to conclude. That Blau and Irving are bad directors (though measurably better than Kazan and at least as good as the hacks who do most Broadway shows) in no way discredits the avant-garde, for they had occupied only a theoretical sector of it. Their notions of what constitutes significant drama survive their incapacity to put it on display; their commitment to serious theatre isn't compromised by their practical inadequacies. Some of the most ironic notes of the year were struck by most of the daily reviewers, who were quite up to detecting the badness of the work set before them but hadn't the slightest awareness of how superior the choice of plays had been. From Walter Kerr, for example, there came a typical sneer for each of the four plays, alongside his perception of how badly they had been done. But then Kerr had also called *The Changeling* a potboiler.

The split in our theatre between idea and action, intellect and technique, is not going to be healed by antiintellectualism of this kind. The drama has always lagged behind the other arts in America precisely because of the entrenched hatred of the risks and pressures of thought among most of its practitioners, as well as its popular commentators. Kazan and Whitehead surely had enough experience; what they lacked were ideas, new ways of doing drama and ways of doing new drama. This year's fiasco at Lincoln Center is not a proof of the impotence of those who advocate thought in the theatre—of those who believe the theatre to be at least as significant a revelation of our existence as are poetry and the novel. It merely demonstrates that such advocacy has to be buttressed with skill and taste, that good intentions are no more guarantees of good work in the theatre than anywhere else. But at least the intentions have been large and demanding. And this is much more than we can say about Blau's and Irving's predecessors, about the "grocers," as Chekhov called them seventy years ago, in whose hands most of our theatre rests, and about the kind of mind for which the debacle at Lincoln Center represents the inevitable fate of anyone who refuses to acknowledge that the pinnacle of dramatic art is *Barefoot in the Park*. (1966)

¶ View from the East

The Tyrone Guthrie Theatre opened on a note of real éclat. The main streets of Minneapolis were festooned with white pennants with a heraldic crimson G, and the monogram was repeated throughout the building, on the tickets and the program and on the blazers of the youthful ushers, where it took the place of a Princeton shield or the emblem of a yachting or rowing club. And in fact there was an air of a regatta or some other clean, wholesome public activity about the event, whose importance is that it brought to the Midwest its first permanent professional repertory company, together with a theatre built expressly for its purposes.

When Lincoln Center's theatre opens here, there will be far less innocent enthusiasm and naïve pride; too many of us are already skeptical of its program and the people who are running it, as well as of the very possibility of being extricated by any single enterprise from our condition of theatrical derangement. But out in those great new spaces all was optimism and exuberance.

The city, ecstatic with sudden glory, turned out in tuxedos and evening gowns, cheered the theatre, the performers, the directors and the occasion, drank champagne at two successive open houses and felt itself to have entered the big time overnight. For the visitor, sophistication was a burden; if you couldn't jettison it all, if you kept making distinctions and applying criteria that in the general euphoria weren't being applied, there was nevertheless an infectious quality to the enthusiasm.

And there was reason for it. To begin with, there was the theatre itself. That it should have been built where it has been is the most impressive, although also the most precarious, fact of all. For what is being tested in Minneapolis is of course the idea of decentralization; if the Guthrie Theatre takes hold and works, if its standards are high and the response to its efforts substantial and continuous, then it may be the fountainhead of a new era in the American theatre. But if it fails, we are all going to have to get right down to our skins and start all over again in a barn.

The building, which one feared might have been ugly or unuseful, is the answer to a great many prayers. Modeled in basic ways after the Shakespeare Festival Theatre in Canada, it is quite beautiful and admirably suited to a classic repertoire. Around its spacious open stage there is a steeply rising orchestra and a narrow balcony running five-sixths of the way; the seats (the capacity is 1,437) are covered in pastel-colored burlap, the acoustics are good and there is ample space for intermissions and easy access to every section. The whole thing gives rise to an atmosphere of bright, self-confident, noncompetitive vigor and casual expertise—a theatre open to whatever degree of technical ingenuity and dramatic imagination wishes to be exercised on its stage.

The resident company is another matter. Guthrie has assembled an extremely uneven group of performers, strong in places, adequate in others and lamentably weak in too many more. The women are especially below the standard one would think minimal for such an undertaking. If the situation is likely to improve in time, as the actors settle down to their tasks, it would still seem that some major changes are going to have to be made if the building is not to remain a more impressive phenomenon than the life it displays.

The same thing is true of the production and direction. The two openings were *Hamlet*, directed by Guthrie, and Molière's *The Miser*, which Douglas Campbell staged, and the difference between them was startling. Whatever can be said for a modern-dress *Hamlet*, Guthrie's was a boon to traditionalists, an exceedingly unpleasant production, gimmicky, heterogeneous, inconsistent and without any style that derived from sources other than a vulgar, obvious theatricality. Campbell's *Miser*, on the other hand, was unified and full of style; it took advantage of the open stage as *Hamlet* didn't, it was lively and vivacious although a bit superficial, and if it, too, suffered from the inadequacies of many of its performers, it managed to rise above them as *Hamlet* could not.

From the latter's opening scene, when Horatio, in overcoat and scarf, and the soldiers, in long military capes and gold helmets with red plumes, appear on watch, Guthrie's *Hamlet* is a series of ludicrous mismatings of costumes and properties. Claudius comes on as Kaiser Wilhelm in certain scenes and as a tail-coated maître d' in others; Hamlet delivers his best-known soliloquy in a red velvet smoking jacket; Laertes returns from Paris in a Hungarian commissar's outfit, brandishing a pistol; Fortinbras stands like Bismarck in spiked helmet and breastplate while two Tommies, circa 1945, operate a field telephone at his feet; Ophelia and Laertes bid each other good-bye carrying tennis rackets; her funeral scene is out of a Jean Renoir movie, that of Hamlet's departure for Denmark out of Orson Welles. And when Hamlet, in slippers and sport shirt, refers to a "bare bodkin" or Ophelia breathlessly tells Polonius that the prince's doublet is all undone and his stockings down, the absurdity of taking the play out of its period becomes most flagrant and attention-shredding.

In the midst of the carnage George Grizzard managed to hold out a Hamlet by no means good but better than one feared. If it was tame and well behaved, it was also adequately spoken and properly paced, and it avoided the worst pitfalls that the role is perennially threatened by. Robert Pastene was an acceptable Polonius and Ken Ruta a fine ghost, but almost all the other major roles were badly served. Jessica Tandy was an astonishingly inept and melodramatic Gertrude, Lee Richardson an undeviatingly wooden Claudius, Nicholas Coster a high-school Laertes, Alfred Rossi and Michael Levin a Rosencrantz and Guildenstern straight from the junior prom, and Ellen Geer well, Ellen Geer was simply the worst Ophelia I have ever seen or can imagine.

Campbell's *Miser* redeemed the week. Employing music, ballet and masks, it was high-spirited and visually ingratiating, the liberties taken with the text, such as a surrealist rendering of Harpagon's discovery that his money has been stolen, being entirely justified. Hume Cronyn's Harpagon was a masterpiece of comic invention and physical wit; his supporting cast was two or three notches above Grizzard's, although Miss Geer turned up again and was joined by one Rita Gam, a Hollywood personality with Hollywood equipment for its projection.

The Guthrie Company is going to have a five-month season, adding *The Three Sisters* to the repertoire next month and *Death of a Salesman* the month after that. It has, as this report has indicated, the advantages of a splendid theatre, of permanence, stability and a great fund of good will. But none of this is going to do a bit of good if its *Hamlet* rather than its *Miser* sets its standard and tone. We are going to be watching; Guthrie has announced that the theatre will do only classics (*Death of a Salesman?*—the definition is really being stretched, but no matter), but let us pray that he learns to do them, not do them in. (1963)

¶The Second Season

When the Tyrone Guthrie Theatre opened in Minneapolis last year, the event drew drama critics from all over the country. But when the Minnesota Theatre Company began its second season in its superb plant last week, only a handful of out-of-town critics saw fit to attend. Yet the second season's inaugural was in some ways more crucial than the first: an enterprise which had begun in possibly illusory hope and éclat was being tested for financial stability and artistic fidelity.

It was an important test, indeed. The first permanent classical-repertory company outside New York, the Guthrie, if it proves viable, may point the way to a liberation for the American theatre—the establishment of other companies like itself to break the monolithic rule of Broadway and lift the pressures of a narrow, commercially oriented stage.

Precarious still, its faults still numerous and its philosophy not yet clear, the Guthrie nevertheless gave strong evidence last week that it is on its way to maturity. Last year the novelty, local pride, and some resonant theatrical names might have accounted for the initial success; this year there is a solidity and confidence fed by deeper sources. Although the season-ticket sale is slightly down, the total advance is up, and local interest remains steady. But none of this would matter were it not that in its productions of Shakespeare's *Henry V* and Shaw's *Saint Joan* the Guthrie company showed how able and cohesive a troupe it is becoming.

The Shakespeare was the particular revelation. The directorial temptation of Sir Tyrone Guthrie—around whom, of course, the Minnesota Theatre Company idea was organized and given shape—has always been excess. He is an exponent of nonstop theatre, an indefatigable arranger of stage business, an exploiter of every opportunity for quick effects. But his *Henry* is significantly restrained, which is not to say dull.

On the contrary, by allowing this most direct and yet meditative of all Shakespeare's chronicle plays to reveal itself mostly unhampered by gimmicks, by making its thunder be thunder but letting its thought be thought, he has ushered it into renewed life. There are one or two arbitrary flamboyances, a perversion of character, such as a foolish, W. C. Fields archbishop, and too heavy a hand with the comic characters. But the rest is clean, true and urgent.

Guthrie is immeasurably aided by the performance of George Grizzard as Henry. An underrated actor, Grizzard moves through the play with a clear intelligence, unerring taste and a remarkable sense of his own limitations. The result is a performance smaller and less electric than an Olivier or Burton might give us, but one which few American actors are capable of today. Above all, it results in a Henry in whom the tension between the necessities of war and statecraft and the demands of reason and probity is lucid and sharply seen.

Saint Joan, which Douglas Campbell directed with alacrity but occasionally with uncertain control, is a lesser achievement. At its center it lacks a performer of Grizzard's stature; Ellen Geer, although she has grown considerably since last season's fluttery and paper-thin Ophelia, is simply not up to the role. That she is physically too delicate for Joan's (especially Shaw's Joan) rough, peasant vitality is not insurmountable. There are moments when she manages to transcend even this obstacle. But she cannot overcome her tiny range, monotony of expression—a radiant smile has only so many uses—and inability to transmute raw emotion into the artifice of playing, to *act* and not merely to let us know what she is feeling.

Yet the company which surrounds her, like that which supports Grizzard, is for the most part a strong one. The performers have by now grown accustomed to working with one another, habituated to the theatre's open stage, and able to draw sustenance from an audience which in its enthusiasm and openness must be an actor's delight. In *Saint Joan* Claude Woolman offers an admirably enunciated Dunois; Ed Flanders a complex, gravely responsible Inquisitor; Ken Ruta an Archbishop of Reims finely balanced between pride and sympathy; Lee Richardson a weighty yet resilient Cauchon, and Grizzard an arresting Dauphin—fussy, neurotic, weak yet honorable, with a core of sanity seldom offered in the role. For *Henry* the supporting cast is a shade less competent but everywhere its level is respectable.

Most impressive is the physical beauty of the two productions. Lewis Brown, who designed *Henry,* and Tanya Moiseiwitsch, who was responsible for *Saint Joan,* have employed every resource without falling over into sumptuousness for its own sake.

Perhaps the highest visual point of the two evenings is that moment in *Joan* when, after the coronation of the Dauphin in the cathedral at Reims, a line of black-and-white clad monks passes off the stage, each carrying a tall candlestick and singing the *Te Deum,* and leaving behind them the solitary figure of Joan, kneeling in prayer before a crucifix, light shining from her armor.

If these new productions give assurance of the company's increasing authority, they also raise a central question about the future. For a theatre like the Guthrie to have a real and lasting effect on American drama, it will have to move at some point to the encouragement, and even the creation, of new plays. Any repertory company which confines itself, no matter how zealously and with whatever skill, to the reinterpretation of the past lacks the fullest being and will eventually be threatened with sterility. The crisis is some way off, but it will come; and we cannot speak of a hope for regeneration until it does. (1964)

¶Howl! Howl!

On a stage bare as "ruined nature," whose blank white flats are overlaid by smaller hanging sheets of rusted metal, Lear sits on a rough throne, dividing his kingdom; his left arm, keeping a small, spastic rhythm, beats a prelude to the coming madness. Off to the side of a stage equally bare, Goneril, wrapped in the darkness of her final evil, sways in a trance of isolation. Under a blazing light, with the sounds of battle—projected as abstract clash and distant energy—behind him, blind Gloucester gazes on an inner prospect of total loss. Such moments, and the stripped, merciless action that connects them, make up the *King Lear* of Peter Brook, Paul Scofield, and the Royal Shakespeare Company—a hard, implacable, revolutionary production that can change the face of Shakespeare for our time.

The company, an ensemble in the fullest sense, is also mounting *Comedy of Errors*, which, after a slow start, rises to a second act of prestidigitation: Shakespeare's earliest and slightest play is transformed, through wit, mockery, zaniness, and silent-screen choreography, into something self-sufficient and deceptively major. Its director, Clifford Williams, has proceeded in a manner opposite to Brook's. The latter makes largeness work by peeling off its excrescences; Williams makes the *Comedy* go by filling it out, employing the most far-flung theatrical elements, from pratfalls to smoke machines to *commedia dell'arte* interludes that are exactly imagined and beautiful to see.

But the *Lear* is the story of this first appearance of the company in New York. It, too, is beautiful to see, but in a new mode of beauty which has the effect of making it seem cold and cerebral to the spectator looking for exaltation. For the pivot of Brook's conception is that *Lear* is lost to the mind and eye when approached as traditional tragedy, as the story of a great man brought down by fate and a moral flaw. On that basis the notorious difficulties of the play are insurmountable, since that is simply not the theme of *Lear* and since the expected effects of tragedy—consolation through a "higher" truth, catharsis as the textbooks define it—cannot be made to come.

Standing exactly counter to the tradition of playing *Lear* for its grandeur, moral upheaval and epic sweep, Brook has staged the play outside its age and outside tragedy itself. He has directed it as a "black" drama of relentless destruction, a mighty image of the grinding down of man to his root. In doing this he has released it into contemporaneity, where it links up with such documents of unredeemed man as Beckett's *Waiting for Godot* and *Endgame*. *King Lear,* this stark and pitiless production tells us, is a play about the radical fragility and vulnerability of our lives.

It is also a play about sight and blindness. Lear *sees* wrongly; that is to say, he misunderstands the nature of reality when he thinks that his dignity and power are immutable, and thus his fate is to be divested of everything. Gloucester, the smaller man, is involved in lesser errors—he misreads the character of his two sons—and his is the lesser fate of literal blinding. Both, in the end, come to new sight, or recognition, but it is the inconsolable encounter with existential truth, from which there is no turning aside nor any transcendent deliverance.

From the smallest visual detail to the central confrontations, Brook has made the production hew to this stern and sinewy line. There is a minimum of props and artifacts, and not a primary color to be seen. The costumes are mostly of hard, aged leather or rough cotton, in off-shades of brown, rust, dusty blues and greens, with a slight emblematic distinction—a touch of gold at the breast, a thin chain—to mark off the major characters. This austerity conveys a feeling of order and hierarchy outside specific history.

In the same way the deaths, agonies and struggles with the elements, the mainstays of conventional approaches to *Lear,* are constructed obliquely, with a rigorous exclusion of literalism and the driest of eyes. Edgar and Edmund's duel consists of a single coming together of their swords, held high and frozen in mortal expectation, then sprung apart for the fatal thrust. The storm on the heath is managed by a slight swaying of the metal sheets, Gloucester's imagined leap from the cliff is performed without even a platform as partial illusion. Everywhere there is a forcing of the imagination to see what lies beneath the surface of artifice, rhetoric and extravagance, and in this compulsion of his audience lies Brook's triumph.

It is a triumph he shares with Scofield. As Burton's Hamlet is the finest in memory, so is Scofield's Lear. Disconcerting at the outset, his flat, slow, incantatory delivery and precise, half-expressive and half-withheld gestures are seen in time to mesh perfectly with Brook's conception. An actor of immense intelligence, he is on occasion almost too intelligent, so that one senses him in wary retreat from the great brute force of Lear, but he constantly circles back to engage the role again. When he enters with Cordelia's body, his cry of "Howl! Howl!" is a laceration of the heavens but not an assault on them; when he speaks what is perhaps the central line of the play—"Is man no more than this?"—it is with a soft, musing despair that projects a force greater than any declamation.

Almost all the supporting performances are up to his lead. Irene Worth's Goneril is especially strong, maintaining a superb edge of contemporary indirection and psychological subtlety within the perennial malice of the role. Ian Richardson offers a brilliant Edmund, one whose evil is a principle to be obeyed rather than an impulse to be indulged, and Alec McCowen plays the Fool with greater mind and less buffoonery than the part usually gets. Only Diana Rigg's too vivacious Cordelia and John Laurie's fussily querulous Gloucester seem somewhat out of step with the production.

For his conception of *Lear*, Brook acknowledges his debt to Polish critic Jan Kott, whose book, *Shakespeare Our Contemporary*, will be published here next fall. In Kott's view *Lear*'s theme is the "decay and fall of the world," and its cruelty is a philosophic one: the destruction of man by a uni-

verse without reason or interest in human fate. To charges
that his *Lear* lacks emotion, Brook cites the encounter between
Beethoven and Goethe, during which the composer played the
writer his latest sonata, full of thought and subtlety. Goethe
burst into tears, whereupon Beethoven stalked out in indignation. The point is, of course, that there are experiences which
do reach too deep for tears, and Brook's *Lear* is one.

¶ Yellowed Pages

As the curtain rises on *The Cherry Orchard,* Lopakhin, the peasant turned merchant who will eventually dispossess the owners of the orchard, is seen waiting in tense expectation. Presently the other characters arrive, filling the room with all the gaiety, chatter, and confused energies which surround a return from abroad. The scene should set a tone of lightness and delicate complexity and impart a fluid movement to the play, whose spirit, Chekhov insisted, was that of "a comedy, even a farce." The worst sin against *The Cherry Orchard* is to play it heavily, statically, bludgeoning home Chekhov's sorrowing view of humanity.

Yet that stroke against the heart of Chekhov is exactly the one perpetrated by the Moscow Art Theatre's production; by slighting the farcical and ironic sides of Chekhov they have made him boring. In the light of the legendary history which unites Chekhov with the MAT, it is as if one were to astonishingly hear Wanda Landowska playing Bach clumsily and without understanding.

A year after the MAT's founding in 1898 Chekhov wrote to its co-director, who had become discouraged: "Don't get weary, don't grow cold! The Art Theatre will supply the best pages of the book that will one day be written about the contemporary Russian stage. This theatre should be your pride, and it is the only theatre I love." The MAT went on to figure centrally in a larger book—the history of twentieth-century theatre itself. And Konstantin Stanislavski, its great director, wrote that "the Stanislavski System . . . must be approached through Chekhov."

Chekhov indeed loved the MAT, but he was also distressed by its distortions of some of his plays. "I can't figure it out," he wrote to a friend during rehearsals for *The Cherry Orchard.* "Either the play is no good or the actors don't understand me."

The trouble came about because Chekhov had written a comedy and Stanislavski had staged it as a near-tragedy.

Beyond the current heavy-handed direction of V. Y. Stanitsyn, staged with almost full fidelity to that original misconstrued production, there is the question of the Moscow Art's almost legendary acting. As Mme. Ranevskaya, Alla Tarassova, one of the MAT's great ladies, is simply too old, stiff, and uninspired to do the job. "It is wrong to show her as subdued by suffering," Chekhov wrote his wife. "Nothing but death could subdue a woman like that." Yet Mme. Tarassova moves heavily and lugubriously around the stage, wringing her hands and coming frequently to rest in poses of despair, elbow on table, cheek on hand, like a cameo of "the actress" from the days of the nineteenth-century tragediennes.

As for Lopakhin, Chekhov said that if "he is colorless and is played by a colorless actor, both the part and the play will fail." Despite this admonition, Mikhail Zimin offers a portrait of slow, brooding self-absorption which is entirely amiss. The point about Lopakhin, and one of the things that make the play a comedy, is that he is neither neurotic nor a villain. He is a gay, kind man who cannot help coming into possession of the orchard because he, the energetic man of a brash new class, naturally inherits the properties of the cultured dispossessed.

With a few exceptions, the supporting cast exhibits a standardization of gesture and an absence of nuance sadly reflecting the ossification of what was once a revolutionary acting style. Angelina Stepanova plays Charlotta, the antic governess, with vigor and originality; but it is the great Alexei Gribov as Firs, the aged servant, who shows that the MAT's achievements are not all frozen in history. Firs is one of Chekhov's eloquent ancients who incarnate the erosion of time, and Gribov plays him with subtle, mysterious pathos and a delicate sense of humanity under siege.

Later in the week the MAT offered Chekhov's *The Three Sisters*. Because this play has less overt comic texture and presents a more "serious" surface, it is closer to the MAT's predispositions. The production, therefore, was a great improvement over *The Cherry Orchard*. Yet it too fell a long way short of being revelatory or overwhelming. The ensemble playing which Stanislavski stressed works here to control and shape the play. The members of the company are in touch with one another; the action in this seemingly straightforward but hidden masterpiece flows evenly around the double center that Chekhov molded: a vision on one level of the displacement of a social class, and, on another, of the ordeal of human sensibility in the arena of brute fact—the frustration of dream by actuality.

Grace, coherence within complexity, the relevance of every detail—these are central qualities of Chekhov's drama, and, at last, most of them are present here. And there are some resplendent separate moments: Masha, the artist-soul among the sisters, pacing taut with boredom and repressed anguish in visual counterpoint to her schoolteacher-husband's complacent waddle; Andrei, the brother, lamenting his vanished intellectual hopes as the old messenger impatiently taps a pile of routine papers for him to sign.

Despite such moments, something is wrong. Except for Gribov as the cynical, decaying doctor, and one or two other performances, the acting is too often obvious and operatic; there is too much gazing soulfully into the distance, too little revelation in small gestures. One has the impression of watching *The Three Sisters* being played with such loyalty to Chekhov's more obvious literary values that everything has been placed prominently on the surface, the subtleties of his method ironed out, the underlying emotions and truths thrust forward, rather than emerging silently and gravely through small and subtle actions.

Such faithfulness is touching, as the taxidermy job on *The Cherry Orchard* is not. But it is also saddening. For what the Moscow Art Theatre has shown these two weeks in New York is the institutionalization of what was once a holy terror. Its piety and earnestness are no longer liberating, but blinding and constricting, like devotion to an idol. Stanislavski once wrote that the MAT had "declared war on all the conventionalities of the theatre wherever they might occur." Such a declaration would seem necessary now against the MAT itself; and there are signs that younger, more adventurous theatre people in Russia would dearly love to issue it. (1965)

¶The Risks of Action

For all its erratic behavior and strange lapses, the Living Theatre continues to occupy a space which no other group seems willing or able to fill. It has, whatever one thinks of them, an aesthetic idea, a style and a program, together with the courage to be idiosyncratic and unpopular. If its actors are inadequate to most of their tasks and its directors are given to working out their neuroses in public, the tasks are usually worthy and the neuroses interesting. If its impulse to *épater le bourgeois* is often absurdly misguided, since its audiences are mostly in its pocket beforehand, the energy released in the process manages at times to retain a rough life and value of its own. It falls on its face, but at least it has its own face. It is, in short, a living theatre, with all the crudeness, embarrassing gestures, stridency, rough manners and irreducible specificity of anything that tries to be publicly alive in an age of blandness and smooth evasion.

It is hard to imagine any other company putting on Kenneth H. Brown's *The Brig*. The work is so far from conventional drama, especially from conventional Broadway psychological drama, that only an institution like the Living Theatre, with its freedom from preconceptions about what a play must be—at least from preconceptions about narrative, conflict, development, denouement, etc.—would dare present it. Moreover, having risked something new, the Living Theatre has this time protected its bet; all the loose ends of its style have come together in the production, and the acting company is for once fully up to the effort. The result is the best thing the group has done since *The Connection* a few years ago.

The play takes place in a Marine brig, or jail, in Japan in 1957. Barbed wire stretches between the stage and the audience and behind it, filling half the stage, is a wire cage containing five double-decker bunks for the ten prisoners. There

are four guards in charge of them, and from the opening
scene, when the lights go on at four thirty to begin the day,
the action details the brutality with which the guards treat
the prisoners, endlessly humiliating them, beating them, forcing them to run or do push-ups until they drop. There are
white lines in various places around the compound, and when
a prisoner has to cross one he must shout, "Sir, prisoner number [such and such] requests permission to cross the white
line, sir!" When the prisoners are not otherwise occupied
they must stand rigidly before their bunks reading the Marine
Corps manual.

They are generally addressed as "maggots" or else "worms,"
as part of the attempt to instill in them a radical sense of their
inferiority to their jailers. "You've touched me!" one guard
cries out to a prisoner who has brushed against him, and the
tone is one of awe that such a crime could have been committed. A moment of silent contemplation of the offender is
followed by the inevitable punch in the stomach.

But for all the brutality exhibited, to display it is not *The
Brig*'s chief point and certainly does not constitute its dramatic
existence. It is a self-contained vision, a judgment and an action; its elements are less than its totality. Because the prisoners are not allowed to speak to one another, the only
dialogue is among the guards and, much more important, between the guards and the prisoners, where it takes the form
of incessant, stylized humiliation and mockery. But speech
here is a set of triggers for movement. The entire two hours become a carefully constructed ritual, one which rises at times to
a frenetic, demented intensity as the men move in their
monstrous rhythms of obedience, shouting their requests to
cross the white lines, dressing with frantic speed, being sent
to the latrine according to a split-second abstract system, the
whole thing shaping itself to a terrifying pattern of automa-
ton-like ferocity.

And this ritual, which spreads to include the cool, deliberate, functional sadism of the guards, is the existence of
the play, which is therefore very far from being a simple indictment of the Marines, though it is of course that along the

way. Centrally, it is a narrow but strong and unappeasable image of our general dehumanization, our mechanization; it bodies forth the rhythms and structure of an ideal efficiency, in this case applied to persons who have broken one or another rule—we are never told what the prisoners are guilty of —and who are therefore subject to the automatic vindictiveness and terror by which the guardians of the Rule, of power, reassert its blind sovereignty. The shocking thing of course is that these are Americans, not Nazis, and so the categories by which we protect ourselves—it can't happen here—are broken down.

The Brig, then, is more than a nonliterary drama, it is an antiliterary one, and this is due to its desire to cut through language to a naked political act, which it preeminently succeeds in being at the same time as it lifts political action into a metaphysical dimension. Its repetitiveness, which disturbed so many reviewers, is essential to its effect, just as the looser repetitiveness in Beckett and Ionesco is central to one of their dramatic purposes, which may be described as the cutting away of the spectator's moorings in conventional progression and narrative development. And Judith Malina's superb direction, along with the fantastic, inhuman precision of its execution, insures that *The Brig* is indeed effective.

Yet the effectiveness, I am sorry to say, is badly impaired at one point. In the single departure from the abstract formal pattern a prisoner breaks down, is beaten and is carried off screaming, "It's a madhouse, somebody's got to listen, it's all wrong." It is indeed all wrong, but the scene injures our sense of the wrongness, precisely because it is a flagrant concession to the expected, a clichéd, belligerent editorial inserted into a tight texture of implicit meanings. If it was felt necessary to underscore the horror and the message, then a silent, unstressed collapse would have had vastly more point and force than this piece of melodrama.

The Brig is going to be compared with *The Connection,* but I don't really think it is on a level with that play. While both are anti-explanatory, stripped of investigatory procedures and without denouement, Gelber's play has a greater resonance, the condition it examines and gives dramatic shape to is more complex, its originality is greater. Still, *The Brig* is very much worth seeing. The only trouble is that the people who need most to see it are not likely to. It is one of the sorrows of the Living Theatre that its plays which shock and unsettle are most often seen by people who have already been shocked and unsettled, who believe and are on the side of the angels. To be a minority theatre means to be most often confined to re-addressing and re-inspiring the minority. (1963)

¶APA at the Phoenix

The chief reason for the difficulties repertory theatre has had in this country is most often thought to be an economic one: you either do not have a permanent, properly equipped home, or if you do you cannot keep a company together long enough for it to be adequately trained and fashioned into a true ensemble. But while there is a certain truth to this, there are much more central aesthetic reasons why so many repertory groups die in infancy or, if they do manage to plant themselves physically, turn out to betray the very purposes of repertory.

To begin with, there is the matter of the repertoire itself. What is so outrageous about the new Lincoln Center Repertory Theater is precisely that it should devote so much expertise and so lavish a physical endowment to such unworthy plays as *After the Fall* and *Marco Millions*. But even where the repertoire is sound and principled, what most often happens is a radical failure of procedure, a failure to develop a style, a distinctive approach to texts which elicits new life from them, with every member of the company contributing to that as an instrument. The new Seattle Repertory Theater, with its unadventurous but far from contemptible program—*King Lear, The Sea Gull, The Firebugs* by Max Frisch—and its unbelievably inept and unimaginative stagings—is the most recent example of this delinquency.

The APA (Association of Producing Artists) is a group which is many cuts above the Seattle one. It is in fact one of our better repertory companies, which is what makes it so representative of the general despair. For as it reveals itself in the season it has begun at the Phoenix, the APA has not been able in its four and a half years of existence to create a style of its own. There is almost nothing in the performances it has been giving which serves the unexpected, the inimitable or the restorative. And because in art you must either break into the new or remain strapped to the surface of an exhausted convention, these performances have the effect of diminishing the works they are supposed to replenish.

Pirandello's *Right You Are* is one of his major plays, a bit schematic now, a long generation after it helped revolutionize the stage, but still alive and very much worth seeing again. But the APA is not doing it well, which is not so much a matter of physical capacity or of technical resources as of imagination and of fidelity to the soul of the drama. There is a great deal of fidelity to the skin of the play; the *mise en scène* is just that World War I Italian upper-middle-class environment, with its suffocating protocol and gossipy concern with appearances, in which Pirandello located and anchored his metaphysical inquest into the nature of truth.

The APA production, however, mistakes the ground for the action it is meant to support. *Right You Are* should never be played as a study of manners, and even less as a straightforward farce with, as a concession, a rind of philosophy. But that is the way Stephen Porter has directed it and the way the cast plays it, the result being that the mystery, which should rise precisely from the tension between setting and significance, is dissipated and eventually disappears. Moreover, in playing for laughs, the troupe gives the impression, as an actor friend of mine remarked, of being a mere stock company, energetic, rather talented and certainly well-intentioned, but a stock company nevertheless.

Molière's *Impromptu at Versailles* and *Scapin* are both minor works, the former an exercise in self-defense on the part of the playwright and the latter a classically constructed farce of great mechanical skill but no pretension to high stature. They can both be enjoyed on their proper levels, that is, if they are done not only with vigor and good will but also with precision and inventiveness. But because the APA has not come into possession of any new approach to Molière, the vigor and good will cannot save the production from an aimless, scrambling, arbitrary and opaque quality. A few performers manage to do their work along a line of thought and coherence—Christine Pickels is particularly deserving of mention—but the general effect is of a superior college production.

Anyone at all familiar with the prevailing level of college productions in this country will understand how deadly this evaluation is. Earnestness, stamina and a loyalty to the classics may be the most one can expect from an amateur repertory company, but they are only the preliminary bases for a professional one. (1962)

¶Official Mediocrity

What is repertory? My dictionary defines it as "a theatrical company that performs regularly and in alternate sequence several plays, operas or the like." By this definition the Lincoln Center Repertory Theater is clearly a misnomer, since its productions are presented not in alternation but successively and since, more decisive than that, it has stopped being a company in any meaningful sense. The Theater's last two productions, Peter Ustinov's *The Unknown Soldier and His Wife*, and Lillian Hellman's *The Little Foxes*, were presented by outside entrepreneurs and with commercially put-together casts, and its next offering, *Saint Joan*, is also going to have an ad hoc group of performers. There are some impressive names among them—Diana Sands, John Heffernan, Philip Bosco, Alvin Epstein—but these are discrete names from the individualistic marketplace of the American commercial stage, who will lend the Theater *their* modest prestige instead of the other way round.

The APA, it might be said, is a different proposition. They are a company with a continuing membership who do their plays in alternation and use their own directors, designers and technicians. Yet I think it time to say that if we go on praising the APA as the fulfillment of the repertory ideal, or even as a company on its embattled way to fulfilling it, we are going to end by driving entirely out of sight any notion at all of what repertory should consist in.

The qualities that take the idea of repertory beyond the dictionary's purely physical definition include an imaginative fidelity to texts, a consistency of taste, a discernible style, a capacity for ensemble playing, a sense of continuing growth, a degree of independence from the box office. By all these criteria the APA doesn't begin to measure up, and the fact that so many of our journalistic commentators keep insisting that they do is one of the more melancholy aspects of the theatrical times. On its current productions, *Pantagleize* and *The Show-Off*, which are quite in the line of its usual work, the APA has to be described as a perversion of the possibilities of repertory, a shell of good theatre, an institutionalization of mediocrity and—I don't think it too strong a word—something of a hoax.

An admirer of Ghelderode (and I am one, with reservations) who thinks he is going to see *Pantagleize* at the Lyceum Theatre would do better to stay home and read it. John Houseman and Ellis Rabb, the co-directors, have for some opaque reason decided that this "farce to make you sad," as the late Belgian playwright described his 1929 work, is approximately twice as long as it should be, and accordingly they have cut it in half. The result is to reduce a complex, very energetic, very unschematic work to the dimensions of a conscious fling at theatrical "absurdity," to deprive its farcical elements of their anchor in a rich language and its sadness of its ground in an inevitability of accident and paradox that needs time to make its shape known.

Ghelderode wrote a play about an everyman figure who up to the age of forty has remained outside those fatal processes of society whereby roles are thrust on men in order that they may be identifiable and available to others. One May Day he gets caught up in a revolution in a nameless European capital, and innocently blunders his way to death as a conspirator, after having naïvely tasted love, power and friendship. His is the comi-tragedy of the man of good but unspecific will, of the universalist in an age of partisanship, of the mystic in an arena of facts. With much gusto, drawing on one of the most extensive physical repertoires of any modern dramatist, Ghelderode sets him in motion through scenes that are part pageant, part music-hall skit, part expressionist lyricism and part surrealist nightmare.

The APA goes at the text, or rather its shrunken remains, with all the cautious knowing professionalism of an official theatre, a cultural asset, as the people who write reports for the foundations like to say. The farce they offer is precisely "official," a little far out now and then, a little kooky, rather extravagant at times but never *wild,* a careful rendering of a baroque substance into a cute piece of acceptable fare. A play with a large dramatis personae, *Pantagleize* presents an opportunity for full ensemble work, yet the things that seem to bind this company together are, now that Rosemary Harris is gone, its shared mediocrity and lack of any discernible attitude or aesthetic whatsoever. The only performer who might be usefully singled out for special censure, however, is Mr. Rabb, the APA's artistic director. He has never given any evidence that he is an actor, but he persists in trying to be one: his attempt this time in the central and title role has the effect of converting a holy fool into a simpering idiot.

George Kelly's *The Show-Off* ought to have been left in the archives, or in one of those volumes of *Not Quite Notable American Plays* which clutter every drama critic's shelves. A 1924 success, its trouble isn't that it dates. As a matter of fact it holds up only too well from the standpoint of time, which is to say that it cannot be eroded by time because it was never anything substantial in the first place. A well-made play with just the right proportions of domestic comedy and grief and with a traditional cop-out at the end, it fits quite nicely into the Broadway entertainment structure, although how it might fit with the ideals of any serious repertory company is up to Mr. Rabb to answer.

The APA once performed a minor miracle with a rather similar enterprise, its resurrection of *You Can't Take It With You,* which is the only production by the company I have ever admired. For some reason everything in that production worked well, the group did attain ensemble stature and you had a sense of achievement if not of high discovery. But everything in *The Show-Off* works badly, so badly, in fact, that the play, startlingly enough, seems better than the performance. The direction by Stephen Porter is plodding, utterly safe and what I can only call "club-womanly," which is the quality of being serious about the trivial and giddy about the significant.

The performers offer absolutely nothing of interest, unless

it is possible, as I suppose it is, for certain sentimental theatre-goers to derive satisfaction from watching Helen Hayes in the post-twilight of her career. Miss Hayes ought to be congratu-lated for her willingness to relinquish marquee status for the lesser glamor of repertory life, but I found it painful to watch this one-time competent performer messing up her lines on dozens of occasions (although she did recover quickly each time) and being utterly predictable in her mannerisms, which are those of a grand dame in reduced circumstances, Queen Victoria in the kitchen.

Miss Hayes plays the crotchety mother of the Fisher fam-ily of Philadelphia, whose younger daughter marries a $36-a-week railroad clerk who is a pretentious blowhard. Clayton Corzatte, whose high-pitched voice and deadly monotony of gesture have contributed to a great many APA productions, plays the show-off in a broad "expressive" style. The remaining roles are filled by APA regulars carrying out their orders. As long as those orders go unchallenged, the company stands a very good chance of winning the war. The losers of course will be repertory theatre as something more than doing plays in alternation, and the dwindling public for true drama. (1968)

¶The Theatre of the Poor

At present the theatre's only hope of life-giving heresy seems to rest in the hands of Jerzy Grotowski. A former actor like Stanislavski and Artaud, Grotowski is also, like them, a theoretician and even metaphysician of the theatre who is set upon the regeneration of his art through an ethic of creative zeal and sacrifice. And, like Artaud, he is also a prophet whose visions and calls to order belong to the great tradition of the imagination, of its periodic reawakening and revivification.

Only thirty-six now, Grotowski has made widening circles in the consciousness of theatre people for the past six or seven years, ever since rumors began to stir concerning the strange, rigorous and seemingly unprecedented work he was doing with actors in the small Polish city of Wroclaw. He had established his "laboratory theatre" in an even smaller town, moving it to Wroclaw in 1961. From the start the theatre had been designed for "research." This meant in Grotowski's words "that we approach our profession rather like the medieval wood carver who sought to re-create in his block of wood a form which already existed . . . [we make] a penetration into human nature itself [and] examine the nature of theatre, how it differs from the other art forms and what it is that makes it irreplaceable."

In time, serious people, actors and directors from Europe and America, began to travel to Wroclaw as to the site of a revelation. Meanwhile Grotowski began to move out into the world beyond Poland, participating in conferences and symposia, bringing his group to theatre festivals and for performances in major European cities (and finally to New York this past autumn), engaging in brief teaching stints at universities, being interviewed widely, publishing a book, *Towards a Poor Theater* (Simon and Schuster), containing his major theoretical statements as well as descriptions of his Laboratory Theatre's rationales, procedures and training processes. The force of Grotowski's work has been such that the theatre, starved for new means, for intelligence, and for the kind of morale that is built on certainty about ultimate values together with radical skepticism about sanctified usages, has felt itself in the presence of something very like a redemption.

As one would expect, the arrival of a reputed savior has resulted in a rush to appropriate his person, his aura, the constituents of his method, and the secret he must necessarily possess. Grotowski is very much aware of what this portends and of what in fact is already under way. To a lecture audience in Brooklyn, many of whose members were furiously intent on wresting his secret, he remarked wryly on a "human weakness," that of "always trying to find a solution," announced that he had no "miraculous prescription, no hidden key," and that his was not a method of training that could be adapted as an absolute and used as a Jacob's ladder by a theatre in the mire.

He knows what has happened to Artaud. "We are in the age of Artaud," he has written. "The 'Theatre of Cruelty' has been canonized, i.e., made trivial, swapped for trinkets, tortured in various ways." And he has declared that "real disciples are never disciples; the real disciples of Stanislavski were Meyerhold and Vakhtangov [who split with the master and founded their own opposing theatres]. I do not wish to have any disciples, but collaborators, brothers." In the light of everything in Grotowski's work, utterance and personal atmosphere, only those who find such words alien and unfashionable could doubt their sincerity.

The usable originality of a creative mind always lies more importantly in the spirit of its activity, which is open to absorption by contemporary and subsequent imagination, than in the details of its actual work, which can only be appropriated at the extreme risk of imitation. But there is a particularly great irony in looking to Grotowski to supply not spirit, a mode of evaluation and principle of action, but something measurable and directly useful, a stock of knowledge or clear instrumentalities of efficacious work. For at the center of his method and belief are an ideal of poverty and deprivation, an austerity and even a certain destructive zeal that have arisen precisely from his repudiation of our Western habit of thinking of knowledge as purely instrumental, power as material, and skill as wholly technical. These are ideas which in the arts are especially likely to organize the high road to inauthenticity and debasement. Against them Grotowski has described the chief training procedure for his actors as a *via negativa*, and the title of his book, *Towards a Poor Theater*, exactly delineates the bases from which he sets out.

His starting point is in the theatre's fundamental malaise, its illusion-making, and in its periodic attempts to cure this by efforts in the direction of amplitude, the result of which is the mounting of even denser illusion, a sort of homeopathic treatment. For Grotowski this is the origin of renewed crisis. Ever since the rise of the film as a rival art, the theatre has attempted to compete both by technological and material means and by its claim to be more "lifelike." Yet the pitiless evidence is that film is infinitely more supple and powerful in technical ways, and that when it is being true to itself it is also closer to experience, in the way that true shadows are closer to existence than false bodies. Ideas such as that of "total theatre," the enlisting of every resource of the theatrical arts in a broad assault on the sensibilities of audiences, take the theatre further from its own nature. The aim of Grotowski's Laboratory Theatre has been to do research into what this nature might be.

It has been for the most part research of a strangely negative kind, an inquiry into how to strip away dreams and false notions, how to pare one's way down to essentials. "We found," Grotowski has written "that the theatre can exist without make-up, without autonomic costumes and scenography, without a separate performance area (stage), without lighting and sound effects, etc. . . . This synthetic theatre is the contemporary theatre, which we readily call the 'Rich Theatre,' rich in flaws." At the center of the Poor Theatre he has been working to create is the conviction, the final product of his research, that the one thing the stage "cannot live without [is] the actor-spectator relationship of perceptual, direct, 'live' communion."

By the word "live" Grotowski does not mean to indicate anything so banal and naïve as a trust in the mere presence of flesh-and-blood performers on the stage to be a source of superiority to the "abstraction" of film or to be a source, *in itself,* of the theatre's aesthetic life and truth. In fact, as time has gone by, this presence has become a source of the theatre's lies and so of its near-extinction. The point, wholly crucial to everything in Grotowski's thought, is that such palpable creatures as actors will, like other men, if left to themselves only "live" by the clichés and habitual gestures of an existence that is forever forming itself into inauthenticity, forever repeating its own lies and evasions. If life were original, authentically enacted, true to what is asked and proposed by human experience, then the theatre, that employment of bodies for representation and *reenactment,* would, by reflecting this, be original, truth-giving, a hard and inescapable revelation. But then we would have no need for it.

The reality is that life in the present is inauthentic, the seat of untruth, false acts, spaces between what we are and the signs we make, an arena where all our gestures and languages are full of an energy bent on dissembling, on masking us from ourselves and from one another. Art is a means of discovering and claiming ourselves through the creation of original acts, acts not found in life; it is, Grotowski reminds us, a "compensation" for life, reflecting it but in a new perspective. It is thus one of life's movements, made necessary by the fact that life "doesn't function in this manner." This is why through art "one must go against life to rediscover it, against the temptations, the stereotypes of daily life."

But the theatre, that place where the only necessary thing is the meeting of actor and spectator, finds this going against life to be the last step anyone would want to take. As it has been constituted for hundreds of years, the theatre is increasingly a site for the clinging to impoverished life through a wish to reproduce it by means of "exact imitations of human reactions and calculated reconstructions" of what men think they are like. This reproduction and imitation is not a matter of texts, which may be as unnaturalistic as is imaginable, but of the nature of traditional acting. The dominant theatre of our time is composed, Grotowski says, of "hardened, demoralized professionals" who "hide behind technical excellence, theatrical gymnastics," the kind of person for whom the theatre is "first and foremost *himself* . . . his own private organism." An attitude like this "breeds the impudence and self-satisfaction which enable him to present acts that demand no special knowledge, that are banal and common-place . . . the impudence to walk around, smoke, talk, etc., things anyone can and does do a dozen times a day, and to *show* that and think it great."

Beyond these commonplaces are the stereotypes of emotion and idea, the received wisdom about them and the absence—played as though it were a virtue—of their truth on the natural level. Because, like any men they are enmeshed in clichés and received self-knowledge, Grotowski's actors have, so to speak, to unlearn their lives, to submit to a process of education for authenticity, for a break into new and post-natural being. They have to get "behind the masks of common vision," to rid themselves of "those elements of 'natural' behavior which obscure pure impulses." This education is at the same time the basis for their training as professionals; a regimen that inverts the classic systems, it concentrates not on right ways to do but on right ways to be, and makes technical skills and histrionic knowledge the result and not the goal of training. In other words, the actor is not taught a set of skills for the execution of predetermined and canonized tasks, but educated for the responsibilities of new ones.

In order for this to take place, the actor has to struggle against his impulses to act as he thinks it should be done, to do what he believes is "natural." "The requisite state of mind," Grotowski writes, "is a passive readiness to realize an active role, a state in which one does not 'want to do that' but rather 'resigns from not doing it.'" A heresy, but only to those for whom art is the natural outpouring of exuberant and confident spirits, the uninflected movement toward "enhanced" or mirrored life, a beeline between two assured points. Yet this state of the actor is a manifestation of those phenomena in all artistic creation in which the imagination shows itself fit for work: passivity in the face of what has not yet announced itself, and pressure on the self to resist its desire *to be as before.*

When he sets out to explain, or even describe, the actual work in the laboratory, Grotowski gets into difficulty: his speech and writing, ordinarily wonderfully supple, exact and animate, tend to grow opaque; he seems to be struggling with a language inadequate to the new actuality of what he has been doing. He is, in fact, fond of citing a poem by Apollinaire in which the poet speaks of the need of every new thing to have a new name, and it is a mark of Grotowski's embattled and on-going originality, as well as of the unformulary nature of his activity, that he has not yet been able to invent the requisite new terms. There is this difference, however: his new "things" can be said to name themselves as they unfold in front of us, their language that of the expressiveness of theatrical acts.

As it is, Grotowski's vocabulary is full of words like "autonomic," "ideoplastic," "tropistic," and, at the same time, of a counter-diction heavily religious: "sacrifice," "holiness," "transgression," "profanation," "sacrilege." It is as though he has pitched his camp in a place halfway between the contemporary and scientific and the perennially spiritual, between technique and transcendence, and works there under these pressures whose presence together is in itself something original.

In this light what goes on in the workshop takes on its general outlines. Apart from the constant vigilance about clichés, the discovering of "points where our stereotypes begin," the actor is helped to penetrate *backward* toward creativity through exercises in the extensions of self-awareness and through an unremitting attentiveness to what is ordinarily hidden or suppressed in his being. It is a procedure resembling psychoanalysis and at the same time the Catholic confession, its difference from both being, however, its basis in the acquisition of "bodily" knowledge, to which, during training at least, psychic or moral or intellectual knowledge is wholly subordinated. The confessional aspects of his training, Grotowski has said, are "different from the religious because [they] engulf our entire being and not only our sins."

"To think with the body": this phrase of Grotowski's, which we have all heard before and find wanting by itself, is, naïvely or not, the motto for his training. Since we have acquired our false lives through the mind, we can recover our true ones only if the flesh is allowed to interrogate itself and determine its own truths. But the flesh is to be disciplined, responsible, and ready for the service of a total human environment; it is not to be allowed to enjoy an independent or authoritarian destiny— as in certain proposals of the romanticism of the body—but is to constantly refer itself to the psyche in order to provide it with a true ground. For the actor this means that he must permit the body to discover its own actualities, make its own statements, but he must then be prepared to offer these to the mind for their *use*, their role in expressive consciousness.

The actor is helped, not to *act*, which would mean doing the things the mind full of clichés proposes—"In looking for the result only the brain works; the mind imposes solutions it already knows and you begin juggling known things"—but to *react*. He is not to "conduct the process [of learning to perform] but to refer it to personal experiences and to be conducted. The process mu t take us. The formula 'resigning oneself not to do' is centr al." That is to say, the actor *allows* the discovery in himself of what is blocking him from authentic expression, he summons up what has happened to him outside life as a performer, he resists the effort of his mind to impose preconceived, safe ways of dramatic expression.

The Laboratory Theatre has employed a changing set of exercises, "whose aim is not a muscular development or physical perfectionism, but a process of research leading to the annihilation of the body's resistances." They include experiments in walking, in being upside down or on one's knees, in flight and leaping, in making "masks" with the facial muscles alone. There are also exercises in voice whose aim is the development of a dispersed resonance, a speaking from the whole body. One central activity is something we might call the conversion of the body into polymorphous consciousness, through a sort of anthropomorphism in which bodily parts take on the attributes of entire beings. They are "games with one's own body," which may include "opposing one side of the body to the other . . . during a fight between one hand and the other, the legs might express terror and the head astonishment" or single unparalleled metamorphoses: "the shoulder cries like a face; the abdomen exults; the knee is greedy."

Throughout his training the actor is prevented from trying to achieve "beauty" or "gymnastics," the attributes of an acting grounded in rationalized culture, egoism and commerce. And he is pressed to "surpass" his fatigue, to get past that point of tiredness which has psychic origins, in a protest against going too far; he is "pushed towards the unknown." But this, Grotowski says, does not happen by chance. For the theatre, the unknown, the revelation of which is its aesthetic obligation, is the outcome of its practitioners having been made ready to exhibit it; the presentation of new experience is made possible by the proper forms having been found. This is perhaps the most decisive element in all Grotowski's action: he has prepared his actors not so they will be more "lifelike," but so that they will be ready for new life, and yet except as such new life is the basis for their work it is not a secular enterprise; the actors have been made ready for the purposes of new art.

He has pointed his methods toward the ultimate structuring of new works, dramas, but these structures arise from the research itself; they are discoveries, not plans to be executed. As the self recovers its honesty, it moves in aesthetic realms, to the accession of forms; the theatre is, literally, a "place for seeing," and the new life of the stage, its presentations of the previously unheard of, requires clear artifices: "the imperceptible demands precision." This phrase is reminiscent of a remark of Antonioni's, who described his films as being "about nothing—with precision," by which one understands that they are about nothing we could have foretold, nothing life offers us of itself.

This word "precision" is one of two key ones in Grotowski's vocabulary; the other is "sincerity." These words, which have to be taken up in all their problematic status and to be defended against our cynicism, define by their conjunction Grotowski's aesthetic ideal and define the difference between himself and many other presences in the theatre. With sincerity alone we have phenomena like the Living Theatre and all slack, earnest humanitarians of the stage; with precision by itself we have Mike Nichols.

Grotowski has written about the way his training moves toward the fusion of these two qualities:

> The more we become absorbed in what is hidden inside us . . . in the exposure, in the self-penetration, the more rigid must become the external discipline, that is to say the form, the artificiality, the ideogram, the sign. Here lies the whole principle of expressiveness.

> One cannot achieve spontaneity in art without the structuring of detail. Without this, one searches but never finds because too much freedom is a lack of freedom. If we lack structured detail we are like someone who loves all humanity and that means he loves no one.

"The actor is a man who works in public with his body, offering it publicly." From the laboratory where he has received his reeducation, Grotowski's actor steps out into the world to make a gift of himself. There is a strong religious connotation to this offering, this "self-donation"; it is part of the same world where phrases like "monastic theatre" and "holy action" circulate. But Grotowski is not proposing a sacerdotal art; he speaks of the theatre as a "secular sacrum" and of its true work as a "secular holiness," and his imagination wholly overflows any Catholic or even Christian limits. This language comes into being as an opposition to a theatre in a state of profanation—against its own best nature and against what is necessary for human dignity.

Grotowski often speaks of the "holy" as opposed to the "courtesan" actor, and by this antithesis places his theatre at the throat of the conventional one. The latter lives by the values of the general society, instead of as a source of alternatives, and its typical actor is a "prostitute" who sells his body rather than offering its activity as new perception. In working for fame, money, or even psychic satisfaction, he necessarily corrupts the uses of the stage; any eye on the responses of audiences brings about a submission to their expectations, which are inevitably engendered in their appetite for what they already know and have therefore disarmed and domesticated. "If in theatre," Grotowski has said, "you work for the audience, if the audience is [your] goal, you can justify it by all the moral and social ideas but you are . . . on the road which will lead you to *Oh! Calcutta!*"

That is an extreme example, but prostitution, as we all know, has broader uses than the sexual. What the prevailing theatre betrays is artistic creation, which is an order opposed to the order of the world. For Grotowski the theatre ought to be an arena for the confrontation of these two modes of existence; there the spectator, faced with actors who are working in his presence but not *for* him, has the opportunity to be a witness. In this "place of provocation" he ought to be fascinated but also full of "indignation and even repugnance," the first responses to the necessary aggressions of new art. He should be "stimulated into self-analysis," able thereafter to carry on the process begun in him by this encounter with the "violation of accepted stereotypes of vision, feeling and judgment . . . this defiance of taboo, this trangression [which] rips off the mask." Such a theatre is not for the satisfaction of "cultural needs," nor for the man "who wishes to relax, but for the spectator with spiritual needs."

The Laboratory Theatre's repertoire is composed of "adaptations" of classic texts—Marlowe's *Dr. Faustus,* Calderón's *The Constant Prince,* the late-nineteenth-century Polish playwright Stanislaw Wyspianski's *Akropolis*—although there is no exclusion on principle of new works. But poised in spirit between the exact present and the past that operates in it clandestinely, the Laboratory Theatre discovers in its adaptations, which may leave nothing of the original intact, the kind of tension set up by the confrontation (an ever-recurring motif) of dimensions of time, and therefore of consciousness—past and present layers of the self interrogating and challenging one another. "The events of the readapted play are like mythical events for Homer," Grotowski has said. They are not "expressed" but interpreted, suffused with present feeling—all that we have—and gathered up into an exemplification of eternal experience without contingency or locale. In this way the atomization of consciousness among us is fought:

> Group identification with myth—the equation of personal, individual truth with universal truth—is virtually impossible today. What is possible? First, *confrontation* with myth rather than identification. In other words, while retaining our private experiences, we can attempt to incarnate myth, putting on its ill-fitting skin to perceive the relativity of our problems, their connection to the "roots," and the relativity of the "roots" in the light of today's experiences. If the situation is brutal, if we strip ourselves and touch an extraordinarily intimate layer, exposing it, the life-mask cracks and falls away.

The experience of attending one of the Laboratory Theatre's performances begins with a sense of radical displacement from the ordinary milieu of theatre, from its familiar seductions and claims, its contrived intimacy or aloofness, and the atmosphere it exudes—when it is being "serious"—of a special life for *culture.* Here is a grave circumstance, disturbing from the outset, outrageous even, full of the unknown, something to which you are never able to "adjust," be carried away by, or lose yourself in. The very performing area is fashioned with apparent indifference to your presence. For *The Constant Prince* the eighty or so who are admitted sit on benches overlooking an acting space enclosed by a high wooden fence, to witness events meant to be seen as though taking place in a circus arena or an operating room; for *Akropolis* the spectators occupy various levels of an unsymmetrical arrangement, the actors moving in their midst, almost touching them at times but without acknowledging their presence in any way.

Everything is alien, bathed in an estranging light. In *The Constant Prince* you hear a violently rapid Polish being spoken and should know that even for Polish audiences this rapidity of speech makes much of the dialogue incomprehensible, by design; in *Akropolis* you witness events falling over one another, squeezed back to back or cut off at midpoint. Every step is taken away from traditional theatre, away from verisimilitude and imitation. The costumes and props are specific but mysteriously unlocalized: black capes, a rainhat, anonymous berets, an umbrella, a wheelbarrow, huge wooden shoes. In both works the actors—a small troupe, only five or six men and one woman—carry out their movements in unprogrammatic opposition to every tradition of grace or elegance in histrionic "expressiveness." They walk bent over, scuttling, or with heads thrown back so they seem about to topple; they move in tight little scurrying groups like a single organism; their gestures are harsh, sudden, fractured, staccato, or else dazed, lyrical, helpless. Almost every movement and sound is what can only be described as "pure," without precedent or predictability, yet wholly inevitable, accurate, created, true.

The Constant Prince is a readaptation of a Polish romantic version of Calderón's drama, and thus plays elements of baroque sensibility against several later kinds. It is "about" the torture of a noble figure by anonymous but powerful persons who incarnate society in its self-confidence and righteousness. These torturers vacillate between hatred and strange adoration of the prince, who attains in the end a sort of ecstasy of suffering accepted out of love and humble devotion to the truth of existence. But this summary tells nothing; what one sees is not a narrative but a sustained epiphany of violence, terror, sacrifice and love, whose extraordinary force emanates entirely from the persons of the performers. In having passed beyond all hitherto known means of expression and beyond representation, they place us in the presence of emotion and consciousness themselves, in the presence, that is to say, of a creation and not an image of one.

Akropolis, although not more astonishing, is a much broader and more elaborate work, and one filled with more immediate data. Wyspianski's play takes place on Resurrection night in the cathedral of Cracow, where in this "cemetery of the tribes," this Polish repository of Western culture, the statues and figures from the tapestries come alive and enact scenes from the Old Testament and antiquity. In Grotowski's version, which retains almost nothing of the original but its central action, the scene is an unnamed concentration camp, or rather a "poetic paraphrase" of one. To confront the question of the effect on human nature of the era's total violence and of what this means for our traditional culture, the work throws up a species of terrible dream enacted by the "dead," the actors, before the eyes of the "living," the spectators who surround them.

"We did not wish to have a stereotyped production with evil SS men and noble prisoners," Grotowski has said. (And this is the first source of the work's infinite superiority to plays like *The Deputy* or *The Investigation.*) "We cannot play prisoners, we cannot have such images in the theatre. Any documentary film is stronger . . . What is Auschwitz? Something we could organize today? A world which functions inside us."

The work becomes, then, the projection of the performers' relationship to the memory or knowledge of the death camps. The inmates, dressed in bags with arm and leg holes cut out, nondescript berets, and immense wooden shoes, enact during the pauses from their labor their own versions of the heroic and normative legends of our civilization. "They give a degree of reality to their dreams of dignity, nobility and happiness. It is a cruel and bitter game which derides the prisoners' own aspirations as they are betrayed by reality."

There are no sets, no props except a wheelbarrow, a bathtub, and some rusty stovepipes with which the actors construct an abstract image of the gas chamber's monstrous functionalism. After the "games" are over, after the actors have horrifyingly travestied Jacob's wrestling with the angel, Helen and Paris in love, Cassandra crying out her prophecy, the last pipe is hung in place and the inmates, carrying an ashen-gray dummy they regard as the risen Christ-Apollo, march singing to a wooden box in the center of the playing surface. They lift its lid and swiftly climb in; they seem, in the magnificent phrase of Ludwig Flaszen, the Laboratory Theatre's literary adviser, "to throw themselves out of the world."

We, the living, are left behind, having been reached in our deepest intimation of the appalling world of our capabilities, compelled, in painful recognition, to grant the truth of what we have seen. This truth is not one that could have been uncovered by an argument from "life" or by any reconstruction of history, but only by such imagination as this, pursuing its materials to their roots and fending off with absolute control that "cultured" treatment which turns art into a confirmation of what we already know or wish to.

In the light of Grotowski's wholly unaccommodating proposals and practice, and his truly fanatic advocacy of a theatre radically condemning the ones we have, it should not be surprising that he is far from universally admired. His very person —perpetual dark glasses and unvarying black suit and tie, exceedingly rare thin smiles and no laughter, autocratic gestures, the impatience of a zealot—causes extreme distaste, and the apparently high-handed way his Laboratory Theatre is run in public—the refusal, for example, to admit a single spectator beyond the small figure set for each production and the insistence on complete silence—causes more. On more complex levels, he is accused of being derivative, the beneficiary of a discipline enforceable only in a Communist state, a mind peculiarly and so untranslatably Eastern European and Catholic. And finally there is the criticism by some who admire his purely technical effects that he has nothing ultimately to "say," that he is confined to his brilliant surfaces as a formalist.

His person is what it will be; outside the cult and consideration of personality there are those who will not mind if he resembles Satan or the man next door. That he is derivative is simply untrue; he has acknowledged his debt to Stanislavski, Dullin, Meyerhold, and Artaud, but he has pointed out, with complete justification, that none of these innovators was able to combine the two elements whose conjunction animates his own methods: the search for sincerity of being and the development of precise signs for the creation of new forms. That his theatre is strictly and even intolerantly run is a measure of his artistic integrity: "We do not exclude an audience, we define the number for the structure of each production . . . and we will not compromise . . . the order of creativity must be decisive." That he is profoundly Polish and a legatee of Catholicism is true but not a disqualification; everything in the spirit of his techniques and imaginative accomplishments is translatable, for they belong to that universal language of which, as Walter Benjamin has said, all national languages of art are simply variants.

The charge that Grotowski is a formalist who communicates nothing beyond effects from the surface, that he is all "technique," is the most difficult to combat, for it rests on a misunderstanding of aesthetic reality that has persisted throughout the epochs of Western culture and has in fact been deeply implicated precisely in the conversion of art into culture. Art is a new action for which life has no precedents; culture is the taming of the implications this throws up. "Formalism" is an indictment from the world of culture, an academic implement, an accusation that some kind of "content" or subject matter is lacking, which means something immediately convertible into use: enhancements of life, interpretations, reflections, solutions.

This tiresome dichotomy, which Grotowski has dealt with brusquely—"If we can divide work into subject and form then we've abandoned the possibility of [being] authentic"—but which artists like him never succeed in overthrowing, has its origins in a humanism seeking as many justifications as it can find, but perpetually overlooking the only justification art provides: its testimony to the *fact* of the imagination as life-giver in the teeth of life itself. The wish to have a work finally "say" something emerges from a blindness to what it is actually doing—putting us in the presence of a life our own lives are powerless otherwise to unearth. Such a wish reduces the action of art to pointing and indicating, and converts it from an exemplary mode to an illustrative one. When Beckett said of Joyce that "he is not writing about something, he is writing something," he described what all true artists, among whom is Jerzy Grotowski, do.

Whether or not Grotowski will revive the theatre is the most useless of questions; probably the theatre does not want new life and will resist it in many ways, among them the conversion into formulas of Grotowski's own examples of creative spirit. The process is already under way, and we are likely to see the widest range of corruptions and misuses of his action and thought. The very phrase "Poor Theatre" has begun to function, as he has taken note, "as part of our magic terminology . . . through which we think we touch experience but only draw away." Here and there there will no doubt be actors and other people of the theatre who will know what to do with him: accept him and then test him; work in their own way toward the sincerity and precision for which he has found aesthetic incarnations; understand the necessity for sacrifice the way he does; perhaps above all learn from him what not to do.

But it may be that his influence will turn out to be greater outside the theatre, in areas where institutional pressures toward conformity and mechanical self-perpetuation are less severe. His general ideas about art are among the most liberating of our time, but the liberation is of a strange new kind, or rather of a kind that speaks of a return to something forgotten. At a moment when the notion of the independence of aesthetic truth is thinly held and the harrying of art for immediate social purposes is widespread, his thinking comes to us as perverse, unfashionable, under suspicion. This is why it can teach us a way to get free of the oppression of the age and the ethos, to counteract that tropism toward society and "reality" that has turned so many putative artists into mere recorders. "In art," Grotowski has said, "it is not life itself that makes the context—it is the objects of art. That means to do a great work one must not observe life. That effort is artificial. We observe life as we live it. To say that in order to create I must observe society is wrong. Society is always there in our experiences."

He has also said this: "In life the first question is how to be armed; in art it is how to be disarmed." That there is so much brandishing of weapons in the one order is just the reason for there having to be nothing but vulnerability and saving defenselessness in the other. (1970)

Index

About the Author

RICHARD GILMAN is professor of playwriting and criticism at the Yale Drama School. He has also taught at Columbia and Stanford universities, and was on the faculty of the Salzburg Seminar. Mr. Gilman has been literary editor of *Commonweal* and *The New Republic,* and drama critic of *Commonweal* and *Newsweek.* He is the author of *The Confusion of Realms,* a collection of writings on contemporary literature, art and drama, published in 1969.